ALSO BY ELIZABETH SPENCER

Novels

Fire in the Morning
This Crooked Way
The Voice at the Back Door
The Light in the Piazza
Knights & Dragons
No Place for an Angel
The Snare
The Salt Line
The Night Travellers

Short Story Collections

Ship Island and Other Stories
The Stories of Elizabeth Spencer
Jack of Diamonds and Other Stories

Play

For Lease or Sale

Special Editions

Marilee
On the Gulf
Conversations with Elizabeth Spencer

LANDSCAPES OF THE HEART

A MEMOIR

LANDSCAPES

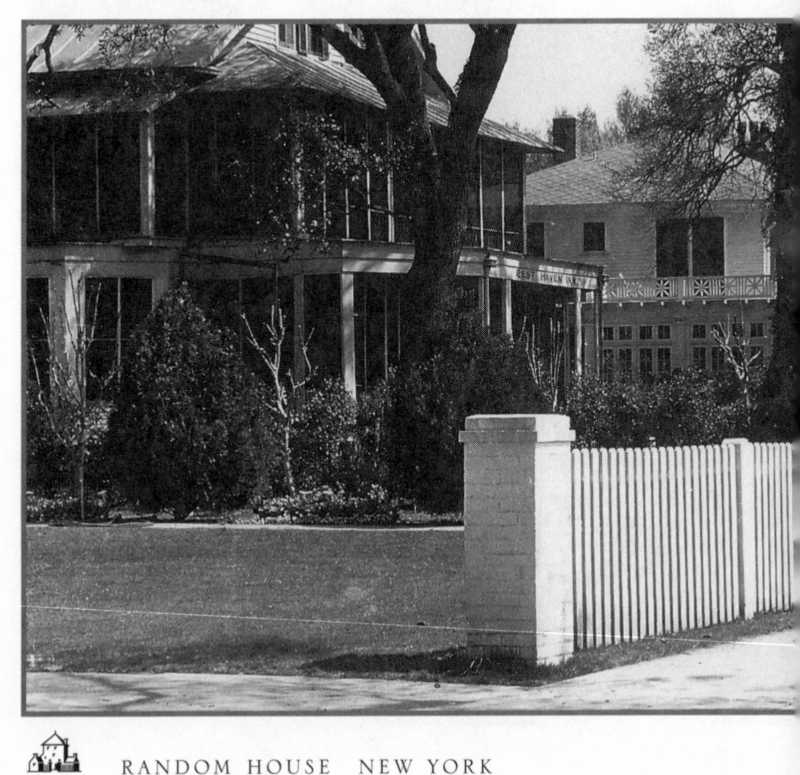

RANDOM HOUSE NEW YORK

Elizabeth Spencer

LANDSCAPES OF THE HEART

A MEMOIR

Parts of this book have previously appeared, often in somewhat different form, in the following publications: *Eudora Welty: A Tribute, An Apple for My Teacher, Family Portraits, Friendship and Sympathy, Mississippi Writers: Reflections of Childhood and Youth (*Vols. I & II*), Mississippi Writers: An Anthology, The Atlantic, Eudora Welty Newsletter, Opera News, The Southern Review, The Sewanee Review, Oxford-American, Brightleaf, Gulf Coast,* and *Carolina Quarterly.*

Grateful acknowledgment is made to the following for permission to reprint previously published material:

The Estate of Lawrence Olson: Four lines from "1941" and six lines from another poem from *The Cranes on Dying River* by Lawrence Olson. Reprinted by permission of Jean Olson on behalf of the Estate of Lawrence Olson. *Farrar, Straus & Giroux, Inc.:* Three lines from "Death of Little Boys" and seven lines from "Ode to the Confederate Dead" from *Collected Poems 1919–1976* by Allen Tate. Copyright © 1977 by Allen Tate. Reprinted by permission of Farrar, Straus & Giroux, Inc. *Harcourt Brace & Company:* Excerpts from "The Exiles Have Achieved Places of Eminence" in *Mississippi: The Closed Society* by James W. Silver. Copyright © 1964 by James W. Silver. Copyright renewed 1992 by Margaret T. Silver, James William Silver, Margaret Gail Silver, and Elizabeth Silver Little. Reprinted by permission of Harcourt, Brace & Company. *Alfred A. Knopf, Inc.:* Four lines from "Old Mansion," one line from "Judith of Bethulia," and two lines from "The Equilibrists" from *Selected Poems* by John Crowe Ransom. Reprinted by permission of Alfred A. Knopf, Inc. *Vanderbilt University Press:* Four lines from "Lines Written for Allen Tate on his 60th Birthday" and eight lines from "Spoken at a Castle Gate" from *The Long Street* by Donald Davidson. Copyright © 1945, 1950, 1960, 1961 by Donald Davidson. Reprinted by permission of Vanderbilt University Press.

Illustrations on pages 38 and 41 courtesy
Mississippi Department of Archives and History

Library of Congress Cataloging-in-Publication Data
Spencer, Elizabeth.
Landscapes of the heart : a memoir / by Elizabeth Spencer. — 1st ed.
p. cm.
ISBN 0-679-45739-9
1. Spencer, Elizabeth—Biography. 2. Women novelists, American—20th century—Biography. 3. Southern States—Social life and customs—1865– 4. Southern States—Intellectual life—1865–
I. Title.
PS3537.P4454Z47 1997
813'.54—dc21 97-9580
[B]

Random House Website address: http://www.randomhouse.com/
Manufactured in the United States of America on acid-free paper
2 4 6 8 9 7 5 3
First Edition

To William and Elizabeth Hamilton Willis,
who know how it all was

". . . and how the night
Came down the hills at Carrollton"

—"Private Poem" from *The Cranes on Dying River*
by Lawrence Olson

". . . I feel the need of a land, of a sure terrain, of a sort of permanent landscape of the heart."

—From "A Southern Landscape"
by Elizabeth Spencer

ACKNOWLEDGMENTS

Special thanks are due to Louis D. Rubin, Jr., who was kind enough to offer advice on the writing; to Walter and Jane Sullivan, who helped me confirm the validity of many memories by fact checking; to Hunter Cole and the Mississippi Department of Archives and History, who provided numerous photographs that would not have found their way into this book otherwise; and especially to Samuel S. Vaughan, my editor, who was supportive and encouraging every step of the way.

CONTENTS

Part Two School

Part Three Widening Orbits

ILLUSTRATIONS

PART ONE

The Circled World

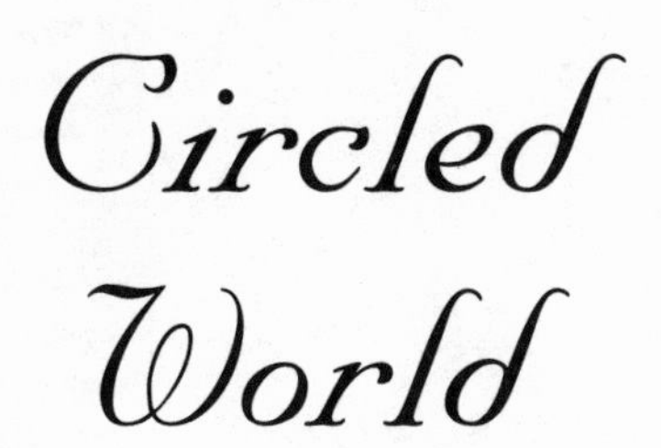

1

RIDING OUT

THAT day they would have brought the horse up for me. Usually I did it myself, dragging out the gear from the barn, catching, bridling and hitching him, brushing him down, throwing on blanket and saddle, cinching girth. But today I had to get an early start before the sun got up too high, so Bill, our handyman, or Charles, my father's foreman, would have caught my horse, Charlie, and brought him round all set to go.

At age twelve, a slight little girl all but enveloped in overalls, a long-sleeved white shirt, and a big straw hat, I had thirteen miles to ride alone over country roads from home in Carrollton to my mother's family plantation at Teoc.

Once there, I was set to stay awhile.

Taylor Browning, the mail carrier, would already have been given my small suitcase, with a dress or two inside, plus shorts, toothbrush, comb and brush, and Sunday shoes. The plantation store was right on his route, so he would leave them for me there.

The horse and I set out for the long ride.

When we were past the iron overhead bridge across Big Sand Creek, Carrollton dropped behind, and "north town," near the railroad, was soon behind us too. Then there were only a few outlying country houses, and the gravel road twisted free and open ahead. The road-working machines would have been through so many times over the years to grade and lay gravel that the roadbed sometimes now might be seven or eight feet below the original surface. Vines and bushes hung over the banks. If a car or truck came past me, yellow dust roiled up in clouds.

The sun was getting higher. It was four miles to the first turn, this one to the left at the crossroads. Taylor Browning came tearing by me in his Chevrolet, spewing dust. He hardly paused for the mailboxes he opened and stuffed, hurrying on, sorting mail with one hand on the seat beside him, driving with one eye on the road. We were always sure Mr. Browning would have a frightful collision, but he never did. He waved to me.

The next few miles were the hardest. The road ran flat and even with the surface. By now the June sun was beating down in earnest. As far as I could see there was nothing but poor picked-over fields, and not much else. No houses at all, and not a sign of anybody. Nobody knew much about this stretch of road. There were pines along low distant hills. "If anybody stops you," my instructions ran, "you say, 'I'm Mr. Spencer's daughter from Carrollton, and my uncle is Joe McCain.' " I don't remember ever seeing anyone to say it to. There was what we called the halfway house, exactly halfway along the road to Teoc. It was an empty cabin, sitting lonely in a field, the sides grown up in trumpet vine.

This stretch was the only part of the long road where I felt afraid. Suppose somebody did appear, suppose they did stop me and I said what I was told to say and they didn't care? Didn't *care* that I was Luther Spencer's daughter and my uncle was Joe McCain? It seemed impossible, but was a chilling thought. Did it worry no one but me? Would they take my horse? I had a dollar and some change in my suitcase, but that wasn't with me. What then?

On to a right turn where a brown-painted house stood in a heavy surrounding hedge, and we were in safe territory, homes of people we all knew—the Longs, the Meeks, the Balls. A sound feeling. Finally we reached the long descent down the last hill before the Delta stretched out, glimmering green and distant in the morning sun.

Teoc Creek was just ahead, where Charlie shied, balked, and worried his way over the iron bridge clanking from his hooves. The wooden floor had been patched so often it was layered in various-colored wood, and the brown creek showed through the cracks and holes from far below.

We were almost to the store. There were willows near it. On either side of the road, young cotton plants, in long rows wobbly as a child's line on a page, ran outward, broken by patches of new corn.

My uncle might be there. If not, somebody I knew would see me go by. Sam Long, the storekeeper, old Dr. Maybry stopping in to play cards or have a Coke, or Miss Lucy Wollard Ball, driving in for the mail. Somebody would wave. The Negroes all knew me—"How you, Miss 'Lizbet." Inside, whether I saw it or not, somebody would be calling ahead, turning the crank on the dusty phone in that still morning hour, when most of the labor was out in the field, to say I had arrived.

The horse made the last turn, toward the house a half mile away. Sweaty withers toiling faithfully on, he was glad to sniff the end, with barns ahead and well water.

There was the oak grove that sheltered the house, and Uncle Joe on the front porch in shirtsleeves, foot on the railing. "Get on down, hitch him there. Hurry up, you limb of Satan. It's close to dinnertime." Later than I thought. Soon, from out in the back yard, the huge plantation bell would ring, calling the wage hands to come in from the fields, time to eat.

Inside, I washed off in cool water. It had been a long ride.

2

THE TOWN

THE town I rode out from, Carrollton, is one of the oldest North Mississippi towns, dating back to the early nineteenth century. Communities around it were also settled before the Choctaw removal and had Indian names; but Carrollton, like others throughout the country, took its name from Charles Carroll, a signer of the Declaration. In college days and later, when I traveled home by bus, my baggage was always being sent astray to Carrolltons in Georgia or Alabama or Missouri or Kentucky.

This one is in the hills, but only a few miles from the Delta, that flat, rich farming area south of Memphis. It is situated pretty much straight down from Memphis, about a hundred miles, though before the new interstate the distance was longer, and a hundred miles north of Jackson, the state capital. In the ring of hills going east of the Delta, the old towns have similarities: fine old white-painted houses, generous yards of flowering shrubs and cedar-lined walks, a courthouse square with places of business—law offices, post office, bank, drugstore, grocery and hardware store.

The land surrounding Carrollton, which you sweep through so rapidly now that the big highways have come to stay, used to be a difficult terrain of bluffs, bottomlands, and wayward little streams we called branches. You reached town by tunneling slowly on dusty gravel roads, worn down into deep roadbeds. The hills were seamed with eroded red gullies, but also rife with dogwood and redbud in the spring, and heavily wooded along the ridges with wonderful oaks, sycamores, and gum trees, hiding hollows where clear springs pulsed up over white sand.

During my childhood in the twenties and thirties, getting in and out of Carrollton could be a problem. The stagecoach to Natchez was the last public transport to go right through, though later the Trailways bus would detour off the highway and stop on the courthouse square. Now that service too is gone.

It is a spread-out town, sprawled over the contours of the hills; its unexpected geography knits itself together by adjacent back yards or narrow lanes, then strikes off, contrary fashion, in another way entirely. You can never see it all at once.

3

THE McCAINS

When I read that happy families are all alike, I get suspicious. Who could find even two to compare?

But in my growing-up time, I thought of our two families, my mother's (the McCains) and my father's (the Spencers), as part of one, which was mine, and believed we were happy. I think that back then we mostly were.

Parents, aunts, and uncles were young, cousins even younger, and the future lay all ahead, promising ease and gaiety, full of hope. Worries, financial and otherwise, seemed peripheral, the dark beyond the firelight easy to forget with so much liveliness dancing around in plain sight.

The first thing I remember was learning to walk. I think maybe it was the second time I learned, for I had been perilously ill and had to start over in many ways.

I am sitting in a large leather suitcase, playing horse with the straps. My father helps me stand up. Then he reaches out his hands. "Walk to me," he says and lets go. I teeter, almost fall, and then step forward, out of the suitcase onto the carpet. After two steps, I fall forward and am caught, but I have done it. Everyone claps.

Another earliest memory is of sitting on the floor at my grand-

father's feet. He is napping in his chair and a fire is burning. It is afternoon. He wakes with a snort, which startles me. He says he was dreaming but does not say about what.

My grandfather was the only grandparent living for me to know. John S. McCain. I called him Gan.

He was a tall gentleman, white-haired, with a neatly trimmed white mustache and wide, honest eyes. He wore brushed dark suits both summer and winter. Suspenders. Bands on his sleeves above the elbow kept his cuffs in place. His starched collars were white as snow, his black bow tie set daily in place. His walking sticks were many, ranging through various woods all the way up to a gold-headed cane, which I, returning from a family funeral many years later, left forgotten in the overhead rack of an airplane. I could never recover it.

To me Gan was that primal image of love which I wish everyone on earth could know. What better thing to wish? Food, clothing, and shelter? Even these basics, possessed without the regarding face of love, are only tokens of survival and do not ensure happiness at all.

It is hard to imagine him except in the way I knew him, sitting in his usual armchair before the fire or in a front-porch rocker or a lawn chair beneath the trees, walking cane propped beside or laid across his knees, reading or conversing with whoever was near. Or walking, swinging the cane briskly before him.

He never trusted cars very much, and would always ride quietly beside my uncle or my father on the front seat, his hand holding on to a strap beside the door. He looked ready for anything to occur. My uncle recalled lecturing him at some length about the safety of motor cars, but about that time hearing him say, pointing out the window, "Son, there goes our wheel." One had come off in the rough gravel and was rolling along just ahead.

He had lived seventy years when I was born, and what a lot had already happened! He was fourteen years old when the Civil War ended. He had tried to enlist for service, saying (the one lie ever attributed to him) that he was eighteen, but no one had believed him. He had gone back to the family plantation at Teoc.

As "the only man on the place," he must have run it as best he could. He had memories of a difficult time. No coffee, no flour, no tobacco.

His brother Joseph had gone off to the war. Joseph had a weakness: he fainted at the sight of blood. At the first engagement, he turned white, fell from his horse, and was left for dead, but later revived and rejoined his unit in the night, scaring everyone to death.

What happened to the many slaves on the family land—two thousand acres in Carroll County at the base of those hills that rim the Delta—whether they ran away when freedom came or not, I never thought to ask. All one knew was that black people were there. Perhaps they never left at all.

All the descendants of slave-holding families I have ever known believe in the benevolence of their forebears as masters. No one has ever disenchanted me of this notion about our own people, though how the black descendants might see it I can't say. At any rate, throughout all my childhood, black people were numerous on "the place," still working the land.

The place lay thirteen miles northwest of Carrollton. Gan had brought his bride there, Elizabeth Young, her family being from Middleton, a town near Carrollton, which has since vanished.

John Sidney McCain. "Mister Johnny."

The name continues, passed down intact through the years to two admirals, son and grandson, and so on to a great-grandson, now in the U.S. Senate.

To his six children, he was "Father." Four boys, two girls.

The original family home, overlooking the flat expanse of Delta land, stood on a hill and was once described to me by my uncle Bill, the eldest son, as "impressive . . . in the old Southern style." By that I could imagine a mansion if I chose, but I now think it was probably a traditional two-story plantation home. It burned down the year of my mother's birth.

My grandmother, proud of her Scots ancestry, had an entire set of Walter Scott's novels, which somehow got rescued from the fire. This and a few items of furniture were all that was saved. My grandmother had named the plantation Waverley, in admiration of Scott's Waverley novels, but the Indian name of that area prevailed, and it was always known as Teoc, from the Choctaw "Teoc Tillila," meaning Tall Pines.

My mother was born soon after the fire, in the only shelter the family had to go, one of the Negro houses on the place.

These houses, as I recall them, having been constantly in and out of so many when I visited Teoc, were simple but comfortable and roomy.

My grandmother had nine pregnancies in all, having miscarried twice and lost one child in infancy. These unfortunate three must have come between the three older and the three younger, for there was a long spread in age. William Alexander ("Bill"), John Sidney ("Sidney"), and Katherine Louise ("Katie Lou") came first, then Harry, "Jimmie," and Joe. My mother, "Jimmie" (p. 12), hated her name. My grandmother had called her James to honor a relative, with Mary before it, but nicknames were a sign of affection and Jimmie she remained to all but my brother and me, he having stumbled onto Mimi while learning to talk.

Pressed for money though they were ever since the comfort-

able days before the ruinous war, the family never spent time discussing the matter. They seemed absorbed in their affection for one another, close to the point of clannishness, knowing pride as a rightful attribute, valuing honesty, integrity, and intelligence. They were all "smart," that is to say, even after a lost war, they could regroup and go on with their liveliness of intellect, their unquestioned traditions of manners and friendliness. They were welcoming people.

The house they took over after the home burned was scarcely a stone's throw away, but at the bottom of the line of hills rather than the crest. They took it away from an old slave Negro I remember well. His name was Armistead Meuks, the surname indicating another master before the McCain connection. One notable aspect was the size of his feet—he wore size sixteen shoes, which had to be ordered specially. The other was his independent nature. He did not want to leave his house. "I'se hyere 'fo Boss was," he said at the time. Only God knew how old he was.

The house, expanded and embellished, became a real home place, plain at first, but tended charmingly, with verandas added. The oaks planted around it grew and flourished, forming a shady grove.

Early in the century, my grandfather, who had held other county offices, ran for sheriff and served for six years. On this account he moved his family into Carrollton, the county seat.

Many stories of his term in office survive. He was said to have dealt justly with black and white alike and to have been averse to violence—lynching and any such lawlessness. Yet I understood he had supervised the hanging of two convicted men. I cannot really imagine this, but duty was what it had to be called. In Carrollton, past the old coaching house, there was a hill known as Hang Hill, where the gallows had stood. Ghosts were sometimes reported.

My grandmother, who as a Carrollton lady busied herself in the church and made lasting family friendships, died the summer I was born. By then my grandfather had retired from public life and was spending time on Teoc or living in town with my mother and father. They had moved into their own house, the one I was born in. My being named for my grandmother may have strengthened his affection. However it was, he seemed to have adopted me as his own.

The whole McCain connection bore an aura of an outside world. They were related permanently to Teoc and Carrollton, but they knew and were known, recognized, skilled, and active in the bigger world beyond.

My grandfather's brother Henry Pinkney McCain ("Uncle Pink") had gone to West Point. He was said to have fathered the draft act, and had commanded the training of the expeditionary force that sailed to fight in France under General Pershing. An enormous rotogravure-type photograph of the entire force, lined up against the Pennsylvania landscape at Valley Forge, hung in our hallway. We could barely make out Uncle Pink in the forefront of the multitude, but my little school chums and I used to stand on chairs and try to pick out individual men as being handsome or "cute," brown-haired or blond.

The next generation followed his lead. Bill and Sidney took competitive exams and entered West Point and Annapolis. What could they do around farms and small towns in an impoverished area, not yet healed from a civil war? The law? The church? Nothing there seemed to challenge them.

I wonder if their dreams were fed by their reading. They favored bold adventure stories and poems—Kipling, Scott, Stevenson, Henty, Macaulay, Browning. Stuck away in trunks in the attic in Carrollton, school notebooks I came across when exploring were full not only of class notes but also of original verses that spoke of heroism and daring deeds. Their Latin texts with Caesar's Gallic Wars were in our bookshelves. They were cavalier.

In Scotland, I feel sure, the McCains, Presbyterian though they were, would have remained loyal to the Scottish crown. The story went that my grandmother's family had fled to the New World because a price had been set on their heads by Elizabeth of England for their loyalty to Queen Mary. I recall that even my mother, whose dislike of Rome ran deepest of all, never failed to praise the beauty and charm of the unfortunate queen.

I thought of my uncles years later, when I read in Henry James's *The Bostonians* how Basil Ransom of Mississippi had gone to Boston in the post–Civil War years because he was bored sitting around a plantation.

As a child, I was in great awe of my two older uncles. Uncle Sidney came home more often than Uncle Bill, and I prized the affectionate attention he fixed on me, ready to praise whatever good he could observe. He criticized as well, but it was a kind of teasing. "When you pout, you're the Duchess. Now smile and be the Princess." His wife, Aunt Kate, an authoritative lady with rich brown hair, had been his teacher, eight years his senior, admirable for her high intelligence, which he, with his love of a keen mind, must have been drawn to.

Once when he visited us alone, I remember, on a warm evening, my father being absent, he, my mother, and I, sat in our wide hallway, and he said that I must have some children's books by George MacDonald. My mother named the many books I loved, which she was always reading from aloud.

"Those are fine," he said, "but these MacDonald books are not like anything I ever read before. She must have them."

They arrived soon after—*The Princess and the Goblin* and *The Princess and Curdie.* They were, as he said, a real feast.

I loved books from the first, imaginative stories and fairy tales, Greek and Roman gods and goddesses, the pictures of Roman legionnaires in the Latin books, ladies in long draped robes, King Arthur stories, Robin Hood. But the MacDonald stories were different, mystical, with walks in the twilit woods, mysterious stairways in the castle, an ancient princess in the tower, spinning at her wheel.

There came a time when all "the boys," my uncles, came home together at one time, no wives with them. This occurred because my grandfather had become very ill with pneumonia and was not expected to live.

I found it incredible that Gan could be sick. From the time I could walk, every day before I was school age, we had taken our walk together, downtown and back. Not liking to stick me alone in the huge "company room," my parents had allowed me to sleep in his room. I loved to watch the shadows from the fire leap on the walls and ceiling. A collie dog named Bob had come out of nowhere and taken up with us. He slept right beneath our window. If anything startling was heard in the night, sounds from the extensive yard or from the fields beyond, my grandfather would say, "Everything all right, Bob?" Thump went the tail. We were safe.

But now came this sickness.

Mr. Johnny loved his boys, and they knew it. They all dropped everything. From far-off Yankeeland, from Washington, Philadelphia, Wisconsin, they came.

By the time they had assembled, however, he had taken a turn for the better, and the visit turned into a joyous reunion. He was still in bed, but the boys—two high-ranking Army and Navy officers, and a third, Uncle Harry, assistant manager of a department store in Wisconsin, and of course Uncle Joe, there from Teoc—all gathered in his room and began one of the world's more curious contests. With my grandfather's great fleece-lined bedroom slippers at either end of the room as targets, with a scoreboard propped up on the mantelpiece, they had begun a game of pitching dollars, always a favorite plantation sport.

Afraid of being in the way, yet eagerly curious to watch them, learn them by heart—these brave, laughing men, wearing their marvelous thick Yankee overcoats for "outside," teasing and joking when their eyes fell on me—I clung about in corners and doorways, but even when farther away than that, I could hear their hoarse voices, while from the bed my grandfather could also be heard: "I gannies! It's a tie score! . . . Pitch 'em, Bill! Missed, goldarn it!"

In summer my grandfather sat out in the yard in the shade of a large tree we all loved, though its particular kind was a puzzle. It had small, hard, bitter nuts, and because only pigs could have stomached them, it got the name pignut tree. But it was too beautiful to be called such a name as that. Some said it was a white hickory, which sounded better. It had a barked trunk, but at about six feet up, great smooth limbs sprang skyward, rising to a fine, satisfying height. I used to climb it, as high as I could go.

Mr. Dave Welch from next door would come over and sit in the shade in the afternoons with my grandfather. When Mr. Dave was absent, Gan would often simply sit there, walking cane laid across his knees, and I would know that he was thinking over some deeply felt thing from the past. He sometimes spoke to me of my grandmother, "Miss Lizzie."

All his boys, to my mother's constant worry, had a weakness for drink. It was told of him that my grandmother would have a toddy ready for him when he came in from the fields on Teoc. One day she forgot to make it and he struck her. He was so overcome with remorse at what he had done that he gave up drinking from that day.

I had a pony named Dan, a calico somewhat larger than I should have been riding at my age. One afternoon I had ridden him far up the road toward town and back. At the head of our road something spooked him. He shied and bolted.

Before I could regain control, he was streaking in a headlong gallop, straight for the drive that swept around our house, and had entered a stretch between two fences overgrown with vines, leading to a high wooden cattle gate that closed off the barn lot. Once he was between those fences there would be nothing to stop a crash into the gate.

My grandfather ran from his chair in front, through the house to the back yard. As we plunged into the stretch, there he stood before us, right in the path of the horse, his arms raised and waving. The horse stopped so suddenly I was hurled to the ground. Gan scooped me up and ran back to the house. I was all right except for a few bruises and a bad scare. But I never forgot the sight, a life risked to save me, without an instant's debate, hesitation, or fear.

4

A CHRISTIAN EDUCATION

It was a Sunday like no other, for we were there alone for the first time. I hadn't started to school yet, and he had finished it so long ago it must have been like a dream of something that was meant to happen but had never really come about, for I can remember no story of school that he ever told me, and to think of him as sitting in a class equal with others is as beyond me now as it was then. I cannot imagine it. He read a lot and might conceivably have had a tutor—that I can imagine, in his plantation world.

But this was a town he'd finally come to, to stay with his daughter in his old age, she being also my mother. I was the only one free to be with him all the time and the same went for his being with me—we baby-sat each other.

But that word wasn't known then.

A great many things were known, however; among them: I always had to go to Sunday school.

It was an absolute that the whole world was meant to be part of the church, and if my grandfather seldom went, it was a puzzle no one tried to solve. Sermons were a fate I had only recently got big enough to be included in, but I had been enrolled in Sunday school classes since I could be led through the door and placed on a tiny red chair, my feet not even connecting to the floor. It was always cold at the church; even in summer, it was cool inside. We were given pictures to color and Bible verses to memorize, and at the end, a colored card with a picture of Moses or Jesus or somebody else from the Bible, exotically bearded and robed.

Today I might not be going to Sunday school, and my regret was only for the card. I wondered what it would be like. There was no one to bring it to me. My mother and father were not in town. They had got into the car right after breakfast and had driven away to a neighboring town. A cousin had died and they were going to the funeral. I was too little to go to funerals, my mother said.

After they left I sat on the rug near my grandfather. He was asleep in his chair before the fire, snoring. Presently his snoring woke him up. He cut himself some tobacco and put it in his mouth. "Are you going to Sunday school?" he asked me. "I can't go there by myself," I said. "Nobody said I had to take you," he remarked, more to himself than to me. It wasn't the first time I knew we were in the same boat, he and I. We had to do what they said, being outside the main scale of life where things really happened, but by the same token we didn't have to do what they didn't say. Somewhere along the line, however, my grandfather had earned rights I didn't have. Not having to go to church was one; also, he had his own money and didn't have to ask for any.

He looked out the window.

"It's going to be a pretty day," he said.

How we found ourselves on the road downtown on Sunday morning, I don't remember. It was as far to get to town as it was to get to church, though in the opposite direction, and we both must have known that, but we didn't remark upon it as we went along. My grandfather walked to town every day except Sunday, when it was considered a sin to go there, for the drugstore was open and the barbershop, too, on occasions, if the weather was fair; and the filling station was open. My parents thought that the drugstore had to be open but should sell drugs only, and that filling stations and barbershops shouldn't be open at all. There should be a way to telephone the filling station in case you had to have gas for emergency use. This was all worked out between them. I had often heard them talk about it. No one should go to town on Sunday, they said, for it encouraged the error of the ones who kept their stores open.

My grandfather was a very tall man; I had to reach up to hold his hand while walking. He wore dark blue and gray herringbone suits, and the coat flap was a long way up, the gold watch chain almost out of sight. I could see his walking cane moving opposite me, briskly swung with the rhythm of his stride: it was my companion. Along the way it occurred to me that we were terribly excited, and the familiar way looked new and different, as though a haze that had hung over everything had been whipped away all at once, like a scarf. I was also having more fun than I'd ever had before.

When he came to the barbershop, my grandfather stepped inside and spoke to the barber and to all who happened to be hanging around, brought out by the sunshine. They spoke about politics, the crops, and the weather. The barber, who always cut my hair, came over and looked to see if I needed another trim and my grandfather said he didn't think so, but I might need a good brushing; they'd left so soon after breakfast it was a wonder I was dressed. Somebody who'd come in after us said, "Funeral in Grenada, ain't it?" which was the first anybody had mentioned it, but I knew they hadn't needed to say anything, that everybody knew about my parents' departure and why and where. Things were always known about, I saw, but not cared about too much either. The barber's strong arms, fleecy with reddish hair, swung me up into his big chair, where I loved to be. He brushed my hair, then combed it. The great mirrors sparkled and everything was fine.

We presently moved on to the drugstore. The druggist, a small crippled man, hobbled toward us, grinning to see us, and he and my grandfather talked for quite some time. Finally my grandfather said, "Give the child a strawberry cone," and so I had it, miraculous, and the world of which it was the center expanded about it with gracious, silent delight. It was a thing too wondrous actually to have eaten, and I do not remember eating it. It was only after we at last reached home and I entered the house, which smelled like my parents' clothes and their things, that I knew what they would think of what we had done and I became filled with anxiety and other forebodings.

Then the car was coming up the drive and they were alighting in a post-funeral manner, full of heavy feelings and reminiscence and inclined not to speak in an ordinary way. When my mother put dinner in order, we sat around the table not saying very much.

"Did the fire hold out all right?" she asked my grandfather.

"Oh, it was warm," he said. "Didn't need much." He ate quietly and so did I.

On Sunday afternoons we all sat around looking at the paper. My mother had doubts about this, but we all indulged the desire anyway. After the ordeal of dressing up, of Sunday school and the long service and dinner, it seemed almost a debauchery to be able to pitch into those large crackling sheets, especially the funny papers, which were garish with color and loud with exclamation points, question marks, shouting, and all sorts of misdeeds. My grandfather had got sleepy before the fire and retired to his room, while my mother and father had climbed out of their graveside feelings enough to talk a little and joke with one another.

"What did you all do?" my mother asked me. "How did you spend the time while we were gone?"

"We walked downtown," I said, for I had been laughing at something they had said to each other and wanted to share the morning's happiness with them without telling any more or letting any real trouble in. But my mother was on it, quicker than anything.

"You didn't go in the drugstore, did you?"

And they both were looking. My face must have had astonishment on it as well as guilt. Not even I could have imagined them going this far. Why, on the day of a funeral, should they care if anybody bought an ice-cream cone?

"Did you?" my father asked.

The thing to know is that my parents really believed everything they said they believed. They believed that awful punishments were meted out to those who did not remember the Sabbath was holy. They believed about a million other things. They were terribly honest about it.

Much later on, my mother went into my grandfather's room. I was silently behind her, and I heard her speak to him.

"She says you took her to town while we were gone and got an ice cream."

He had waked up and was reading by his lamp. At first he seemed not to hear; at last, he put his book face down in his lap and looked up. "I did," he said lightly.

A silence fell between them. Finally she turned and went away.

This, so far as I know, was all.

Because of the incident, that certain immunity of spirit my grandfather possessed was passed on to me. It came, I think, out of the precise way in which he put his book down on his lap to answer. There was a lifetime in the gesture, distilled, and I have been a good part of that long, growing up to all its meaning.

After this, though all went on as before, there was nothing much my parents could finally do about the church and me. They could lock the barn door, but the bright horse of freedom was already loose in my world. Down the hill, across the creek, in the next pasture—where? Somewhere, certainly; that much was proved; and all was different for its being so.

A Final Word

I was fourteen when he died. I had gone to Teoc with my aunt and uncle to spend a weekend. When we got to the house the telephone was ringing. It was my mother, telling us to return at once.

I was frightened as we drove the winding country road back to town. I remember huddling in the back seat, and thinking that though my mother had not said so, we must all know what had occurred. On the front seat they were silent. I think grief was not so strong with me as fear.

I wondered later what I was afraid of. But in a way, I knew. He was the loving companion of days that would never be repeated. There have been many loves for me since then, but none quite like that. I could remember it, but not call it back. This fact, which confronted me that night, is as awesome, as fearful, as anything can get. It's enough to scare anybody to death.

From Teoc Gan once brought a pocketful of acorns from the live oaks near the house. He went around the yard in Carrollton planting all these. I was with him. I remember his bending to dig a sufficiently deep hole, dropping in the acorns, tamping the soil back over them with the tip of his cane.

Those trees now stand tall and strong around the house. It was sold after my parents' death, and though it is in the hands of good owners, I nevertheless dislike going there now that so many have passed away. But when I see those noble oaks, I am cheered. I remember the day, and that planting, and can see the yield which seems to honor it.

5

DOWN ON TEOC

TAKE two anxious young parents living in a snobbish little Mississippi town during the hard times of the twenties and thirties, hoping to please the fine families they had always known, hoping to do the right thing in every way, hoping their children would excel in school, succeed socially, be praised for good looks, dress well, never say the wrong thing, never be criticized, be friendly to all. Furthermore, and most important, those children were rigidly expected to attend church and Sunday school and young people's meetings and read the Bible every day and say their prayers every night and grow up to be good Presbyterians.

Take two lively children with inquiring minds who were not overly anxious to please and who had scant concern about what anybody thought.

Help!

Something, obviously, had to come to the rescue.

The something that did come for my brother and me was what an attentive guardian angel or, more likely, a wise and witty fairy godmother might have had made to order. He was not a something but a someone, and was there all the time: our uncle, our mother's youngest brother.

Joseph Pinkney McCain was charming and funny, full of jokes, songs, and teasing. But he listened with care to what peo-

ple said, and people to him did include children. He was irreverent, tolerant of sins, and friendly with sinners, was happily married to a pretty woman who loved him completely, and by some inexplicable curse, which was for us like a final touch of miracle, he was childless.

The outline is enough to let you see it all.

But wait. There are wonderful things to tell.

The house I went riding thirteen miles to find was not to be seen from a distance. In blistering July heat, the oaks spread a depth of cool shade; their giant shallow roots crawled and sprawled, breaking through the surface of the sandy soil between the cattle gap and the front gate, pushing up close to the broad front steps. In the still of night, an occasional oak ball banged on the tin roof like a fist. In winter, too, the oaks made an evergreen shelter in a swept landscape.

Coming there in a car from town, as we so often did, navigating those crooked roads heavy with dust or sloppy with mud, we we would take the familiar turn at the plantation store, a plain brick building with gas pumps out front, and then for the last short drive, past a hill slope with a cemetery among the trees on the right and a long spread of infinite flat fields on the left. Then we would see the grove. Just over a small bridge, we would enter it.

Uncle Joe would be waiting. He'd have seen the cloud of dust the car made from the time it passed the store, watched it advance, heard the rumble of the cattle gap, and come out to stand on the veranda, waiting, one foot on the porch railing, wearing seersucker trousers and rolled-up shirtsleeves, ready.

Squeezing past our parents, my brother and I were the first ones out; the way I remember it, we couldn't wait. Cars stopped habitually in the wide sandy space between the cattle gap and the front fence. In my memory we were through the gate before the motor died. What joy in that sand beneath our shoes, or maybe we were even barefoot, though Aunt Esther would not be too happy about it.

"Come on in! Come on in!" my uncle would call. I always had bandages. "How'd you skin yourself this time? Lord have mercy. Can't you learn to stand up?" And hair to pull straight over too large ears. "A little more and you could use 'em to fly." And new tennis shoes in an ever bigger size. "How firm a foundation, ye saints of the Lord." All this for me, with another store for my brother. Whatever he said, we were happy to hear it. Though it couldn't be called complimentary, we would stand there anyway, grinning in mindless delight at his ragging and railing. He picked us over like a hound with puppies; he carried us in his teeth like cubs.

Our parents would have come in, standing back and admiring us, glad to be there, my mother especially—her home, after all. Her brother, her children. I think, too, that, like us, what they felt was freedom. Away from it all. A long sigh.

Aunt Esther was coming. Out through the shadowy hallway with its comfortable chairs and sofas and gleaming tables, or in from the screened-in half of the veranda with its rugs and ferns and rocking chairs, and the glider, so nice to nap on in the afternoon. The oak boughs lifted in the breeze.

"That was quite a storm last night," says my uncle. "I thought it struck one of the oaks."

"Which one?" asks my mother, proprietary.

"Don't think it did. Just sounded like it."

"I was scared," my aunt says.

"She was callin' on the Lord to save her," he says. He lifts one finger in a mock sermon. "The day of repentance was at hand." We all laugh. It is nice to be friendly about the Lord.

Maybe we were all there only for the day, but maybe one of us would be staying on. "I can't let them both go at once," my mother would say, so we had our separate lengthy visits. Perhaps it was better that way, we were so different.

Joe Pink, he sometimes called himself, for Joseph Pinkney, his full name. He was of medium height, with rather broad shoulders, one held higher than the other, a family trait, and the lean limbs of all the McCains. The hands were large-knuckled: we attributed big joints to our Scottish ancestry; we had come from Scotland way back when. His hair was sandy brown, getting a little thinner and grayer with the years, though he never got bald; and his face was florid, burned scaly from exposure, and maybe from the occasional bouts of drinking Aunt Esther frowned on, holding him down. His expression was changeable, serious and inward to the point of somber meditation in repose, but more often broken into a dozen planes with foolishness and affection. He loved to rag people, observe them carefully for what he could draw out as material for his stories about them, lie in wait for their more embarrassing moments to occur (sometimes prearranged little traps they were bound to blunder into). Then he was off, relentless. Cries of protest. General aggravation. Yet no real anger. How did he do it? I don't know. It was said that everybody loved Joe McCain.

He did not like everybody. He liked attractive women, but he often disliked "ladies." He disliked properness and put-on, pretense. There was a good bit of that sort of thing around, especially in Carrollton, and a number of my mother's models of fine behavior bored him. He would sit in their company with his hat in his lap, saying the right things, but you knew the small boy in him was counting the minutes till they left. He hated hypocrisy, and these mincing ways smacked of it to him.

He loved his friends in the Teoc community. Back then it had a rural delivery service; a church four or five miles distant from the McCain place; and a number of farming families, who came to the store to get gasoline and groceries and were in lively touch with one another.

Aunt Esther was social in the fashion of the times. She was by general consensus very pretty, with chestnut hair drawn into a chignon, large brown eyes to match, and delicate features. She loved pretty things and often drove to Greenwood, a Delta town about ten miles away, to shop for materials, sewing supplies, spices, gloves, and many other items on her list. She often left time to go to the picture show. She worked hard. She crocheted spreads and afghans, embroidered linens, briar-stitched throws in velvet and satin. She canned and pickled and preserved in late summer, and raised abundant flowers in beds outlined in native rock, reached by winding sandy paths. Here in this garden beside the house she gave evening parties with Japanese lanterns hung from the oak branches. The ladies wore their fragile dresses; their husbands or bachelor friends, dressed in shirts and ties and summer-weight coats, standing around, eating and talking; a fine evening. At her bridge parties, she set tables out in the open hallway. Organized, and a bit sharp-tongued, with so much to do, she bossed us around. "She thinks my children belong to her," my mother used to say, but without resentment at first—a little, maybe, later on.

As for Uncle Joe, there was no debate. He knew in what ways we belonged to him, knew it all along, knew what a difference he could make and was making. Occupied with business, my father spent a lot of time worrying.

A part of my uncle's love for my brother and me was rooted deep in his clannish family feeling. He could and did get mad at you for hypocrisy, or churlishness, or what he called "welshing," failing to do what you'd promised. You had to measure up. But he never rejected you. Thirteen miles away, along twisted roads almost but never quite impassable, he was always there, through the years, foot on the porch railing, looking out, waiting.

He rode the place in those days. The big reason to bring my horse was to ride with him. Those were pre-jeep times, and no car could maneuver the plantation roads. They were swampy in places, broken by drainage ditches, or heavy with dried mud from the winter.

Uncle Joe would get up before day, while I was still asleep. My mother, complimenting my aunt, often said of her, "She gets up and dresses at four in the morning to eat with Joe. She'll never let him eat alone." Harvey Hoskins, the overseer at the barns, would bring up my uncle's mare in the dim light, and he was off to the fields. Later, when I woke and ate, I would walk down to the barns for my horse. I would ask along the way, riding out through the huge wooden gates of barns and lots, out onto the land, "Where's he got to? Where is he by now?" and whoever I passed would tell me, or guess at it. I would find him not long after. A little at a time, out in the dazzle of full sun, we covered the immense fields, stopping for a while where a tractor might be broken down, or to pass the time of day with the cotton choppers, who would come close and talk about the crop stand, or to look in on a cabin where somebody might be sick. Sometimes we got off to pick blackberries from bushes along a drainage ditch, or to drink water that gushed from the iron pipe at one of the artesian wells scattered over the place. We watered the horses from the concrete trough, and drank right from the pipe, letting the water run over face and neck to wash the sweat away. The water tasted of iron and was clear and swift and so iron-cold it hurt your teeth to drink it. The Negroes came to these wells, usually in the evening after work, riding a mule-drawn slide with a barrel on it to fill for daily water at home.

In the late morning we would wind up at the store. The mail, a Coke or Nehi if not too near dinnertime. I might get to watch a quick hand of cards with Sam or Rosewell Long, or Dr. Maybry, or Arnie Meeks (the men sitting on the smooth bare oak counter, dealing from a deck worn to rags). The loser paid for the drinks. Then back to the house, maybe hearing the great bang and bong of the dinner bell along the way.

I've tried to think back, tried earnestly to remember if there were evidences of bad feeling between my uncle and the many black people, descendants of the original slaves, for the most part, who worked on his land, lived on it year-round, and were furnished out of the store. As best I can recall, they were exceptionally good-humored around him in a way that seemed to make their dependency a reassurance to them rather than a burden. I can't to this day believe I would not have noticed any deep-seated animosity.

It was slightly different with my aunt. I knew the house Negroes often felt themselves ordered around, and I knew that some of them resented her. She railed at them for laziness, for forgetting, for doing what she wanted less than perfectly.

Her story is interesting in itself. She was married quite young, at eighteen, and at that a year older than my uncle. She had come from being a small-town teacher (French and elocution), and found herself, a "town girl," cast up in the midst of a plantation with an entirely black population for miles around to see to daily and call on for everything she couldn't do herself. In addition, she had the running of what amounted to not just a house, a home, but a whole system of providing year-round food and civilized living, from the raw material of sheep shearing and hog slaughtering, milking, separating butter and cream, cutting and hauling wood for fires, to keeping well, or nursing the illnesses of, all and sundry around her.

As if that were not enough, she also, in the first days, felt it her duty to "educate" the blacks, and so called them into classes and gave them, among other subjects, "moral instruction." Her pupils agreed with every word she said but went straight about living as they pleased. Very soon she gave it up. There were episodes, later to be laughed at, of her running in from the garden in tears, apron flung over her head, of stormy vexation and despair. But she turned her corner. "She had grit," my uncle often said, adoring her, though there had been a lot of quarrels too, and still were, for they were two spirited fighters. And lovers, too: we never doubted that.

By the time I came along she was very much the chatelaine, a demanding mistress, quick, with a no-nonsense way of making sure she was listened to, obeyed, obeyed on time. She kept the keys tied with rawhide thongs to small cedar boards, labeled "smokehouse" or "pantry" or "woodhouse" or "tools." These had to be returned by nightfall. From a country house, a cabin hastily enlarged after the old home burned, added to in haphazard wings and tacked-on porches, she fused and embellished a gracious, welcoming plantation dwelling, never a mansion, but beautiful to look at, serene to stay in. For this she had to have help in plenty, and her help admired, obeyed, but sometimes resented her. They did not cling to her the way they clung to him.

Out on the place, riding with my uncle, I noted how Negroes came to find him, sometimes in pairs, trouble on their minds. "You go on ahead, Lizzie," he would say. So it was a marriage dispute. He wouldn't think it suitable for me to hear. Nor would they have told it before me. I would ride ahead and wait. He would sit his mare, leg up perhaps, with loose reins, and they would stand near her head or at the stirrup, and he would listen, take off his cork helmet at times, scratch his brow, nod, following everything. Something would be, if not settled, advanced by the time they left, what I don't know, but they would look more at peace, would have agreed maybe to come back and talk again. At other times, some scrawny woman would come up, or rather grow up, right out of high weeds, the pernicious Johnson grass that cursed that particular region, and complain that she didn't have food to get through the month. He would stop his horse. "Lord have mercy, I done furnished you twice already," he would say, but then the story would come up, rising up in all its detail. "Well, go on up to the store. Side meat and cornmeal . . . put it on the books."

I also loved riding in wagons and got to do this frequently down on Teoc in the summer. The Negroes indulged me. They would let me take the reins and teach me to hold the team together for an equal pull. I knew all their bridling and harness, and how they were hitched up. An empty wagon is fun to ride because the mules are happy with the lightness of the load and enjoy trotting along in unison.

I may be the only person still alive who can ride standing barefoot in an empty wagon driving a team without getting pinched toes. Wagon boards are never nailed to the bed because the motion of the wagon jostling over uneven roads would split them. You have to take care to keep your bare feet centrally on the wider boards. I was once good at doing this.

In the late afternoons on Teoc, I would watch for the return of a man named Gold, whom I especially like to follow around. When he came clattering along toward the barns in an empty wagon, I would run out and call him. He would stop the team and pull me aboard. He would sit on the board seat so that I could drive alone to the barn gates, where he would spring down and open them wide for my triumphant entry.

Those were happy days.

Yet it was an ugly system, of course, enslaving, grown up after slavery and not possible, apparently, ever to lose. But in that childhood time of enchantment and love, it never seemed to me anything but part of the eternal. Might as well question why the live oaks were there, or the flowers in Aunt Esther's garden, or the stars in the sky, as to say that Teoc could be run any way but the way it was, always had been, always would be. I myself was a slave more willing than any.

Once or twice, when invited, my aunt and I attended Negro services at the plantation church. We were solemnly made welcome. Later, during the thirties, the blacks on the place collected enough money among themselves to build a new church. It was neat, of wooden construction, with a modest white steeple and sturdy front steps. They named it St. Joseph's Chapel for my uncle. Some left Teoc, but wherever they went to, they were apt to write him, either for money or about some problem. I remember one well, a field hand named Joe Willie, who left and went to Memphis. I saw him a year or so later, back at the place. "I thought you left us, Joe Willie," I said. My uncle told me later that he had got into some scrape and got hit in the head. "Yes'm," was Joe Willie's version, "I went up yonder, but they tried to keel me, so I done come on back home."

We rode all summer, often as much as twenty or thirty miles a day. Sometimes in late afternoon, when the shadows grew long, we'd race our horses along the levee road near the creek, and often my uncle would suddenly turn his mare and drive her straight up the levee to the very crest, where he would halt, take off his hat, and catch the evening breeze, looking out and all around, while I came trotting up behind to join him.

All the time, the life of that land and those people was going on all around us. There is nothing like it I know of today, and though we took it for granted as usual plantation living, I know now that even then it was rare. I have come now to see that my memories have more in common with country life as described by Chekhov, Tolstoy, and Turgenev than with the America of that time as we read about it in Dreiser or Sinclair Lewis. Enlightened as to its ills, as one would have to come to be, I could never deny that I loved it, or cease to look back on it with the greatest affection. I still claim joy as a good portion of its quality, and I love it still.

Uncle Joe was a great one for discussing books he liked. The McCains were brought up around books, always had books, talked about books, took characters from books into their lives. They enjoyed fiction mainly, though they had studied history in the schools and academies they attended, and everyone had taken Latin. Also mathematics, said to "improve your mind." My aunt Katie Lou McCain, the elder sister, even taught Latin, in a town to the south.

Come to think of it, it may have been books which, if they didn't teach us our traditions, had much to do with reinforcing them. Behavior and manners came to us from an eighteenth-century code of life. People in Carrollton often seem to have stepped out of Jane Austen. Authorities from the past stood in austere ranks—the Bible, the Romans, the Greeks. Our finest houses looked like classical temples. Our lawyers quoted Cicero. Our ministers knew Hebrew.

Books at Teoc and at home in Carrollton stood two deep in the bookshelves, and most of them were good ones, would be thought so to this day. It's true that my uncle liked adventure tales, Rafael Sabatini, for instance; and my mother confessed to liking such books as *V. V.'s Eyes* and *Queenie's Whim*, but for the most part the shelves were solid in their Dickens and Thackeray and Jane Austen and Hawthorne. My brother's favorite book, read many times over, was *Moby Dick*. He persisted in believing it is about a whale hunt. I agree.

My uncle saw to it that I read every word of his favorite book, *Les Misérables*. When I was as young as twelve he sent me plodding through this tome, well over seven hundred pages long, in the edition he had at Teoc. His own enthusiasm spurred me on. He kept me at it. Fantine and Cosette, Marius, and most of all Jean Valjean himself were objects of his comment. He had thought of them a lot. He admired Valjean for his courage, his endurance, his masculinity, and his ability to grow, become greater than he was at first. He dwelt with some amusement on the love of Marius for Cosette. "He couldn't eat or sleep. He grew thin and pale. Look what love will do. That's how it is, Lizzie." "Poor things," my mother would chide. "It's such a cruel book. They were all so poor. It can't be good for her to read all that." "It's life," he would say. "She ought to learn about it."

He also admired Dickens, especially *A Tale of Two Cities;* the Evrémonde story was a fascination to him. Where did all this Frenchness come from? I've no idea. My grandmother admired Walter Scott, but Uncle Joe confessed that Scott bored him with long descriptions. Perhaps Hugo by comparison was more interesting, and the same went for Dickens when he didn't try "to put in too many characters."

During rainy days we sat and talked about these things. He liked Mr. Darcy in *Pride and Prejudice* and thought that Becky Sharp in *Vanity Fair* was "a mean little devil." He smoked Target cigarettes and let me roll them for him on a little orange-colored machine. The tobacco was spread in a small canvas trough, the fine paper set in place, and when I pressed the lever, one rolled around the other. I made them for him fifty at a time, and he kept them in a humidor on the hall table.

Nothing gold can stay.

I grew, entered awkward adolescence, suffered through growing pains, made everybody as miserable as possible, including myself.

Aunt Esther developed a malignancy. Incurable. She died during my first year away at college.

For a long while Uncle Joe was blindly depressed. There were the drinking, the late nights, the gambling, the women.

But a discovery emerged.

Still in his forties, he was not only charming but desirable. He was a "planter." Prestigious: a McCain. Slowly, he reawakened to life, but this time that life was himself, a new revelation.

Things were never as before, but they were similar enough still to be clung to, and many times to be enjoyed. He would take me out to his favorite restaurants at times, showing me off as his "latest girlfriend." The owner of one came out to peek at me. Back in the kitchen she scolded him. "You robbing the cradle now. Shame on you."

He had some questionable acquaintances. My mother got wind of one and reproached him at some length. He checkmated her easily. "She's a good woman," he said. What he meant by that phrase was not at all what she meant. But she couldn't go further with it. There was a family meaning he had put to use—"a good woman" would certainly be approved. My mother gave up.

He took trips to New Orleans. He had sometimes gone before in the company of his older brother Sidney, whenever he was home from the Navy. Together they had created for me the vision of a glowing myth-city long before I had ever had a chance to see it for myself. When I first went there, early in my college years, I fully expected magnolia-scented air, walls draped in perpetually blooming bougainvillea, violet orchids opening by the light of scarlet moons. It was almost true. Uncle Joe often named his favorite restaurants and what he liked to order. Pompano *en papillote* at Antoine's, shrimp Arnaud at Arnaud's, and trout Marguery at Gallatoire's. Don't neglect Tujogues's for lunch.

He still danced about at bedtime in his old pongee dressing gown, his "deshables," as he said. Sang the old foolish songs. Enjoyed movies, books, pretty women.

And married again.

Had two boys, his pride and joy. General happiness.

Then, the accident.

How did it happen? His second wife, Rebecca, afraid of possible tornadoes, had got him to build a storm pit, a below-ground refuge. Water had got into it, and some snakes. Alone, he had gone out with the gun to shoot them. She had driven up to meet the school bus bringing the boys home. Midafternoon in winter, no one around, even the kitchen empty. He evidently slipped on some broken steps. A shot rang out over winter-quiet fields. A bloody period.

Teoc was never to revive. He had recovered its life once, along with his own; but without him there was no new life possible. Rebecca left, moved to Greenwood with the boys. I'm told the house was rented first to one family, overseers, then to others. The oaks were cut down. I never went there again.

My brother, bolder, or maybe more nostalgic, drove there once with his wife, to see it again. In the old days, on a happy afternoon, he and my uncle had buried a small store of articles inside the concrete support to a water tower—coins of that year, stamps, some newspaper clippings, statements they had written about themselves, all to reconstruct that time and place for whoever might come after, like capsule testaments shot out into space if time, say, is the space shot into.

But the house had fallen to ruins, and growth had come up so thick my brother could not force his way through to reach that spot and reclaim what they had so hopefully put there for the future to find and know them by. He came away with nothing.

6

MALMAISON AND THE CHOCTAW CHIEF

An upbringing in the neighborhood of real splendor is a gift of fortune. No matter how that splendor came to be there, whether from kin or not, its presence is always with those who ever saw it and knew it for what it was.

Malmaison. It was a house that was also a home, and takes its place among the great mansions of Mississippi, which, though mainly centered in Natchez, are scattered throughout the state. But it was different from all the others. Here comes history.

All I knew in my childhood was that Greenwood Leflore, last chieftain of the Choctaw Indians, had built the house for his wife, Priscilla Donley. Was there a need to know more?

First and foremost, it was there to be looked at, and look with astonishment and wonder was what you had to do, having followed a winding gravel road through thick woods for some miles from our own family place, also at Teoc, until a curve and climb swirled us upward, and a drive led us over a cattle gap, flanked by entrance pillars. And there it stood, rising up immense and palatial on its low, flat hilltop.

Two stories and a cupola. Massive white columns. Elaborately carved woodwork beneath the eaves. A grand entrance portico. A porch so large that rocking chairs set out on it looked to belong in a children's playhouse. Long galleries for both stories ran along either side. There were many wrought-iron balconies. And the cupola! It was like a small ornate house set atop the mansion like a crown. Its doors and windows matched those of the house below. A walkway surrounded it, enclosed by wooden railings. It could be called an observatory, and perhaps the chieftain thought of it so, for from it one could look out over the whole of the Teoc country, most of which he owned.

What was inside? Leflore, himself three-quarters French, had a great admiration for French style. He had named the house Malmaison because, it was said, he admired the empress Josephine, who had so called her own home when she was put aside by the emperor. The doorway, when you entered, simply swallowed you. A majestic hallway opened gleaming before you, parlors on either side. The parlor furnishings were in gold leaf, upholstered in crimson damask. They had been designed and executed in Paris. There were enormous gold-framed mirrors, murals of foreign scenes, linen curtains painted with scenes of Versailles, Saint-Cloud, Malmaison, and Fontainebleau. There were Sèvres vases, glittering chandeliers, tapestries, and an enormous rose-colored carpet, Aubusson, without a doubt. The china and silver, when set out for dinner parties, were so sumptuous it was hard to imagine them actually in use.

Who was this man, this chieftain? Why had he not only wanted all this but also been able to have it?

Greenwood Leflore was only one-quarter Indian, the son of Louis LeFleur, a Frenchman who came up from the Gulf Coast and founded LeFleur's Bluff, a trading post which was later renamed Jackson and made the state capital. LeFleur married an Indian princess who was half French, the niece of the great Choctaw chief Pushmataha. Their son Greenwood was attractive, intelligent, and lucky. As a boy he caught the eye of a certain Major John Donley from Nashville, who ran a stage-coach route along the Trace from Nashville to Natchez. Donley adopted little Greenwood, took him home, and saw to his education. Years later, Greenwood returned to Mississippi with Donley's daughter Rose as his bride. After she died, he married another Donley daughter, Priscilla.

Leflore's portrait shows a narrow sensitive face, black hair, a fine straight nose, and remarkable large black eyes. It is the total *awareness* of those eyes that strikes the viewer. They express no sense of inferiority; they penetrate; they certainly command and may demand, but they would never beg. And so he must have been.

His father, Louis LeFleur, had been dashing, a heartbreaker, it was said. Greenwood might have been a bit like that too. There is an air of romance in all the stories about him. A will he left, witnessed by two McCains, his neighbors, provides for some various black children, though whether his own or not is unknown.

Among the Choctaws he had seemed at first a hero. He was elected chief while the tribe lived in their native lands of northwestern Mississippi. He was ambitious to lift their standards, and thought it best for their future to encourage them in white man's ways. I read that he sought to stamp out witchcraft,

stressed education, encouraged democracy. But the Choctaws were already, by all accounts, civilized. They made excellent farmers and knew how to prosper. Their customs were already democratic. They became bitter enemies only when mistreated or betrayed. In general they lived peaceably, and in the early days they got on well with the white settlers.

But the settlers who were pouring in wanted everything. Promises were made and treaties were drawn up by the dozen, but all were broken. Removal was obviously in the future, and all that had gone before was nothing but delay.

Leflore, it was said on local authority, "got the best deal he could get." Negotiating with emissaries from Washington, he won one concession after another from the U.S. government. Indians could stay if they wanted to. They would be given(!) some land. As the land was theirs already, this bit of generosity seems totally astonishing. Yet in the Treaty of Dancing Rabbit Creek, they were forced to cede it to the United States, which allowed them to have a portion of it back. The ones who decided to stay usually found themselves cheated out of what they had been allowed, but so it went, in treatment of the natives, way back then. The white race said, "It's yours but I'll take it anyway." And they did.

What of the ones who left, moved by promises of a new rich land in far-off Oklahoma? The story of their removal is pathetic and shameful and need not be retold here. The uncertain winter weather played a large, unexpected part, and many white officials acted nobly, but on the whole their westward trek was a horror story.

After the cession of land and the removal of the tribe, the Indians turned against their hero. Rejected by his own, Leflore chose to enter the planter society of Mississippi, to establish an opulent lifestyle and take a prominent place among the white hierarchy. Did the naming of the house Malmaison touch on his sorrow at being thought a traitor, cast aside by his fellow Choctaws? I never heard it said, but have often wondered.

Leflore was proud of his standing with President Andrew Jackson and others he had negotiated with, face-to-face. The coach that had once taken him to Washington stood housed at

Malmaison, a prized memento. During the Civil War, he refused to abandon his U.S. citizenship; he would not betray that, at least. The neighboring McCains were all Confederates, yet respected a neighbor's right to choose. There was hostility toward Leflore, attempts on his life, threats to burn the mansion. Some from the McCain place came to stand guard at night. This story was told in our family with pride. We felt for his independent spirit; friendship made us obliged to honor it.

I, of course, never laid eyes on this remarkable man, dead long before my time. Faithful to the Union, but acting for his tribe with such disastrous results. Seeing them march impoverished away to an uncertain future, yet staying put himself with handsome bounties awarded by the federal government for his aid in negotiation. Hero or opportunist? One cannot finally say. He was now owner of fifteen thousand acres of some of the best land in the state and a thousand slaves, plus a grandiose residence second to none. He was noted for good business sense, and traded in cotton and lumber with great success. His portrait is worth pondering. Those eyes are looking at reality.

We all knew his descendants. In my childhood, with Uncle Joe and Aunt Esther at our plantation nearby, we often went to Malmaison. There were annual fairs on the extensive grounds around the mansion; country produce was displayed in the two "garçonnières," small houses which stood flanking the drive on either reach of the front lawns. Leflore's daughter Rebecca Cravat had married the architect of Malmaison, a man named James Harris. Harris took his payment when the house was complete by asking for Rebecca's hand. It was their granddaughter whom I remember best, a pretty, pleasant lady named Frances ("Miss Fannie Eva") Montgomery. Of Mr. Montgomery I remember little being said; he must have died early on. Miss Fannie Eva's two sons were William and Andrew.

Andrew Montgomery was one of the handsomest young men I ever saw. His Indian blood must have been minimal, but some of it was certainly in his makeup. He was of average height, very strong-looking. His hair was black as coal, his eyes dark. I was a gangly little girl one hot summer afternoon when we were all at Malmaison. He must have seen that I was restless with grown folks' talk, for he said, "Would you like to go up and see the lookout?" He meant the cupola. Of course I said yes.

Together we climbed the stairs to the second floor, then some narrow stairs that ran steeply upward. Reaching the top, Andrew opened the doors of the small house, stiff from disuse, and, telling me to be careful of the railing, led me to look out over the extensive lands on every side. I could see Teoc Creek, a winding ribbon, edged with sand. I could see, I thought, all the way to our own family place, and the oak grove around the house. Rolling country, with wooded hills and open fields, breaking down toward the flat stretches of the Delta. How Indian on that summer afternoon it all seemed! One could know the sense of ownership the proud chieftain must have had, as the Frenchman in him took pride in the furnishings and portraits in the rooms below.

Ostracized by Indians and under a cloud among Southern whites, Greenwood Leflore ended his life in solitary pride, seated on the front veranda at Malmaison, wrapped in the U.S. flag, awaiting death. All these facts, which I learned through the years, have filled in around his name. But I still have no clear image of the man himself.

The handsome Andrew Montgomery was killed in battle during World War II. I was off working in Nashville when Uncle Joe wrote that he was "going today to a burial service for poor Andrew," whose remains had been shipped home. I recalled the evening Andrew had burst in on my uncle and me dining in a booth at Lusco's, the famous restaurant in Greenwood. He was with his fiancée, a lovely blonde, whose photograph had recently been chosen out of thousands for the cover of a national magazine. They were both so happy, talking excitedly. Like the few minutes on the cupola when he waved his arm out over all of the Teoc country, that memory has no darkness in it at all.

In 1942, the unthinkable happened. Malmaison caught fire and burned to the ground. I was not living in Carrollton when it occurred, but the shock was something I feel to this day.

The evening of the tragedy has been reported in great detail. It was during the war, the last day of March, a blustery, windy evening. Miss Fannie Eva had driven with her sister Florence to a neighboring town to hear firsthand news of Andrew from an Army buddy who was visiting home. When she returned at dusk, two other ladies had driven out from Greenwood to see her.

The four women were alone in the house, talking together in a downstairs room, when they heard a mysterious knocking and cried out to know who was there. After a pause the knocking continued. They called out again, but no one replied. They took up guns. Soon they heard footsteps walking in upstairs rooms above them. Going each to a different entrance, they fired into the night to call in neighbors. They never saw anyone. Smoke alerted them to what was happening.

The women set about at once to rescue what they could. The nearest fire truck was in Greenwood, fifteen miles away. They hauled out china and silver, pictures and chairs, and grappled with heavy furniture, but the mansion was catching fast.

What a blaze it must have been! The windy night grew bright as noonday. A full moon rode high overhead. Word spread quickly and crowds drove out from Carrollton but could only watch. Malmaison died blazing with Indian fury, like a final flamboyant gesture, funeral pyre and warlike signal. In my mind's eye, the cupola sends up a defiant blaze as high as the moon; then it plummets downward.

William Faulkner wrote a great many stories with Indian characters, based on Indian life as he imagined it to be. Because he lived in Oxford, northeast of the Choctaw country, one has to surmise (without knowing positively, for I think he never says) that his Indians are mainly Chickasaw, a related and equally strong tribe, which lived in the Oxford and Holly Springs area. However, one of his stories, it seems to me, is clearly Choctaw, and so named; and the home mentioned in it—Contalmaison—is undoubtedly Malmaison.

The story is "Mountain Victory." In it a stranger comes to a remote mountain cabin in Tennessee. He has been a major under General Longstreet, and is now on his way from the surrender in Virginia to his home in Mississippi, mounted on a thoroughbred bay, attended by a dwarfish black servant. From the twisted events that follow, a violent story surfaces. The mountain family is pro-Yankee; one of them has fought against the Rebels. Judging by his skin and intense features they take the stranger to be a "nigra." He then tells his history—a grandfather who was François Vidal, a French nobleman, an émigré to New Orleans. Vidal married a Choctaw woman. Their son, Francis Weddel, had once driven to Washington to entreat with Andrew Jackson for better treatment of the tribe. The parallels to Leflore are too obvious to miss, yet the allegiance here is to the South.

The officer's name is Saucier Weddel, a corruption of Vidal, just as the name Leflore had sprung from LeFleur. Weddel wears a worn, mended cape, lined in sable. He has cut pieces from the fur to wrap the feet of his servant. The daughter of the mountaineers and the younger son recognize and revere Weddel's obvious aristocracy. They want to go with him, the daughter as his wife, the son as a servant. But the father and the older son react with a jealous hatred. The black servant, drunk on mountain whiskey, scorns them volubly as "white trash." On these emotions the tale spins toward a tragic end. Readers of Faulkner are on familiar ground: the noble personage is trapped and doomed by his own nobility.

What strikes home to me in the story is—precisely—*home.* Both the black servant and the chieftain's son (how can I not see Andrew?) want to get there. It is their consuming passion. The servant speaks of it: " 'Ain't you never hyeard tell of Countymaison? His grandpappy named it Countymaison caze it's bigger den a county to ride over. You cant ride across it on a mule betwixt sunup and sundown.' " Weddel speaks of it: " 'I am a Mississippian. I live at a place named Contalmaison. My father built it and named it. He was a Choctaw chief named Francis Weddel.' "

That night, trying to sleep in the barn loft and awaiting sunup, Weddel "lay rigid on his back in the cold darkness, thinking of home. 'Contalmaison. Our lives are summed up in sounds and made significant. Victory. Defeat. Peace. Home. . . . It's nice to be whipped; quiet to be whipped. To be whipped and to lie under a broken roof, thinking of home.' "

Like Andrew, he is never to reach it. Do any of us ever get there?

. . .

When I was a child, we were always conscious of Indians, in a peripheral sort of way. The boys at home used to search for arrowheads in the pasture, and would bring them to school. I would ask my family if I had Indian blood. I was firmly assured that I did not. On the most distant points of the plantation at Teoc, riding with Uncle Joe, we would sometimes stop to talk with a saddle-colored man, who would be sitting on the porch of his house and would come out to speak with us. Uncle Joe would explain as we rode on, "That was a gentleman of color. One of the Leflores," he would add, but I scarcely caught on at that time.

There are natural open spaces in the wooded hills around Carrollton, going south toward Coila and Black Hawk, where, in the scarcely breathing quiet of a spring afternoon, one can feel the Choctaw presence still. They are about to walk through—silent, following some ancient path.

Many people at home are said to have Choctaw blood, and have more recently begun to claim it, and journey out to tribal reunions in Oklahoma.

Black Hawk itself, once a village, now not much more than a site, is said by those who have discovered artifacts there to be the oldest town in Mississippi, perhaps in the entire United States. It dates far back into prehistory, first home to an obscure tribe.

The passing of Malmaison returned a plainness to that country, and along with the decline of our own family, at least in that place, leaves me with no wish to return. Teoc is gone in the old sense and something workaday, unadorned, has taken over. It is dispossessed. We "must grieve when even the Shade / Of that which once was great is passed away." It is a very good thing to have grown up as neighbor to splendor.

7

THE SPENCERS

ON the one hand there was Teoc and the McCains, on the other McCarley and the Spencers. McCarley was a community rather than a town, though it did have a store, a post office, a cotton gin, and a church or two. Like Carrollton it was in the hills, five miles to the northeast. It was a stop on the C. & G., the Columbus to Greenville railway.

My father's family were all from McCarley. They had property there, and were kin to half the neighborhood and beyond, but never owned any large acreage, my impression is, nor did they ever own slaves. They were always, however, connected with the railroad, the C. & G., and by extension the Southern Railroad. They owned the one store in McCarley, also the gin.

My mother came to McCarley as a young woman to make a living for herself by teaching piano lessons. She had always been a prizewinner in musical contests. The traditional routine for proper young ladies accomplished in music was to find a room with a nice family who had a piano in the parlor and who would not mind the noise of scales being run and beginners' pieces stumbled through during the afternoon hours. The place she found was with a certain Mrs. Redditt.

My grandfather had driven her the five miles from Carrollton in the family buggy, to talk with the Redditts and set up the arrangement. As they were crossing the railroad track, she saw a young man standing down from the crossing, toward the station stop. He lifted his hat (I envision a straw boater) and waved it at her. She turned to my grandfather. "Can I wave back?" He told her yes and she did. She was waving at her future husband.

James Luther Spencer—"Mr. Luke," as he later became—was one of four or possibly five surviving brothers, though a number of other siblings had died, and one brother, Willie, had simply walked away and never returned. My parents being the last born or next to last among offspring who began arriving in the 1860s, I was, extraordinary as it seems, only one generation away from the Civil War. Both my grandfathers were not only alive and active during that tragic time, but my father's father, who died long before I was born, had actually fought in it. He must have been through some of the worst of it, for he lost an arm at Gettysburg. This was Elijah Harrison Spencer. After the conflict, he worked as a rural mail carrier, as well as a farmer, I suppose, and did whatever else there was to put food on the table. Times were hard, everybody worked hard, but the sons seemed to have happy, affectionate memories to talk about.

There were Thomas Harrison, and Louie Clyde, and Eddie Gray. Tom, the eldest, married and lived in Winona, another ten miles to the east, but Louie stuck around McCarley, and Luther, the youngest, who would become my father, must have started out working in the station agent's office and in the store as well. Eddie Gray soon moved on to a "connection" with the Southern Railroad.

Louie and Luther, working in tandem, were absolutely bound to clash for one simple reason: there was never but one authority in the world, and that was Luther Spencer. Perhaps this quality was what attracted my mother, for she had a Victorian admiration for strength and worthiness in men, shading toward "worth," which in turn shades toward "amounting to something." She was said to have been very pretty, and photographs prove it true. As a girl she had a number of admirers back in Carrollton. Her health was never robust, and at some point she must have left McCarley for Teoc.

My father persisted, and would drive a buggy all that long way, a good fifteen or so miles over country roads, to spend Sun-

days with her, though he was, of course, visiting the whole McCain family as well. In a way he was courting them all. My grandmother was said to have liked him. She told my mother he was going to "amount to something." He always recalled the long journey back to McCarley on Sunday nights, falling asleep in the buggy while his trusty little horse kept up a steady gait home.

They both wound up in Carrollton. My father, raised a Methodist, became a Presbyterian before he knew it. My mother's classic phrase of persuasion, often quoted, was "I will respect anything you want to be, but I can't raise anything but a Presbyterian."

He had a store by then, down in North Carrollton, the separate village that had sprung up across the creek, near the railroad. I have an old photograph of him leaning on a counter, a bright-faced young man, his shelves stocked with goods behind him. He was known as a go-getter, and probably liked being called that.

He seemed to have always had the same character: an indefatigable angler after whatever would earn money, a person of community spirit who helped others at such a breakneck speed they may have often wondered what hit them, a man who demanded total and absolute purity in womankind. My mother often wore white, and all his life he loved the virginal look of it. She would never wear even a touch of makeup.

Dad became an authority on everything within five minutes after he heard it mentioned. He had no interest in it if he could not control or manage it, or if it could not make money. He disliked men who taught, at whatever level, because he judged them not good "b'inessmen."

Finding a pretty girl of a good family must have been enough for him, because why Dad ever liked a music teacher is a mystery. He had no love for music or feeling about it and could never carry a tune. He believed that made-up stories, poems, paintings, and so on through the whole lexicon of artistic endeavor, were simply foolishness, a waste of time, all right for women to indulge within limits, he supposed, but out of the question for a real man to take seriously.

In this attitude he was different from his brothers. While not especially well educated, as they would have been if times had been different, and as they took care to see that their children were, they did not condemn differing tastes, and showed affectionate interest in what others could do. They were humane and comforting sorts, long-nosed and hazel-eyed, easy to be with, rational and practical, and they told innumerable stories. I know now they all agreed that Luther was different—in a sense one of them, but set apart by a compulsion to compete, to "get ahead."

Yet they profited from his generosity. If one needed money to tide over a misfortune, he could borrow it from Luther. If a son needed a job, Luther would give it to him, letting a secretary go to provide it. If a daughter needed a place to live while she taught grade school in Carrollton, Luther's house was to be her home.

Eddie Gray, next to the youngest, had done a curious thing: he had gotten a *divorce*! Divorce in those days was practically unheard of, especially in our connection. Uncle Ed had two boys, who by court order were his in the summers, and with Spencer practicality he simply brought them over to McCarley and Carrollton and parked them with the relatives. He did indeed visit from time to time. He had something of the air of a dandy, dressed handsomely, and distributed large wet kisses. He called me his "little ole sugar." In the swing on our front porch, he would sit alone, admiring the sunset.

His boys were wonderful fun. The arrival of Edward and Jamie in June of every year became an advent breathlessly awaited. When they came, our summer *began.*

Everybody liked them. Jamie was my age almost to the day. Edward, older, was a small boy, but what made him the interesting equal of those taller than he, such as my brother and his friends, was his skill at tennis. He was a class act.

We had always had a tennis court at the far side of the property, and on the first day after the boys arrived, with never a warning word to anyone playing there, my brother would take him out and introduce him, "our cousin from Tennessee," and Edward would wait his turn to play. He would amble onto the court. Toss for serve. Then: Wham! Pow! Wow! Soon all the afternoon crowd turned from wherever they were straying and began to watch. Edward was dynamite, a wonder.

As evening fell and the shadows of all the pecan trees grew longer, my father might show up from work with an enormous chilled watermelon in the back of his car. Between the house and the tennis court, under the trees, we had built a Ping-Pong table out of the casing for a new gin stand. On this table, when the older crowd took over the court, the younger ones, like me, would slap at the hollow white ball, hoping it wouldn't hit a crack where the table was nailed together and bounce back-

ward. Dismantled of Ping-Pong gear, the table was grand for watermelon cutting.

The best melons, known to weigh around forty pounds and to be so green as to seem almost black, were stored for chilling in the downtown icehouse as no refrigerator could hold one. Thump one with a knuckle, and a hollow sound would say it was ripe and ready. The granddaddy of all our knives had been sent for from the kitchen. ("Hold that knife away from you when you run!") Smaller knives were fetched as well, along with every last saltshaker.

All gathered around, watching as the great dirigible shape was readied for cutting—the ritual turned sacred and a hush would fall. The knife went in. One shallow cut straight along the length, then another, deeper one.

Jamie and I had long arguments. Is a watermelon red before you cut it? If a tree falls in the woods with nobody around for miles, does it make a sound? We were annoyed to learn there were no answers.

Leaning over on tiptoe, like the audience for some star performance, we could all watch as the beautiful monster let out an all but human groan and split in half, could see the crêpe-myrtle red of the chilled flesh, pushing close to the white rind, studded with black seeds (sign of a good one), and the oval of the seedless "heart," large as a football. We all but burst into applause as the split occurred, then crowded in for the juicy cuts that instantly smeared faces, stained shirts, and dribbled on bare legs and feet.

Dad was terribly proud to have given all this pleasure. My mother would have come out in the cool of the day, wearing one of her voile afternoon frocks, lace at the collar. She would also go to watch the tennis, still, amazingly, in progress. Edward would be out there, his shirt drenched with sweat, as one by one the town champions came to oppose him. My brother, a crack player himself, sometimes even won. Then, the last match over, they too would join us, warriors come in from victories in the field.

Everybody in town came down our road on those long summer afternoons. At other times, the bunch of kids my age and Jamie's would gather and hike through woods to a place called Shaw's Pond, a good three or four miles from town. It was a cold, clear swimming pond, spring-fed, shaded by pines, so that the water was always black. There was a rough pier there and a diving board, and in those days anyone who wanted to walk or drive out there was free to come.

Tiredness came with twilight. "Go take a bath before supper. Be sure and wash your feet." The cook would have left dozens of biscuits in long pans ready for the oven, and there would be ham or a mountain of cold fried chicken, with potato salad, sliced tomatoes and cucumbers, a wealth of peach preserves and blackberry jam, and tremendous appetites, much laughing and joking and good feelings, everybody cleaned up, the boys' hair slicked down with water. This was as good as it got.

Consider those four men—the Spencer fathers. If the McCains resembled Highland Scots, it would take Dickens to describe the Spencers. They had sharp noses and double chins, amiable faces but strong opinions. All but Uncle Louie, whose dark hair held its place, were bald, or getting there. When together, they would sit in a rough circle on interminable Sunday afternoons in the living room in McCarley or Carrollton, wherever they were. They would be in their brown business suits with vests, their good quality "low quarters," different from high-top shoes.

They would talk. But unlike the McCains, who thrived on exchange, not a one of them ever listened to the other. In fact, as Jamie and I have often recalled, they all talked at once. It was much like the chanting of some ritual in Latin, or a bunch of frogs on the edge of a pond. You never could hear what they were saying. Perhaps they were each on a different subject. They did not even look at one another. Some voices would rise above others for a moment, then fall back into the chorus. Only one thing you could be sure of: No one ever agreed with anyone else.

I believe all of them had revered their mother. I never saw her, but her picture shows her with long brown hair, upright, in high-cut dark silk, smiling with a firmly controlled friendliness. She gave birth to nine children, and in the nineteen years between their father's death and her own, she must have had her hard times bringing up the five who lived. Because times, beyond any gainsaying, were desperately hard.

The McCains also, along with so many other Southern families in those times, had very little money. (In fact, if any family was known to "have money," the immediate question, spoken or not, was, How did they make it? Where did it come from? The Snopses had yet to be invented to supply an answer.) The McCain plantation at Teoc was still mortgaged following the war, and so would remain until my father and my uncle combined to put it on a paying basis in the late 1940s. But the large property itself, the numerous black tenants, plus the prestige of relatives in distant places, gave my mother's family a higher social level than my father's, felt but never mentioned.

But family talk continued on both sides with prideful reference, and beyond a doubt the boys, my father especially, had adored their mother. The main quality he admired in women was sweetness, and he always said she was the sweetest woman he had ever known. When she developed tuberculosis, it was thought that another climate would help her improve. The older boys made up a sum and rented a whole bedroom compartment on a train out to Texas. My father, as youngest, was sent along as her companion.

They went to San Antonio and stayed there some months before she died. He never forgot the trip. At age eighty-eight, a lone widower, mentally crippled by a series of strokes, he used to recount to me for the thousandth time how he had brushed her long hair for her, holding it over his arm until every tangle was gone, and then helped her pin it up. "Do you remember her?" he would say, forgetting both when I was born and when she died.

I once in the early fifties drove my parents across the Southwest to spend Christmas with my brother and his family in San Diego. When we reached San Antonio, my father raced about seeing places he remembered from those long-ago times—the Alamo, Buckhorn Saloon, the river walk.

The Spencers had revered their father as well. Gettysburg and his amputated arm must have lived eternally in his memory, but I heard no stories he had passed down. Uncle Louie related that Grandfather had been present when Stonewall Jackson died, accidentally shot by his own men, but my uncle was so old when he told this, I had some reason to wonder if it could be true.

Our grandfather had invented a device for opening gates without alighting from a buggy. This, he figured, would save rural mail carriers many hours along the route. He had sent off for a patent, but automobiles were closing out buggies and the product was never manufactured.

They called him Papa. Though they all remembered the day of his funeral (it was raining), they felt it a pity that no one could remember where his grave was.

When I used to come home to Carrollton to do whatever was needed for my father in his last years, we regularly took the car and went searching all over Carroll County for "Papa's grave." We must have explored every tiny out-of-the-way cemetery in those hills, the big Buick easing in and out of unlikely places, but I think we never knew if this or that broken and mildewed fragment of marble was really his or not.

In one cemetery there was the grave of a tiny boy, Elijah Lee Spencer, born in 1891, four years after my father, who had scarcely made it to six months old. "My baby brother," Dad would say, for he remembered him. But there had been others: Julian, who had died at birth, Lou Ella, who lived only to age three, and Clarence Wilson, who lived scarcely a year.

Then there was Willie. As noted before, William Henry Spencer, the firstborn (1869), had simply left. Nobody ever knew where he went. He would have been a young man then. There were various sightings, usually somewhere out West, but no one ever heard from him and all leads proved false.

It was said of my grandmother that she would walk to the edge of the front yard each afternoon when the train pulled into the McCarley station, hoping that Willie would be on it. He never was.

Jamie says the true story is that Willie went out West and changed his name to Howard Hughes. Proof of this theory is to this date lacking. Another cousin proposed an elaborate explanation involving a severe sunstroke, which had produced amnesia.

My own theory is that such a disappearance comes of living near a railroad. The whistle sounds, the engine is heard from far away. Approaching, growing awesomely ever nearer and larger, it seems to bring knowledge of marvels it cannot speak to tell. Departing, it draws a young man's yearning to follow after it, as long as it can be heard.

On still nights in our country town, I used to hear trains on that very track, passing through driving rain, or darkness thick with summer heat, or frosty starlight. The feelings evoked were many, not necessarily the same as Willie may have had, but never failing to awaken. There is a little bit of Willie in us all.

Willie's departure left the four brothers—country boys who moved from that little railroad community out into the world of business and affairs. They had all planted, chopped, and picked cotton, had known farmwork, milking and feeding, plowing mules, and driving wagons, slaughtering and butchering, firsthand. They had worked in country stores and knew the value of products shipped in by train, bills and invoices from distant centers passing through their hands.

Uncle Ed wound up in Birmingham, a leading executive for Southern Railroad. Uncle Louie, while content to be with country friends around McCarley, built a new house, the finest for miles around, bought land in the Delta, and ended life better than well-to-do, a respected man of business.

Uncle Tom, aspiring to no great prominence, was a friendly "traveling man" for speciality advertising products. Our own house abounded in fancy shoehorns, leather-backed clothes brushes, calendars, and diaries, all stamped with our family name, as they might have been with names of businesses and companies if sold on his route.

His marriage to Mary Beard, on the other hand, was a great success. Perennially smiling at all who came their way, he and Aunt Mary took sly account of each other; to be around them was to feel shined on. They were never well-off, and their four children may have caused various anxieties. They were the only part of the family who lived in half of a house. It was over in Winona, a hill town to the east of us, located on the main-line Illinois Central and the highway to Memphis. The house had once been a church, now deconsecrated and turned into two spacious apartments.

I loved going there. When Uncle Tom was away on his selling travels, and the children, older than I, were away at school or work, Aunt Mary would sometimes invite me over to spend the night with her—"just the two of us," she would say. We would talk a blue streak—visiting, she called it—and eat suppers of chicken salad, hot rolls, iced tea, and one of her fancy gelatine desserts. Then we would walk up to the picture show. She had a slight, charming stutter, and my father criticized her fluttery ways, but to me she was fun to be with, fond of prettiness in life, the pleasure of living.

Uncle Tom had a weakness for miracle cures. Medicines said to cure everything from arthritis through constipation and asthma were always about to be produced from among the samples in his car. He once brought us something called Crazy Water Crystals, packaged from one of the many natural phenomena over in Arkansas. The crystals were supposed to cure any number of complaints when drunk dissolved in water, but the main thing they did was cause gas. My brother delighted in drinking large quantities and pestering everyone with the resulting explosions, which smelled. He thought this was terribly funny; I suppose we all did, except my mother, who thought it was coarse.

Stopping by for a visit one morning when passing through Carrollton, Uncle Tom asked my mother where I was. My mother laughed. "She's writing a book," she said, as indeed I must have been, up in the main living room, where it was quiet.

"I read a book once," said Uncle Tom. "I've forgotten what it was about. Something about some chickens . . ." He tried hard to recall but could not. His daughter May became a brilliant student and eventually a lecturer in history. He applauded all her work, and spoke of it with the greatest pride.

May loved him. After Aunt Mary's death he spent his time largely with her. Knowing he was probably in his last illness, she asked the minister to call. She had never once heard her father use a single word of profanity, but when the minister left, she bent down to hear what he was saying.

"Looks like the son of a bitch could have said a prayer."

8

RELIGION

OH, my God!

The entire family on both sides of our house were brought up as strict Protestants, believers in God, Christ, the Bible, the devil, heaven, and hell. All retained their early beliefs, except for Uncle Sidney, who was said to be an atheist, though no one exactly called him that. "He just says he doesn't believe in anything," my mother would explain, adding, "He says that but I don't believe it." She could not conceive of a world or a day or a minute in which her religion was not only totally there but also functioning on all cylinders. It was woven into all she thought, said, and did.

The Spencers were brought up Methodist, and were, I think, churchgoers, except for Uncle Ed, who claimed to tune in sermons on the radio. Uncle Louie was the main support of the Methodist church at McCarley. His daughter Virginia sang in the choir or played the piano, or sometimes both, just as my mother, if the organist did not show up, could be found at the little Presbyterian church organ, valiantly pumping away, playing and singing for both Sunday school and church.

Carrollton was crowded with churches. There was first and foremost to our way of thinking, since we had to go so often, the

Presbyterian church, white and plain (they liked everything plain), with cedars in the front, a white steeple, and a bell, its rope hanging down in the vestibule. The old front walk was brick, with moss grown in the cracks.

The hours on Sunday one had to spend in that church I scarcely would choose to consider to this day. Sunday school! Some good things could be said for it. We memorized Bible verses.

I always liked the cadence of the Bible. The verses we were taught stay with me still, especially as Miss Jennie McBride, our Sunday school teacher, was giving us the same ones in primary school. I loved hearing that the Lord was my shepherd. I loved also seeing the cards with pictures that were handed around, in that case pictures of sheep and a man in a purple robe with a tall shepherd's crook, carrying a little lamb. I collected cards like these. "Suffer little children to come unto me," said one. They were sitting in His lap. That would be nice, I thought.

Art was in short supply, one had to realize from going occasionally to the beautiful Episcopal church across the street, where there were images of a religious nature in the stained-glass windows and graceful carvings on pulpit and lectern. At the Presbyterian church the stained glass bore no images, and the light that came through the windows looked livid, as if bursting through storm clouds.

The center of attention was the chancel, and central to that, the pulpit, where the enormous Bible sat upon a white cloth with a single lily embroidered in golden thread. From up there came the interminable sermons. Some went on for nearly an hour. The shortest could generally be clocked to run forty-five minutes.

Once the church elders met and agreed that the minister, a lean, gray, long-faced man named Mr. Harris, preached too long. It was thought that someone had to give him the message. Dad was selected to do so. He called on the minister and let him know that his sermons were learned and contained fine thoughts but should be shortened. Mr. Harris then went the rounds and asked the other elders if they agreed with this. Everyone denied ever having considered such a thing. We were back to square one.

After services, what a joy to be back home! To squirm out of Sunday clothes, socks or stockings, tight shoes, scratchy petticoat, and, in later years, proper white gloves and the necessary hat. To leap into any old thing and grab up the funny papers. In summer to run around barefoot.

At Teoc there was yet another Presbyterian church, serviced by the Carrollton minister on off Sundays. It was an unadorned white building on a low hill, standing lonely in all weathers during the week, but on Sunday a magnet, drawing its members from all directions for services.

When our minister was at Teoc, we went to some other church, the first choice usually Episcopalian, though its pulpit was often empty as well, being served by the rector at Greenwood. Then we had to choose Methodist or Baptist, and usually took Methodist, since my father had once been one. The Baptist church, an imposing brick structure, stood along the main route from our house to our church. We had to maneuver through scores of cars parked there for services. My mother expressed weekly dismay: "The Baptists are taking the earth!" She felt a certain curious competition about other denominations, I guess because our congregation was always a small one. (Not so small as that of the Episcopalians, who were originally a handful, though they enjoyed some converts, suspected of trying to upgrade themselves socially.)

Presbyterians were known to be fanatically strict, upright to a fault, their Scots origins showing through in such traits as emphasizing "stewardship" (meaning money) and clinging rigidly to beliefs in predestination and eternal punishment meted out for no particular reason other than having been born. The sermons we heard were often on texts from the Old Testament. God's awesome judgment was always at the ready. Methodism seemed to me much kinder, but Dad took to Presbyterianism like a duck to water. It might have been invented with him in mind. He gave liberally to the church all his life, and the Carrollton church came to depend on his largesse so much that he could get his way about everything. There was nothing he liked better than that.

Taking me over to the Episcopal church was something I suspect my mother in later years came to regret. I fell for the Book of Common Prayer right off the bat. I liked hearing those well-phrased *brief* supplications instead of having to fidget through wearisome petitions thought up on the spot. One prayer especially that my mother praised was said each time we attended. Speaking of the Lord God, a phrase went: ". . . whose service is perfect freedom . . ." My mother would remark on this on the drive home. "It seems a paradox," she would say, "that service can be freedom. But if you think of it, it's true." This remains with me, and having long since joined up with that church, I say it often and think of her words each time I do.

In the back of the Episcopal church were benches for Negroes, and some at times attended. I found this remarkable from the first. "They" were never in our church at all, except that we had a Negro janitor to clean it. I don't know when I first questioned this and was told in an offhand way, "Oh, they have their own churches." But I was born questioning everything. I think I said that we might at least have benches. "They wouldn't come," I was told. "Not many of them are Presbyterians anyway." I suppose I may have said, "Why not?" and was finally told to hush. I was told to hush about any number of subjects I thought were discussable, but had to learn were not.

The above exchange from my childhood, when my curiosity met a gentle correction, in no respect resembled the kind of heated dialogue that would savagely spring up and gigantically bloom years later. Then, even an unspoken thought would be heard as loud as a gunshot, and a rage would foam, with no regret or second thought, up to the very chancel, engulfing the Bible as well if the Good Book dared to stand in the way.

But more of that later. In my early years, I could easily be argued down and would even accept whatever I was bidden to, because deep down I believed that God was in his heaven and our two families belonged to all that was good on this earth.

Every summer in Carrollton we had the tabernacle meeting.

The tabernacle was an open-air structure across Big Sand Creek. It had a wooden platform wide enough to hold a piano and benches for a choir, grouped on either side of a lectern. The denominations took turns inviting some silver-tongued preacher, or, if not a great orator, at least someone who could revive the flagging Christian spirits of the entire community. Revive meant revival. We all naturally had to attend, though I squirmed out of it whenever I had the slightest chance.

The meeting was always held in August. The crops were laid by then and whole families could come in to listen. The Baptists and Methodists were the ones who took to all this; they were ready for it. The Presbyterians did their best. We "brought in" the sort of democratic, easygoing divine who went down well with people in general; and the Episcopalians also cooperated, in a low-key, superior way.

But the real firestorm "reviving" was right up the Baptist/Methodist alley. The meetings may have started out low-key, but they rose up and began to walk about the third or fourth day and by the first week's end were fully charged and running strong. I don't recall any seizures or speaking with tongues or healing sessions, but I remember the rhythm of impassioned shouting from the platform, and repeated calls for coming forward to "give your life to Christ while time remains."

"While time remains" had a dual meaning: (1) life might end between one breath and the next and the unrepentant pass, right off the bat, into torment; or (2) Judgment Day might arrive, when Jesus would come to take over all worldly affairs. Jesus could do this at any given moment. It could happen next week, next year, tomorrow morning. It could happen *tonight.* There was a threat in everything. The message was *Watch out!*

Once, the Presbyterians engaged a real revival preacher, who went around doing nothing else, a pro. His name was Howard Williams. To our family's extreme good fortune, he came to hold the meeting the summer we had all planned a trip to the Ozarks.

Everyone in the McCain branch of the family was in on this vacation, one way or another. We had rented a house in Branson, Missouri. It was said to be cool there. Heat in Mississippi was so terrible in July and August that all the indoor strategies ever devised could scarcely do more than lower it by five or six degrees. Mountains in those pre-air-conditioning days seemed about the only answer, New England and Canada being too remote to consider.

My aunt Katie Lou was sent ahead by train with my brother to open up the house. The rest of us followed some days later: my grandfather, Uncle Joe and Aunt Esther, Annie, the cook from Teoc, my mother, and me. Annie had to ride in a different car, but we saw her at station stops. We were joined at various times that summer by different McCain relatives, went daily to a lake to swim and row a boat, took drives into the Ozarks, and felt that the weather was not as cool as advertised.

My father was back at home seeing to b'iness. It was during that period that the Howard Williams revival meeting shook Carrollton, Mississippi, to its very foundations. Nothing like it had happened before or would again. The stories were many.

For one thing, Mr. Williams was "charismatic," a term that was not used then. What we might have noted was that he was sexy and that the women who got worked up about that meeting were not altogether thinking of religion. He also, it seems, had a first-rate singer to lead the choir and congregation.

They came in pairs, these annual visitors, singers being only slightly less important than preachers. Whole choirs were formed—women's for the mornings, mixed for the evenings, children's for special numbers. The best singers from all the congregations joined in. The songs had to be the old ones everybody knew. To hear them in the night from home, where I frequently stayed, was to feel the whole night had become filled to the brim with their message.

Blood! It overflowed the music, drenched the clouds above, flowed in the creek that lay between our property and the tabernacle; it was not to be confined to veins, where it belonged.

In our church we periodically, four times a year, drank wine or (after Prohibition took firmer hold) grape juice from tiny crystal communion glasses held in hardwood trays and passed around by the elders. At Grace Episcopal Church, you went up to kneel at a railing and took a sip of the real thing from a silver cup. But these polite formalities, relating to blood, were minor little dribbles compared to revival-meeting blood that came booming through the songs like the Mississippi River at flood crest.

There is power, power, wonder-working power
In the blood of the lamb . . .

There is a fountain filled with blood, drawn from Immanuel's veins
And sinners plunged beneath that flood lose all their guilty stains . . .

Just as I am without one plea
Except thy blood was shed for me . . .

Mr. Williams, we were told on our return, would dress in a snow-white suit. In those hot, expectant nights, he would wait in back of the audience, out in the darkness, while the singer and choir worked the crowd. While the last verse was being fervently sung, he would come dashing in, run down the sawdust aisle, and leap to the podium.

Before the two weeks were over, many in town had wept and repented in public. They had openly confessed their sins. Those who managed to keep a cool-enough distance would remember having heard an earful. Suspicions were confirmed; whispered scandal declared out loud.

The tide swept on till the very day of departure, when a crowd gathered at the station to bid a tearful farewell. Still singing mightily, they thrust wads of money into hands and pockets of minister and singer. The train was held up for nearly an hour—one more prayer, one more song. More and more dollars changed hands.

I always wondered how they felt when the train actually chuffed away and gradually dwindled from sight around a distant curve. No secrets left and not much money either.

We missed it all, praise the Lord, being in Branson, Missouri.

9

THE OLD LADIES

ONE afternoon, when I was a little girl, my mother and I walked up to see old Mrs. Scott.

It was quite a way to go, from our house at the far eastern end of the rambling old Mississippi hill town, up through town and beyond to the west, up to the old Scott place. We reached the town square by climbing a slope up to the level of the school, then winding up beyond the school building and the Somerville house to the McBride house on the corner, then turning left, straight on to the courthouse square. Past the Merrill store and the old Stansbury place another climbing road took us up along a string of spaced-out houses. All were different, set far apart along the right-hand side of a concrete walk.

As house followed house followed house, it seemed the town was holding on, lingering, tenacious. There on the left stood the standpipe, a Tower of Pisa without leaning, soaring up above trees, both landmark and necessity. It held the town water supply, and was placed at this high point of terrain so that water, pumped up each day from the powerhouse down near the creek, could run downhill to supply the thirsty faucets of every household. Finally there was the turnoff lane to the old Scott place, the last before the town let go.

The house gave only a glimpse of itself to anyone passing, for it was set back from the road and reached by a lane flanked in shrubs and trees.

The Scott place was said to be the oldest house in Carrollton. It was once a stagecoach stop, I was told, on the road down to Jackson, Vicksburg, and Natchez. I remember a large rambling weathered house with a big porch running round about it from front to side, giving entrance by a side door. Ethel Vinette Wallace, Mrs. Scott's granddaughter, welcomed us. She had thick, dark hair.

We entered a large room with a fireplace. I saw a chair by a window and an ancient face all but lost in the setting of afghans, quilts, and throws. I held my mother's hand as she led me forward. "It's Mrs. Scott, Elizabeth. You must say hello." A tiny old hand reached out to touch me. It ran along my arm. "So this is Elizabeth." The face smiled. A small voice came up out of the pile of coverings. I remember it as a happy voice, brimming with a deep affection that didn't need to be stated. I sat down when I was told. I never said anything unless spoken to.

During the visit my mother's eyes would fill with tears. She was full of love for this old lady and the family, one prime reason being that they were Presbyterians. They were not only Scotts but also (by descent) Scots. Old Mrs. Scott's daughter had married a McEachern (pronounced McCahan). Mr. McEachern had built a house next door. It was phenomenal for its roof, which slanted down from a dizzy height at something as near the perpendicular as you could get and still slant. It was said that Mr. McEachern had wanted it that way to let rain pour down so rapidly it had no chance to leak.

I was happy walking home in the late afternoon beside my mother. The way back was downhill and easy. Mimi (as we called her) liked to walk and went along briskly, always in her dark coat with the rich silver fox collar, her worn leather handbag in one hand, my own hand in the other.

I was delighted when these visits to old ladies were over. I could talk, I could chatter. I didn't mind that Mimi laughed at me. I could skip and pick up whatever caught my attention. I could ramble on and off the walk. The sidewalks were marked all over town by hoofprints because cows had got out before the cement was dry and had wandered around in the night.

Clouds overhead were like marvelous long scarves of deep pink. We were favored with glorious sunsets over our town. They seemed spread out above the whole county and made the sky seem bigger than any that ever was.

That day I was wearing a pair of brown kid gloves with a small button at the wrist. I can still recall the thin leathery texture of them, like a second skin, and how, when we reached home and I took them off, my mother noticed that my nails needed to be trimmed and did so, with tiny curved scissors. I recall this because my nail-biting started later for what now seems a good enough reason.

Money.

We were always worried about it, as my father had to work very hard to get it, to keep it or use it well, and so the talk ran to it, and it brought its usual freight-train load of anxiety along with it. In my father's talk, just as in that of my mother's family, men were said to "amount to something" or to be "worth something," but he invariably meant work and its cash reward.

My mother's idea of reward, however, lay in doing the right thing. She had a real love of this notion of life and of the people included in it. Outside her own family—home, children, and kin—she kept herself going on the thought of the loving approval of those friends her own mother had held dear.

Another old lady remains involved in my early memories, though there was never the need to visit her, as she was there all the time, right next door. Her name was Miss Henrietta—a real "Miss," for she never married. She lived with her brother, Mr. Dave Welch, in a one-story antebellum house that had been left her by her aunt, a certain Miss Baugh. Miss Baugh had beautiful furnishings, many of which eventually came to us, given out of gratitude.

Miss Henrietta, like many people in Carrollton, had a "place," this being not a productive Delta farm but a little property up in the hills, about two or three miles from town. Whether she rented this farm or not, I never knew, for though she was all but impoverished herself, she was always giving things away. An entire family named the Littletons lived out on the property. There were any number of Littleton children, and Miss Henrietta used always to be carrying them anything she had to spare by way of clothing or food. My aunt once gave her a warm sweater as a Christmas gift, but said, "Just tell me which one of the Littletons you want to have it, and I'll give it to them."

Miss Henrietta was a small lady who bundled herself in an old coat in winter. A belt wrapped around her, midway down the coat at something no one could call a waistline, made her look like a little walking bale of cotton. Each day she would go trudging off up the hill to go to town, where she had a small store just half a block downhill from the courthouse square. I was always welcome to come into this store and sit perched on the counter talking to Miss Henrietta, who would give me a peppermint out of the glass-front display case.

To increase her income from practically nothing to a pittance, my father got her appointed agent for an insurance company. He would go up and spend a number of hours with her each month, to get her books straight, for I think she had no idea how to keep them properly. She kept house, after her fashion, with her brother. They were our only neighbors. The house, with its long concrete walk, broken by steps in pairs and threes, sloping down to the front gate, and flanked by cedars, had a lovely pillared porch and triangular podium above the broad front steps.

During the Civil War, a ship named *Star of the West* had been sunk by Confederates on the Tallahatchie River near Fort Pemberton to block passage of the Yankee forces who were moving on Vicksburg. A large pier-glass mirror framed in ornate gold leaf had been among the things salvaged and had somehow found its way into that house. It stood leaning in the hallway, prominent from the moment one entered. I would see myself coming in, first thing, and when wearing a frock, could see if my petticoat showed.

The Welches, sister and brother, were always happy to see me. They liked having children around, first my brother, seven years older than I, and soon to be sent off to an academy, then myself, always ready to have someone to trail around with and talk to.

Mr. Dave had spent time in Guatemala, where, it was said, he had had mining interests. Though he almost never spoke of his time in that distant place, he kept woven baskets that had to have come from there, and large prints of native men chopping what looked to be sugarcane, native women carrying baskets loaded with tropical fruits on their heads. He had wicked-looking curved knives racked up on the wall of that back room.

In the parlor, however, all was ornate, with antique mahogany, cherry, and walnut furniture. There was a framed black-and-white picture I remember of horses in a field, frightened before a storm. Black clouds were rolling, lightning streaked the sky. The horses' heads were flung up, their eyes and nostrils wide, manes streaming in the wind. I thought it must be of Scotland because there were mountains in the background and what looked to be open ground with low bushes—heather, perhaps. I liked hearing names of things in far-off places.

Mr. Dave raised prize tomatoes, grew watermelons, made hot tamales he would bring across to the fence in autumn. They were wrapped in corn shucks and warm to touch, pleasantly spicy to eat. He also had two Airedale dogs, named Pet and Beauty, and kept a tall horse, blind in one eye, called Ole Dick. His saddle was a modified Western one, with two girths, and to have me with him, he made stirrups from the cinching straps of the second, so I could ride behind the cantle, holding on to him if he went fast. We would go through town and out to the Littleton place. He was a small man with a tubby stomach and white hair. He rode very straight, very proudly.

One spring afternoon we turned from the main road and followed a path to a stream. It was running clear and shallow over a bed of flat stones, colored orange, brown, white, and gray. Mr. Dave dismounted and helped me down. He left Ole Dick with bridle hooked to the saddle horn. He sat down in the cool willow shade and took off his hat. It was summer. I took off my shoes and waded in the blissful water. The stones were smooth. We did not talk about anything. The horse cropped grass. The water murmured.

Mr. Dave usually spent his days doing work around the garden while Miss Henrietta was uptown minding the store.

Back in those days no one thought so much about driving everywhere. From earliest times I can remember we always had a car, but often we walked to town or to visits, and many people walked all the time. They did not think of it as anything to complain of. Mrs. Elizabeth Glenn was one lady I never knew well (she was not in our church), but she was remarkably present in our town, as she walked in such an exemplary way, her back straight, her head high, the way Mr. Dave rode. How not to find this an example? ("Stand up straight," they told me. "Look at Miss Elizabeth Glenn.")

Miss Flora Nelson, a redheaded lady who was known to be highly educated and could carry on talk of books and current affairs with whoever wished it, could be seen hustling along, bent over; her thoughts got there before she did.

Miss Recie Gee, of one of the richer families, had a built-in chauffeur, one of her sons, to drive her places. In the South, married or not, a lady can be Miss Something all her life.

Miss Edith Erskine (another real "Miss") never went out at all, that I can remember. She lived up on a hill in an old house, again furnished, as I was to learn, with beautiful things. Her means of visiting was the telephone. She was the town's one and only Roman Catholic.

During the summer revival meetings, when people got filled up with religion and were enjoined by some visiting Bible-pounder to "bring someone to Christ," thoughts turned to Miss Edith. Miss Edith was ready for them. She told them on the telephone that she took her orders from the pope (just what they were expecting to hear) and that the pope himself had been on the phone to her that very morning. The pope had told her she could play cards—it was not a sin—and that she could also have a glass of sherry and smoke cigarettes.

Thus did she conquer. I suppose whoever had called her may have resolved to pray fervently for her salvation, but she may have scared them off even that. A small, thin, upright lady, Miss Edith wore her head in a silk scarf, wound round like a turban. Her sister drove over from Greenwood, a large town nearby, to take her to Sunday mass.

Miss Edith decided one day to give a children's party. I believe this occurred before I started to school, but I am not sure. The memory has a "before school" feeling to it—that is to say, it is one of those timeless ones. For to me, Miss Edith Erskine will always be there. Through all the ages she will go on talking amiably on the phone to the few she favors, dismissing those she does not, deciding on one day, though not on others, that she will give a children's party.

I remember being dressed to go. I always had a party dress. It usually had some fancy touches, a ruffle, smocking, a lace collar. I was expected to wear patent-leather shoes with a cross-strap that buttoned, and white socks. I would be reminded to speak to Miss Edith about how nice everything was, and to eat whatever was offered.

Miss Edith did well. She had decorated with crêpe-paper streamers and had looked up some games she had us play. They were mainly quiet games, such as turning children into animals and asking them to act out what they were. A pony would trot around the room, a dog would bark, a cat would mew, a lion would roar.

Another game was called Go In and Out the Window. We always played this at children's parties, but I have never found anyone outside Carrollton who has heard of it. You form two circles, boys in one, girls in the other. One must move to the right, the other to the left. Clasping one hand after another you begin to sing, weaving in and out. "Go in and out the window," you sing, then some words I forget, but always ending, "For we have gained the day." Stop! Does some adult drop a handkerchief? One child is always left without a hand to catch. A single ring forms. The left-out child must stand in the middle and the song changes. A boy must go to a girl (or vice versa) and kneel. "I kneel because I love you" goes the next, followed by "I measure my love to show you," arms extending wide as a tape measure, "for we have gained the day." These two drop out and the round begins once more.

In repeating familiar phrases I never stopped to question their meaning. So I learned dozens of Bible verses in Sunday school without any notion of what they were saying. To me the *sound* of words, like those in this chant, was what the words were *about*. I think now that this game must relate to some courtly dance or ritual come down from long-ago days. Later on, when I came to memorize poems, I loved their sound so much I hardly thought of what the words meant.

That day at Miss Edith's, when the games were done, we were led into her dining room, where we had some sort of punch in small glass cups and were allowed to cut a cake. There were cookies, too, and we all said what we were supposed to at the door and walked out down the long front walk between the cedars. Other trees enclosed that property high on its hillside corner and masked the house from being seen by any but those who climbed up from the street to go there.

The hill is still there, and though the house either burned down or was demolished years ago and another, new house now stands on the property, itself hidden by its high position on the hill and by trees, I still persist in thinking of Miss Edith and her house as right where they always were, and will remain. Where Carrollton is concerned, it seems a desecration to recognize that time exists at all.

What Carrollton ladies lived on, many of them, like Miss Edith, from fine old families, some of them widows or unmarried ladies, was often a mystery. It is to be supposed that most everyone was not as well-off as they would have liked to be. They had manners and a standard of behavior that suggested they should never give a thought to money. Discussing it was not approved of. "Po'-mouthin'" was downright common.

Many had "places" in the Delta. The hill towns were older than the Delta ones. Except for river towns like Greenville and Yazoo City, the Delta through the ages had held little but swamps, mud, mosquitoes, moccasins, and alligators. Cleared land there was incredibly productive, but who would want to live on it? Better to buy it up, hire it out to an overseer, let black labor plow it, plant it, and harvest it, and take the annual proceeds. "He's over at the place" was as familiar a phrase, almost, as "He's gone fishing."

Whether they had money or not, the ladies of Carrollton maintained a way of life. I think of huge old bathtubs with ball-and-claw feet, of multiple petticoats, silver dresser sets, talcum powder, and afternoon naps. Recipes and ladies' auxiliary meetings. Dictums and preferences. "I would never walk by the barbershop; no telling what those men might say." "Don't go in Tardy's store in the morning or in Herbert's in the afternoon—the sun shines right through your slip." "Always speak. Even if you don't know them, you must always speak." "Don't ever laugh at country manners. You might hurt somebody's feelings."

"Remember who you are. People will criticize your behavior. It will reflect on your home." "Don't scratch. Even if you're sitting barelegged on Miss Beaurie's horsehair chair, don't scratch. . . . And don't bite your fingernails, either."

It all seemed gentle and soft, loving and tolerant, but it was as rigidly bounded as a high-security prison, guards on the watchtowers, dogs trained for hot pursuit. Manners and behavior, what one wore and did not wear, what talk was allowed and what was never to be mentioned (though everybody knew it). Gossip and confidences. I was warned against "talking out." Whatever I said would be repeated; a secret might get loose, or worse, an attitude toward a secret might not be the accepted one, and might suggest that our family was in some way "out of line."

Of course, even among the ladies there were the rule breakers. Gossip sprouted up around them like weeds. They pretended to be all they were supposed to be, and everyone pretended that this was indeed true. So a state of what was pretended by everyone gradually took over, and the hidden life marched right along its way as the life of expected propriety spread over it, like the caterpillar ride at the county fair.

Among the more fabulous old ladies of Mississippi, Mrs. Lizzie George Henderson ranks high. She actually lived in Greenwood, but had inherited Cotesworth, the home of her father, Senator J. Z. George. This beautiful home, in all its white-columned classical simplicity, is set just outside North Carrollton, on rolling farmland.

Between Carrollton in the hills and Greenwood in the flat Delta comes Valley Hill, a wonderfully steep drop from hills to Delta, a correspondingly steep climb from Delta to hills.

Miss Lizzie George had an electric car.

I saw her once gliding around in this thing. I was in Greenwood with my mother and my aunt, who had doubtless gone over to shop at Fountain's ("Big Busy Store") and must have had some business, too, around at Whittington's (dry goods), for I remember she was passing down Main Street near the Leflore County Court House. She was sitting up straight and wearing a hat with a veil tightly drawn down under her chin, and my aunt said, "It's Miss Lizzie George Henderson in her electric car," and my mother said, "Don't stare."

Staring is not a good thing—I was always being warned against it—but how was one not to? When I hear of the "horseless carriage," I think of the vision I had that day (I think I did well to stare, for I never had it again); I do not think of country carriages, obsolete but in my childhood still around, stuck away in the barns of relatives, with the stuffing coming out of the cushions and the glass broken out of the lamps, which we used to play in by the hour with the Negro children, crying "Giddy-up" and "Gee" and "Haw" to our hearts' content, and never going anywhere.

No, indeed; I think of Louis XVI, had Franklin or Jefferson or somebody visiting the court devised a motor for him on a dull afternoon when wearied of piquet and high diplomacy and all those ladies, and how, having had the royal coach brought round and the horses sent back to the stables, they might have hooked it all up and then advised, "Why don't you just try it out around town?" Versailles is a flat town too.

The lady herself was remarkable; if not royal, she would do until the real thing came along. She was just sitting there, being borne along at a decorous, silent rate, her back straight as a plumb line, not noticing anyone (though if she by any chance *did* look your way, you'd better speak, and quick); she touched no visible control (or so in memory it now seems).

And she was famous. She owned a huge Victorian house in Greenwood. It was carefully shuttered, with a butler and others engaged in intricate service. She had the whole of it painted mustard yellow, and as if that weren't enough, what with the electric car, to produce a state of marveling and bemusement in Greenwood, which has not to this day gone away, she also had a carillon installed in the courthouse and gave it to the city. For years you could be reminded of her by the chimes, which rang every fifteen minutes. (They recently broke down, but are being repaired.)

She came out to Cotesworth and caused a Spanish walk, in variegated colors, to be run the long way up from the drive, right to the pure white façade. But she did not come out in that car. She tried. But I don't think she succeeded. The story has it that she got halfway up Valley Hill and then couldn't make it. The royal coach did not have the power for that relentless climb, and Mrs. Henderson in her electric car passing through the courthouse square is one vision at least that Carrollton missed. *Dommage!*

I do not really think we should dwell on how she felt, this handsome and imperious woman, so much the mistress of all she surveyed, when she stalled on Valley Hill, and stalled, and stalled again. There are moments of defeat too painful to consider.

Of course, she had her long car back in Greenwood and her chauffeur—maybe even two or three cars and chauffeurs—but that's not the point. It was not a practical matter, after all. And the weather was probably hot, and there were all those petticoats, those stockings, those layers of various embroideries, and the long sleeves and the mitts, and the face powder and the hat and the veil. For we do know she would never have ridden through our little hill town without being flawlessly dressed. Ladies of her sort measured up to an excessively high standard, which they themselves had set; and any defeat they encountered was, as it should have been, a matter of terrain.

10

FIELD OF BATTLE

MISSISSIPPI, summer of 1861. There was excited talk in the parlor. The Confederacy had won a great battle against the Federal forces at Manassas, presaging general victory and an early end to the hostilities. General Beauregard was mentioned so often as leader and hero that a little girl who was crawling about on the floor got to her feet and stood firmly before the company. "My name is Beauregard," she said, and from then on would never answer to any other name.

I wonder what people in Carrollton, Mississippi, find to talk about now that just about everybody who remembers Miss Beauregard Somerville has passed away. She herself died many years ago, during the thirties, but that in no way stopped her being spoken of as a living presence.

On the rainy winter evening when we got the news of her death, my father "went up there." She lived only a short distance from us, up the street that led to our house, past the school campus. The house still stands, its construction definitely in the grander post–Civil War manner, gables on the roof and bay window in the façade, a wraparound front porch, stained-glass windows. A long concrete walk ran up to sheltered front-porch steps. The steps from the street were imposing beyond the ordinary, flanked with scrolled cement, like banisters. Elephant ears were always growing in the round plot in the front yard. They spread out their great green fronds, where raindrops would linger, large and white as pearls. You walked softly as you entered the house, minding your manners. You would be judged if you did not.

She was not a "Miss" any more than her name was Beauregard. Beauregard was soon shortened to Beaurie and the Miss attached early on, I can only imagine.

Miss Beaurie was my grandmother McCain's best friend, and when my grandmother died, Miss Beaurie lived on as a supervisory spirit to my mother and, by extension, also to us. She dispensed the authority of her approval or disapproval to any number she judged worthy of notice: approval was assumed, thus infrequently mentioned; disapproval was dreaded, and was often called into play. The times were changing; danger was everywhere.

Miss Beaurie was the custodian of manners. She couldn't have invented them herself, so she must have got them from those before her who knew best. Wherever the rules came from, the families she accepted had to obey them. All their children and kin came under her surveyance, and were fair game for comment. Was a girl seen uptown without stockings? "I must speak to Nora," she would say. "Augusta must not go uptown looking like that." She never wished to hear about a lady smoking, but if she did, watch out! Drinking for any woman lay beyond the pale: banishment was the only result possible.

My mother related how, as a girl herself, she was once afflicted with persistent hiccups, which went on without stopping for two whole days and nights. The family tried every known remedy: dropping a cold key down her back, sudden scares, having her swallow down a glass of water while holding her breath. My grandmother was about to call the family doctor, but was inspired to say to my mother: "Beaurie told me what you did." The hiccups stopped instantly.

Did some girl begin to go out with a young man "not of good family"? The telephone call would come; the mother or aunt or both would be summoned. Miss Beaurie served tea to her visitors, I believe, or maybe coffee, teacakes as well. I don't remember vividly, perhaps because I never liked going there.

The house did make an impression. It was lined with wood panels and rich wallpapers. The carpeted stairs ran up from an entrance hall into a mysterious upper floor I was never asked to explore. The dining room was on the right, to the left the parlor. This was the best room, I suppose, as there were open windows, and more light coming in.

The lady herself sat in her long black skirts, summer and winter, with her high lace collar and her fan. Long widowed—I never heard very much about Mr. Somerville, whoever he had dared to be—and childless, she knew better than anything else exactly how to be Miss Beauregard Somerville.

My mother always dressed me carefully for these visits. I had to wear my black patent-leather shoes with the strap that buttoned, my white socks. My dress had to be clean, pressed, starched in summer, and never too short. (The Keenan girls wore short dresses; you could see their panties; I expect their mother got her reprimand.) My proper dresses, however, were never long enough to come between my bare legs and the horsehair upholstery on the straight-backed chair. I would sit, sternly forbidden to scratch, and wonder how long before we could leave. My feet dangled down with nothing to rest on.

I don't remember Miss Beaurie's face as well as I wish I could. Long, vertical wrinkles, a pursed mouth, and gray-black hair with curls across the brow, features whitened with rice powder. Feet in neat black laced-up shoes, small crooked hands. The high lace collar. The cameo. A stream of talk directed at my mother, who always supplied the right answers, the appropriate questions, the expected nods.

Although my mother all her life professed the deepest admiration and devotion to Miss Beaurie, I do wonder how much of all this was what she thought she ought to feel. I remember that when we finally paid our respects and left—walking decorously down the front walk to the steps, turning at the obligatory place to wave goodbye up to where she would be at the door, ready at a precise moment to return inside—once freed, once out of sight, my mother, a young woman herself back then, might begin to sing or skip and talk in a carefree way, holding my hand as we went along down the sidewalk back home, and laughing at one thing or another. Once by some unaccountable chance we found two kittens by the sidewalk, no houses near. She picked them up mewing, put one in each pocket of her coat and took them home. One died (I smothered it, I think, with affection), but the other lived.

Miss Beaurie had a car and a chauffeur. She made long trips to Memphis to shop. These took place, I believe, twice a year, and only a chosen one or two of the ladies she regarded highly were asked to go along. I remember the car well, for Miss Beaurie was what is known in Mississippi as a "big Presbyterian," and for church functions I was sometimes allowed to be driven in it, along with my mother. "We'll just drive up to the church together" was what she said by telephone. I don't quite recall why we had to go with her. We, too, had a car, though you could never be sure something wouldn't go wrong with it. It had to be started from the outside with a hand crank and sometimes would not turn over.

Once or twice I traveled to Memphis with the ladies in Miss Beaurie's superior auto (I also went on trips there with my parents). That auto! It must have just missed being a limousine. I believe it had jump seats like old-fashioned taxis. Often I had to sit by one of the ladies. (I could not ride backwards long without getting carsick.) One of them wore a fur piece, a black silver-fox fur with its head left in place, wicked glass eyes set in above its narrow snout. The mouth was hinged to bite the tail, right above one paw—the paws were also intact—and so to hold the pelt in place. The lady would open and close the mouth, pretending it would bite me. I never liked this. One of the other ladies was a marvel for the long black line that I observed coming down the side of her mouth. I asked my mother about it, and was told she "dipped," meaning took snuff, but not to mention it. She believed her habit to be secret, though everyone knew it.

"Everyone knows it, but don't mention it." It was easy for any child to see how such a regulation about one thing extended to multiple others.

Through the years, stories emerged. The Somerville cousins,

girls of a likely age and beauty, came to visit from Oxford during my mother's girlhood. They came for a "house party" at Cousin Beaurie's. When I taught at the state university, which is located at Oxford, I became friends with Ella Somerville, who many years before had been one of these girls.

"Oh, yes," she recalled, "we were invited for buggy rides with the unmarried young Presbyterian minister. Cousin Beaurie doted on him. I think one of us was supposed to marry him. And of course you knew about the murder."

"Murder!"

"Why, yes, in those days, she would tell about it. You must have heard it."

No, I hadn't but I heard it then. It began like so many stories: It was a dark and stormy night . . .

Envision for a moment Carrollton, Mississippi, an old town of scarcely five hundred souls, set off from any railroad, run through by one narrow, graveled highway. White houses perch on hills surrounded by enormous yards; crooked roads wind outward from the town square, out from the courthouse, past the jail, churches, law offices, post office, out from shaded walks on the square that went past the hardware store and drugstore, bank and lodge hall. On a rain-lashed night, who or what could or might or would want to wander around there? Somebody did.

A man, neither young nor old, no kin to anyone, came out of the rain and knocked at a door. It was the side door of the Somerville house. He was asked in.

Only Miss Beaurie and her husband were there. She always had a cook and a butler, also a gardener and the chauffeur, whose name was Fox. But none of them lived there, and evidently no one other than the two Somervilles was present when the knock came.

The nameless man was appreciative and cordial, well-mannered and full of the right things to say. Food was brought him and dry clothing, and he was invited by these Christian folk to sit and talk. What the talk ran to has not been passed down, but the Somervilles were impressed enough and good-hearted enough to ask him to stay the night. One can know the phrases: "You can't go back out in this sort of weather. You'll be sure to catch pneumonia!" One can all but hear the heavy pounding of rain on the gabled roof, the rumble of thunder, the shifting pressure of wind. Cozy within, they talked of beliefs so devoutly held, the Bible, the church. Oh, yes, the guest himself, despite his misfortunes, was a believer. The family Bible appeared and passages of encouragement were read aloud. There were prayers. The Somervilles opened up a guest room. How happily they must have gone to bed.

But in the night they heard noises from below. The two of them got up and crept down the stairs. Their guest was in the dining room relieving them of the family silver. He was putting it in a sack. Evidently there was enough light to see by, for nothing was done to disturb what he was up to. Their cousin Ella remembered and told me what it was Mr. Somerville took up for a weapon, but I have forgotten. Maybe a poker? A flashlight—one of those bold, eighteen-inch-long nickel-plated monsters, with a wheel-like enlargement at the head? No, to the best of my belief, Miss Beaurie herself held the flashlight and beamed it on the thief at the appropriate moment. With poker or tongs, gold-headed walking cane or whatever was handy, the guest in the house, the unfortunate Christian believer come in from the cold, was bashed in the head and brought down on the dining room floor, silver cutlery falling all about him, stone dead.

I asked my mother if this could possibly have really happened the way I had it from Ella. She evinced no surprise or regret. But then it was a long time later.

"Oh, yes," she said. "They hated it mighty bad. Of course, Mr. Somerville never meant to actually kill him."

"But then what happened?" I pursued.

"What do you mean, what happened? They buried him."

"Wasn't there any inquiry, any inquest? Didn't anybody ever know who he was?"

"No, they never found out," she said. "He wasn't from anywhere around here."

"Wasn't from anywhere around here." Key phrases like this

extend infinitely into the social order, of no help at all to a nameless stranger.

Of the trips to Memphis when I went along I recall less than I would like to claim. The ladies talked a great deal, but it was not the kind of talk I was interested in. I do remember Fox, the chauffeur, though. In good weather, Fox would efficiently arrange the isinglass windows so that we could get fresh air without being blown apart. If it rained, he would halt the car, get out, and snap them all in place. Fox himself was a well-built tan-colored man, exquisitely polite, and well trained in helping ladies in and out, in being on time to the second.

Memphis, our major shopping town, was all of one hundred and thirty miles away on Mississippi roads that well into the late thirties were completely unpaved. Tennessee had pavement; when we bounced across the state line, everyone sighed with relief. In Mississippi there were dust, curves, hills, and tiny towns to pass through. One of these was called Polk. Miss Beaurie had discovered a filling station in Polk with a sandwich shop that made excellent sandwiches. We would select what kind we would like—chicken salad or ham—and Fox would take the list inside. The sandwiches eventually came out in a bag, each wrapped separately in wax paper, and were distributed. A thermos of iced tea came open. Cups were passed out. These were our "refreshments."

In Memphis we stayed at the Gayoso, which Miss Beaurie for some reason preferred to the Peabody. Hotels to me spoke of adventure, though of what sort at that time I could not say. The hotel lobby was fascinatingly paved in small hexagonals of white marble, as was the bathroom. And there were big white towels and soaps wrapped individually and a strange enticing smell.

Underneath all the shopping and talk, I lived a small but intense life of my own. I liked to pass through the revolving doors, go to the desk with whoever asked for our key, mount upward in the elevator, follow the carpeted hallways. Trailing the ladies through the streets from shops to department stores, I ogled at window displays and marveled at Mr. Peanut, who strolled about the main business streets advertising Planters Peanuts. His helmet was an enormous peanut shell painted with a face. He wore spats and carried a walking cane. I think my mother took me to the picture show one evening but I fell asleep.

It was understood that on the way home from Memphis Fox was to be granted the favor of going by his sister's house. She lived in the black section of Memphis, and we would regularly stop before a small low house with a fence around the front yard. Fox left us to sit in the car while he passed within the house carrying a large bundle. "Fox brings presents for his sister," Miss Beaurie would explain with approval, "and she always remembers to send some things back for his wife and children." The things sent were all in a large box, which Fox deposited in the trunk of the car. I don't recall that we ever saw the sister. However, Fox resumed the trip without comment. He was not the talkative kind of servant who invited questions.

Years later it came to light that Fox, season after season, had been running whiskey into the dry state of Mississippi in Miss Beauregard Somerville's car.

When my parents were away, I was sent over from the school to Miss Beaurie's house to eat dinner—"dinner" meant the midday meal. I had to sit at table with her and with whatever relative might be staying there. I answered questions that were addressed to me. She gave me a fine enough lunch but insisted that I drink hot water out of a china teacup. Some idea of hers made this the perfect thing in winter for the digestion. If she said it, you had to do it.

The rustle of taffeta. Long skirts in hot weather or cold. Petticoats. Black shoes. High lace collars. And no one to doubt that she was right about everything.

She had a greenhouse covered in glass at the side of the house. It was the only one in town. In winter it was nice to venture in there, especially if the day was sunny, but in summer it was unbearable, stifling. One summer a hailstorm rudely smashed many of the panes.

Miss Beaurie had a butler, whose name was Aaron. Long after she died, he showed up at our house one day. He was slight, stooped, light-colored, and, like Fox, not talkative. He had considerable dignity and used no wiles on us, simply was there and, in some inexplicable way, ours. We were expected to find work for him, to provide. We did. He did some garden work for my mother and whatever odd jobs could be found for him. He ate there, received clothes, and was paid the meager going wages of that time. He was with us until he grew too old to work, and then, in his last illness, my mother went up and nursed him, she said, meaning, I suppose, that she brought him what food he needed and saw to it that he was sheltered and comfortable. He asked her once for a fruitcake at Christmas "to put in his trunk." She made it for him, with the others she cooked each Christmas, and he did, I am sure, as he said, store it in his trunk for eating a little at a time.

The edicts of Miss Beaurie thus continued through many years and lives. You did what was expected of you, in the way it was expected for you to do it. Ella Somerville in Oxford had much of this same nature. In her last illness from cancer, she received her visitors in the hospital, I am told, propped up in a splendid negligée, conversant and interesting as if in her own parlor, where I had been welcomed so many times.

Carrollton was part of the Oxford Somervilles' past. Their mother, a Vassar, had come from there. Though the old Vassar home had fallen into disrepair and at last disappeared, it had stood on the highest hill in Carrollton, where also stood the standpipe. Ella and her sister Nina Cully used to joke about owning our town's water supply. Connections are what you'd better have in Mississippi in order to mention anything.

The night of Miss Beaurie's death my father, as I said, went up there. "Sitting up" with the newly dead was the custom in those days. When one group had served out a sufficient number of hours, others would come in to stay, and so on through the night. My father came home late. "She left you her diamond," he told my mother. My mother burst into tears.

It seemed the gift of the diamond was not altogether based on old family friendship, though certainly that was the major part of it. Miss Beaurie had a place over in the Delta. My father, being well-known as a good businessman, had given free advice to Miss Beaurie through the years. I don't know if he went so far as to interview her managers, or personally see how well they attended to their work, but he knew what she should be realizing on the farm, and could offer a firm hand if needed, and help her with expenses. She was recognizing his services, as well as the long tie with our family, by this legacy. She was doing, as usual, the right thing.

At the time of Miss Beaurie's death, a curious detail emerged. Searching through her house for some necessary article, my father opened a closet door and hundreds of small empty paregoric bottles fell out on the floor. Paregoric was used a lot in those days for easing pain. It was measured out by the teaspoonful in a small amount of water for swallowing down. What painful health problem was going on beneath all those skirts and petticoats, with those arms and legs never exposed, that long neck sheathed in lace? Or was it another sort of pain? Paregoric is also a derivative of opium.

Miss Beaurie's diamond was an exceptionally large one. My mother had it set with her engagement diamond, which my father as a young man, before he met her, had bought for fifty dollars from a nameless wanderer who had ridden the rails down from Memphis and needed cash. This one, too, was large and fine, well over a carat, and the pair looked well when mounted together.

All links join the world, or did join in the world where I grew up. Once when driving through the South, my husband and I noted a sign in northern Virginia that indicated a battlefield nearby—Bull Run, or in other words, Manassas. We drove to see it. I recall it vividly now—a treeless long green meadow, sloping upward toward a cresting hill.

I thought of Beauregard: General Pierre Gustave Toutant Beauregard, C.S.A. *Beau regard* . . . beautiful glance.

How easy to visualize him, his ornate New Orleans name worn easily, the noble head, the straight bearing. He holds his fine horse firmly reined beneath him—arched neck, ears forward, rich mane and tail furling in the breeze. See him so poised at the crest there, looking outward on his field of victory. Nothing is before him now but the sweep of tall green grass, bending softly in the light wind. The moment is one of triumph and beauty and silence. There are no dead.

11

SOME OLD GENTLEMEN AND OTHERS

MR. Walter Johnson was a singular citizen of our town. I've no idea where he came from. He was just always there. He was an elder in our church, white-haired, with longish white mustaches and a sonorous voice, which I remember because elders were often asked during services to stand up and lead us in prayer. I connected him with the smell of paint because, among other lines of work, he was a painter by profession and would come down to the house whenever we needed painting done. I was scared of him.

For a time, he ran a picture show down across the bridge in north town. It was in a large shedlike building among the business houses, and had long wooden benches like the tabernacle, also sawdust floors. We went there to see silent movies. Someone up front banged on a piano, making appropriate noises during chase scenes, when horses galloped, or crooks ran from the law down city streets, or cars sped over country roads. Frilly sentimental tunes came flowing out during love scenes, reunions with long-lost children, the dying of loved ones, and other such occasions. We used to sit on our hands, leaning forward, enthralled. These were the days of Rin Tin Tin, the valiant police dog, and Silver King, the marvelous white horse. There were serials. Pretty girls got tied to railroad tracks with trains chugging around the bend about to cut them in two. Cars shot over the edge of a cliff. Then you had to wait till next week to see how they got out of one predicament and into the next.

The movie house was useful for other occasions, one when I was five being an appearance of Santa Claus. My mother took me downtown to see Santa Claus and there he was, bright among a crowd of other children and their mothers, wearing a red suit, trousers stuffed in boot tops, and thick white whiskers, handing out candy and small wrapped gifts. I was scared to death and cried. A devout believer in everything I was told (I had been crushed with disappointment to come across some dyed eggs before Easter, thereby having to face the fact that the Easter Rabbit was not real), I began to cling to my mother and resist going up for a gift. She whispered to calm me, "It's just Mr. Walter Johnson." But I was scared of him, too, and the combination with Santa Claus, with whom he must have had some secret contact, only added to my terror. I wanted out of there.

Another time, when I was walking alone on a town street, I saw come toward me a figure clothed head to toe in a flowing net. His face could no more be seen than his feet. He seemed a god, a daylight spook, a boldly walking apparition. In one hand he held a mysterious large globelike object that seemed to be warping, then shrinking and swelling. I wanted to run, but only had time to step aside into the ditch by the sidewalk. That, too, was Mr. Walter Johnson. What he was holding was a swarm of bees. He knew how to rob hives; so he must have known bees as well as Santa Claus. It was said they did not sting him.

He must have been married more than once; he had a daughter named Vivian, who I understood was a missionary. Once she came home to visit and it was reported that she dumped the church records down a well, but her motive for doing so was not told me. The latest Mrs. Johnson, estranged, was named Lavada, but was known as Mrs. Newspaper Johnson because she delivered the Memphis paper, *The Commercial Appeal,* all through town. She came daily, wrapped up summer and winter in something with long sleeves, and wore black mitts to protect her hands from newsprint and the weather, also a hat.

Since our house was at the end of our road, with nowhere to go beyond it, she would sometimes come in and sit down for a talk with my mother. Once she did this very thing while Mr. Walter Johnson was up on a ladder in the far back of our glassed sunroom/side porch, which ran the entire length of the house, doing some painting. My mother sat listening to Mrs. Johnson and hoping neither Mr. J. nor Mrs. J. would notice the other, as they apparently never had any wish to be in the same world with each other, let alone the same room.

Inevitably, there came a paralyzing moment of recognition. Mr. Walter Johnson tilted on his ladder while Mrs. Newspaper Johnson jumped up and rushed out the door. No word had been spoken. Mimi claimed to be sorry it had happened but could not help it. What on earth they were so permanently mad about, I never undertook to ask. Maybe she was scared of him, but then why marry him? He was a scary man.

Two other old men were Mr. Philip Shaw and Mr. Lee McMillan. I think they lived together, or shared parts of a house in the country, several miles out of town. Shaw's Pond, where we swam so happily in the summer, was on Mr. Philip's property.

Mr. Philip was blind and walked along tapping with a cane. He made scuppernong wine and brought it to the church in a jug to use for our communion service. Since some heavy drinkers were on the church roll and might someday attend, as they were always being besought to do, and as the ladies were always praying that they might, the fear grew that if prayers were answered, a real binge might get launched out of that one little swallow of communion wine. So grape juice was substituted. I pointed out that the Bible said Jesus drank wine, but was told it was unfermented, that is to say, the equivalent of Welch's grape juice. I did not believe it.

Mr. Lee McMillan had fought in the Civil War. Some evenings he would walk down all the way to our house and sit on the porch talking to my grandfather, loudly cursing everything about Yankees and the North. President Lincoln was a favorite subject of hatred, also Reconstruction, and a long list I forget, though I heard it all a few times, having gone to bed in the room inside the front-porch windows. I can still hear my grandfather's admonishing voice, like a chant: No, you don't mean that, Lee.

No, Lincoln was not such a bad man. If he'd lived it would have been a different story. No, the Yankees mainly did what the generals said. No, Lee, you don't mean that.

But the hatred had got to saturation point in Mr. McMillan and I suppose it never cleared out. A good many when I was growing up had this sort of fervent despising of all things Northern in the grain of their natures. It was passionate, and ran a neck-and-neck race with religion.

We sometimes drove out to the Shaw place for grapes and other produce. It was a big house, country-style, with a wide yard and the usual cedars. A long way into town for two old gentlemen to walk. I would ride my horse alone out that way on some days. I can think of the road now, bare, smooth earth with beautiful foliage on either side, and the many times the two old gentlemen must have walked it, one tapping his way along, the other marching to martial thoughts.

The Shaws were an exceptionally fine family with connections at the state university at Oxford, where one had been a noted professor. I remember the Shaw house in Oxford, an upright brick structure, reached by steep steps from the street and overlooking a sharp drop into a gulch where heaven trees bloomed in the spring.

Several children, I among them, are playing in the hayloft of the barn. Hide and seek? Burying someone alive? Suddenly from below, one of the bigger boys, James Edgar Turner, high-school age, comes charging out of nowhere. He climbs up the barn ladder. He has a large fruit in his hand and a knife. "A quince," he says. "It's a quince." He cuts off small slices. Hands go out for them. Then he cuts a larger slice and, smiling down at me, says, "That's for you, you helped me . . ." Helped him where? I don't know. I am proud to hold the fruit, take his notice, eat.

The barn is where the mules are and the cattle. Bill, our handyman, comes to build fires in winter, to milk every morning and evening, all year round. He tries to teach me milking but my hands are not strong enough and the cow, peacefully munching at the stall, knows better. She won't let go. He lets me mix her feed—cotton-seed hulls and a cup full of mustard-yellow meal stirred in. She munches in a leisurely way, nuzzle pushing my hands aside. Cows have four stomachs—I have been told that. I carry a large aluminum cup. Bill squirts in some warm milk, foaming, and I drink it. My mother's voice calls from the porch across the back yard. *"Amos and Andy!"* It's my favorite radio show. I run in through the cold. All of us gather at the radio to listen and laugh.

My father wants me to be a tomboy. He wants me to shoot a gun. I graduate from a BB gun to a .22 rifle. I do target practice and am not bad. A shotgun—.410 gauge—is next. I walk around the property aiming and shooting at birds and squirrels. I think I want to kill anything that moves.

My head by then is full of Tarzan books. I yearn to swing through the trees and leap down on the backs of unsuspecting lions far below. Without a doubt I would know just how to conquer. I have read all about it. Finally, I hit something. A jaybird. I follow after the fluttering creature. There it is, bleeding a little thin blood, down among the leaves in a little ditch. I feel like crying. I want to take it home and splint up its broken wing. But its head is broken into as well and so is the flesh of its neck. Its eye is still open, glazed, disbelieving, frightened. I have to kill it, not leave it to suffer. Oh, no! Somehow, I finish the job. That's all it was—a job. I hated it.

Guns and I about parted company then and there. But no, Dad says next I must learn to shoot a .20 gauge. All women should learn to shoot. Out in the garden, he hands me the gun. It's relatively small, single shot. He has several .12-gauge guns that look too heavy for me to heft. "Hold it to your shoulder. Aim high." I get the nerve from somewhere to pull the trigger. The roar explodes in my head. The kick is so strong I land on my back among the tomato plants.

I will be a disappointment, as my mother is already. Fishing she will accept. Hunting leaves her in despair. "Those pretty things!" she cries, feeling no triumph at a brace of quail with bloodstained feathers, a sack of stiff gray squirrel carcasses.

There were doves and ducks as well. Whatever the pity of the fresh kill, when cleaned and cooked they were good to eat. We had to mind not to break a tooth on shot. Deer came later. Their proud heads were mounted, their glassy artificial eyes looked out at the world. Neither Mimi nor I liked to see them there. "Poor things," we said. But the hides make wonderful bedside rugs.

Hunting is a sign of dominance. Too busy in his younger years, now with money and leisure worked for and earned, my father became a passionate hunter.

Roller-skating right through town with schoolmates on afternoons after school, we used to see Lawyer Tandy Yewell asleep in his office window. One warm day he was leaning way over in his swivel chair, all but falling out. We had curled-up paper whistles with feathers on the end, and skating by would blow the feathers into his ear. By the time he jumped awake, slapping at what might be a wasp, we were gone. Scolding at home when foolish enough to tell about it . . .

A spring day with a riot of dogwood and redbud in the woods. We played in the yards and romped through gullies eroding in back of houses, broke off flowering branches and ran through town, shouting something about a dogwood show. My mother telephoned my father at work. He came home early. There ensued a family gathering of the severest kind. Had I lost my mind? What did I think I was doing? "Celebrating spring" seemed an answer as silly as the crazy mood had been. Though at the moment it had seemed the right response to a world so wildly beautiful with heavenly sight and smell.

Horses.

The first wasn't even a horse. She was a gray donkey named Phoebe. Phoebe would let herself be bridled, but never had a saddle. Someone would lead her out from the barn lot into the yard for me and I would get on her back. She would walk a few reluctant paces but the minute she was alone with me she would stop dead still and go to sleep. I would sit on her, growing angry and frustrated, beating my bare heels into her ribs. Phoebe slept on.

I would slide off, go in the house, wake my mother out of her afternoon nap. "Phoebe is 'sleep," I would say. Mimi was not so happy about this, but would get up, put on her dress and shoes, come out into the yard and find a long limb fallen from the pecan trees. I would get back on Phoebe and she would wham the limb over her rump. Then she would throw it down and go into the house to resume her nap. Phoebe would trot a few steps down the drive, but as soon as the door closed, she would stop dead still and go to sleep again.

Following the brief dominance of the calico who ran away came the era of Dan Patch. He was named for a famous racehorse, whom he did not resemble. He was way too fat, a low Shetland with a heavy mane and a large stubborn head. He had a broad, flat back, and a number of us could get on him at one and the same time. In summers we would simply park him under a chinaberry tree where we were busy building a tree house, and use him as a stepladder, climbing up to hand boards and tools up to those among the branches above.

He was never in a very good humor and at times would take a notion to walk away a few paces and separate the lower workers from the upper. We would have to dismount and lead him back.

He was my pony, however, and I spent considerable time with him. I would ride him down in the pastures that lay in front of our house, reaching toward the creek bank, and take him also into our woods, where I would sometimes go with a book to read in private. He seemed to be patient, but once for no reason he turned and bit my bare leg. I wore the precise shape of his enormous teeth in purple bruises for weeks.

Stabled among mules in the barnyard, Dan Patch would steal their food, and when they turned on him to kick him, he was so low the kicks would go over his head, as he knew they would. They couldn't hit him. But positioned to great advantage down below, his own kicking leverage was superb. He battered them ruthlessly in the belly.

I would ride him across the bridge down to north town. My father in those years had a Chevrolet business there. Its wide showroom space was all cement floor, sectioned off at the side for the office where Miss Willie Moore, his perky redhaired secretary, sat at a desk. I would ride Dan Patch straight into the showroom to say hello. One day when I wanted to go to the drugstore, Miss Willie told me to hitch the pony there, she would watch out for him. On my return, she was surrounded by

an inch-deep pool, her face as red as her hair. The salesman, the mechanic, and my father spent that whole day trying to keep straight faces.

There were horses later, usually two or three, nothing so remarkable, until Cousin Ernest Spencer from Jackson began sending good Tennessee walking horses up for me to enjoy. These were fine animals, and I wished for a life where there could always be a horse or two to turn to.

There is something soothing about being able to get on a horse and ride out of town. They go best on country roads, hard-packed dirt without gravel. Trees and bushes go by, and open fields. They like to ford streams that are not too deep, and stop midway across for drinking, nudging aside whatever trash may be in the way. They also will drink at well troughs. They enjoy water. If alone, you can talk to them and they listen, or seem to, ears flicking back. There is real companionship.

Throughout the fall from September on, the cotton gin went pounding. It was a sound all from the South of that era will remember as a part of the air they breathed. Dad owned a gin in north town, and after school I played in all its parts and divisions throughout the lingering summer heat that refused to let go.

The wagons would line up, sometimes for a half mile, loaded to the top railings with cotton picked by hand in the hill farms out from town. With the tall white load looming up behind, the mules looked small and patient as they waited to move forward. Someone was perched up top to drive, and there was usually a small boy sound asleep on a lofty bed. This slow progress led to the big suction pipe, two feet across, which drew the cotton up into the vortex of the gin. There was every year the story of the little boy who slept through it all, but had his hat sucked up in the process.

Above, the floors were throbbing with the beat of the machines, the noise so loud you could not be heard. Finding someone to speak to with confidence of who he was would be hard anyway; all were covered with fleecy lint, as though just out of a snowstorm. They had whiskers they had never grown and heads of white hair, were frosted all over like cakes, but waved at me and swung me bodily aside when I got in the way.

Three gin stands stood on revolving circles of flooring. You could see the picked cotton coming into the first, metal teeth working through the first process of combing out the seeds, discarding the trash. And in the last, what joy to watch the pure white cotton emerge. Waved out in silent generous bunches and batches by polished wooden blades, combed, pure, almost shining, a docile triumph, the end of so much hope and labor. *Cotton. Here I am!*

The press then descends on that gorgeous fluff. Down it comes with authority, pressing and rising time and again, until the blades shed out the last shreds, and all the motors in the building hush down to a muted throb. The gin stand revolves on its base. I ride it round. Around the new birth, the hemp baling drops in place from above. Flexible metal bands gird the whole.

Then, sudden release. They open the frame—out she comes. Four, five, or even six hundred pounds in one package, code-painted in purple letters, ready for weighing on the outer platform, for tossing down to lower levels with all the others, bouncing in to find a place. The same wagon that had brought in the load might be down below to carry it away, the mules waiting, the driver seated low before an empty bed, a hatless little boy perched beside him. But other bales stayed, sold on the spot, ready for taking to the compress.

Falling from above, the bales always landed in irregular piles. I would climb over them, these soft boulders, bulky, with a musty fragrance that stays with cotton fabric, wherever it appears.

A small house across the drive from the gin was the office. Farmers went there to settle up, and Cot Sanders, Dad's right-hand man through the years, would be within, back of the ledgers. This was the business end.

But in the other direction was a large building connected to the gin by a long metal pipe. This was the seed house. Once detached, the seeds were valuable, yielding cottonseed meal, cottonseed oil, cottonseed hulls. It was mysterious, gloomy, in there, with a huge gray mountain of seed hulking in one corner, and long draperies of dust hanging from lofty rafters.

It was quiet, immense, cathedral-like. I used to feel poetic, and loved burrowing into the seed mountain, half-burying myself, though it must have been as stifling as a quilt in July.

One day I heard a distant rattle which quickly turned into a roar. Seed in a deluge poured from the gin pipe. I was peppered all over, half-buried, and had to struggle free. I never told. It seemed a silly thing to do, thinking poetic thoughts in a seed house, and those friendly men who, up at the gin, tossed me around like a minuscule bale would certainly have told my father he'd do better to keep me at home.

12

THE DAY BEFORE

WHEN I started to school, my grandfather and the neighbors next door—Miss Henrietta, Mr. Dave, also another brother, Mr. Dick, who sometimes stayed there—took a great interest in the event, so important in my life, and tried to do everything they could think of for me. One bought me a lunch basket; another planned just what should be put in it, and Miss Henrietta had made me a book satchel out of green linen with my initial embroidered on it in gold thread. Somebody even went uptown to the drugstore where the school books were sold and got me a new primer to replace an old one, still perfectly good, which had belonged to my cousin. And there was a pencil box, also green, with gilt lettering saying PENCILS, containing: three long, yellow Ticonderoga pencils, an eraser—one end for ink, the other for lead—a pen staff, two nibs, and a tiny steel pencil sharpener. My grandfather laid the oblong box across his knees, unsnapped the cover, and carefully using the sharpener, began to sharpen the point. After doing one of them and dusting off his trousers, he took out his penknife, which had a bone handle, and sharpened the other two in the manner that he preferred. Then he closed up the box and handed it to me. I put it in the satchel along with the primer.

Mr. Dave, having made a special trip uptown in the August heat, came in to say that copybooks were not yet on sale as they had not arrived, but they could be bought for a nickel from the teachers on opening day. "Here's a nickel right now," said Mr. Dave, digging into his trousers' pocket. "*I'll* give her one," said my grandfather. I was spoiled to death, but I did not know it. Miss Henrietta was baking ginger cakes to go in my lunch basket. I went around saying that I hated to go to school because I would have to put shoes on, but everybody, including the cook, laughed at such a flagrant lie. I had been dying to start to school for over a year.

My grandfather said that the entire family was smart and that I would make good grades too. My mother said she did not think I would have any trouble the first year because I already knew how to read a little (I had, in fact, already read through the primer). "After that, I don't know," she said. I wondered if by that she meant that I would fail the second grade. This did not fill me with alarm, any more than hearing that somebody had died, but made me feel rather cautious. Mr. Dick called me all the way over across the calf lot to his house to show me how to open a new book. I stood by his chair, one bare foot on top the other, watching him while he spread the pages out flat, first from the center, then taking up a few at a time on either side and smoothing them out in a steady firm way, slowly, so as not to crack the spine, and so on until all were done. It was a matter, he said (so they all said), of having respect for books. He said that I should do it a second time, now that he had showed me how. "Make sure your hands are clean," he said. "Then we can go eat some cold watermelon."

I remember still the smell of that particular book, the new pages, the binding, the glue, and the print combining to make a book smell—a particular thing. The pencil box had another smell altogether, as did the new linen of the satchel. My brown shoes were new also, a brand called Buster Brown. The name was invariably printed above a picture of a little round-faced child with straight bangs and square-cut hair who was smiling as though he was never anything but cheerful. Certainly I didn't look like that!

Could I wear my new tennis shoes to school, and if not new ones, then old ones? My mother said no to tennis shoes of any description, and when I proposed going barefoot, she said not to be crazy. My grandfather said I had to mind her. I felt that he was only saying what he had to. My parents never seemed as intelligent as my grandfather, Mr. Dave, Mr. Dick, and Miss Henrietta.

After dinner that day it was hot, and when everybody lay down and quit fanning themselves with funeral-parlor fans because they had fallen asleep, some with the fan laid across their chests or stomachs and some snoring, the two Airedales that belonged to Mr. Dave had running fits. If a relative was visiting, or any stranger to our road, which was a street that didn't go anywhere except to us and the Welch house, they were liable to get scared to death by those Airedales because the way they sometimes tore around in hot weather, it looked as if they had gone mad. It was something about the heat that affected their brains and made them start running.

It all happened silently; they would come boiling out of nowhere, frothing at the mouth, going like two balls of fire, first around Miss Henrietta's house, then up and down the calf lot between their house and ours, then all around our house, finally tearing out toward the field in front of the house, where, down among the cotton and the corn, they would wear it all out like the tail of a tornado. Eventually the foliage would stop shaking and after a long while they would come dragging themselves out again, heads down and tongues lolling, going back to where they belonged. They would crawl under the house and sleep for hours.

We had got used to their acting this way, and though it was best, we agreed, to keep out of their way, they did not scare us. The Negro children used to watch them more closely than anybody else, saying "Hoo, boy, look a-yonder." White people had sunstrokes or heat strokes or heat exhaustion—I did not ever learn quite what the difference in these conditions was, and don't know yet. Dogs had running fits instead.

The Airedales were named Pet and Beauty, and only Mr. Dave, who owned them, could tell them apart. He took their fits as being a sort of illness, and as he loved them, he worried about them. He gave them buttermilk out of dishes on the floor and got them to take cobalt-blue medicine out of a spoon, holding their jaws wide with his thumb, pouring in the medicine, then clamping the jaws shut right. It must have tasted awful, for the dogs always resisted swallowing and tried to fight free, their paws clawing the ground, heads lashing around to get away and eyes rolling white and terrible. They could jump straight up and fight like wild ponies, but he always brought them down, holding on like a vise and finally, just when it seemed they weren't ever going to, they would give up and swallow. Then it was all over. I never knew if the medicine did them any good or not.

They had one of their fits that very afternoon, the day before school started. We had a friend of my aunt's from out in the country who had stopped by and been persuaded to stay for dinner, and she saw them out her window and woke everybody up out of their nap. "Those dogs!" she cried. "Look at those dogs!" "It's all right!" my father hollered from down the hall. "They've got running fits, Miss Fannie," my mother cried. "It's not rabies," she added. "At least they don't bark," said my grandfather, who was angry because she had waked him up. He didn't care much for her anyway and said she had Indian blood.

I don't know what I thought school was going to be like. It was right up the road, and I had passed the building and campus all my life, since I could remember. My brother had gone there, and all my cousins, and still were recognizable when they returned home. But to me, in my imagination beforehand, it was a blur, in the atmosphere of which my mind faltered, went blank, and came to with no clear picture whatsoever.

After I actually arrived it was all clear enough, but strange to the last degree. I might as well have been in another state or even among Yankees, whom I had heard about but never seen. I could see our house from the edge of the campus, but it seemed to me I was observing it from the moon. There were many children, playing on the seesaws, sliding down the sliding board, drinking at the water fountains, talking and running and lining up to file inside to the classrooms. All of them seemed to know one another. I myself did not recognize any of them except occasionally one of the older ones who went to our tiny Sunday school. They stopped and said, "Hey," and I said, "Hey." One said, "I didn't know you were starting to school." And I said, "Yes, I am." I went up to a child in my grade and said that I lived down that street and pointed. "I know it," she answered. She had white-blond hair, pale blue eyes, and very fair skin, and did not look at me when she spoke. The way she said "I know it" gave me to understand that she probably knew just about everything. I have seen sophisticated people since, and at that time I did not, of course, know the word, but she was, and always remained in my mind, its definition. I did not want to go away and stand by myself again, so I said, "I live next door to Miss Henrietta Welch and Mr. Dave and Mr. Dick Welch." "I know it," she said again, still not looking at me. After a time she said, "They feed their old dogs out of Haviland china." It was my turn to say "I know it," because I certainly had seen it happen often enough. But I said nothing at all.

I had often lingered for long minutes before the glass-front china cabinet on its tiny carved bowed legs, the glass, not flat, but swelling smoothly forward like a sheet in the wind, and marveled to see all the odd-shaped matching dishes—"Syllabub cups," Miss Henrietta said, when I asked her. "Bone dishes," she said, "for when you eat fish." There were tiny cups and large cups, sauce bowls and gravy boats, and even a set of salt holders, no bigger than a man's thumb, each as carefully painted as a platter. It was known to me that this china, like the house itself and all the fine things in it, the rosewood my mother admired, the rose taffeta draperies and gilt mirrors, had belonged to the aunt of the three Welches, that certain Miss Baugh, dead before I was born, who had been highly educated and brilliant in conversation, and whose parrot could quote Shakespeare.

I did not find the words to tell any of this to the girl who knew everything. The reason I did not was that, no more than I knew how to do what she had so easily accomplished in regard to the dogs' being fed out of Haviland china—which had often been held up to the light for me and shown to be transparent as an eggshell—I did not know what value to give to what I knew, what my ears had heard, eyes had seen, hands had handled, nor was there anything I could say about it. I did not think the child was what my grandfather meant by "smart," but I did know that she made me feel dumb.

I retreated and was alone again, but a day is a long time when you are six and you cannot sit opening and closing your new pencil box forever. I went up to the other children, and things of the same sort continued to happen. In the classroom I did as I was told, and it was easy. I must have realized by the end of the week that I would never fail the second or any other grade. So everything would be all right.

From then on, life changed in a certain way I could not define, and at home in the afternoons and on weekends I did not feel the same. I missed something but did not know what it was. I knew if I lived to be a thousand I would never do anything but accept it if an old man fed his dogs out of the best china or if a parrot could quote Shakespeare. At home when I looked up, I saw the same faces; even the dogs were the same, named the same, though they, as was usual, had stopped having fits once the nights got cooler. Everybody, every single person, was just the same. Yet I was losing them; they were fading before my eyes. You can go somewhere, anywhere you want—any day now you'll be able to go to the moon—but you can't ever quite come back. Having gone up a road and entered a building at an appointed hour, I could find no way to come back out of it and feel the same way about my grandfather, ginger cakes, or a new book satchel. This was the big surprise, and I had no power over it.

Life is important right down to the last crevice and corner. The tumult of a tree limb against the stormy early-morning February sky will tell you forever about the poetry, the tough non-sad, non-guilty struggle, of nature. It is important the way ants go one behind the other, hurrying to get there, up and down the white-painted front-porch post. The nasty flash and crack of lightning, striking a tall young tree, is something you have got to see to know about. Nothing can change it; it is just itself.

So nothing changed, nothing and nobody, and yet having once started to lose them a little, I couldn't make the stream run backward, I lost them completely in the end. The little guilt, the little sadness I felt sometimes, was it because I hadn't really wanted them enough, held on tightly enough, had not, in other words, loved them?

They are, by now, nearly every one dead and buried—dogs, parrot, people, and all. The furniture was all either given away or inherited by cousins, the house bought by somebody and chopped up into apartments; none of this can really be dwelt on or thought of as grievous: that is an easy way out.

For long before anybody died, or any animal, I was walking in a separate world; our questions and answers, visits and exchanges, no more communicated what they had once than if we were already spirits and flesh and could walk right through each other without knowing it.

Years later, when home for a visit, I was invited to play bridge with some friends and on the coffee table saw a box of blue milk glass, carved with a golden dragon across the lid, quite beautiful. "That came out of the old Baugh house," my friend said. She had got it in a devious way, which she related, but had never been able to open it. I picked it up, not remembering it, and without my even thinking, my finger moved at once to the hidden catch, and the box flew open. It wasn't chance; I must have once been shown how it worked, and something in me was keeping an instinctive faith with what it knew. Had they never been lost then at all? I wondered. A great hidden world shimmered for a moment, grew almost visible, just beyond the breaking point of knowledge. Had nothing perhaps ever been lost by that great silent guardian within?

A Note of Caution

The above was a story, a sort of "given," like "A Christian Education." When I wrote it, I believed it all happened, though I had changed Welch to Thomas and Miss Henrietta to Miss Charlene, her second brother to Mr. Ed. Miss Baugh became Miss Bedford. But now I think of it, I wonder if all these little events—the lady coming for dinner, staying to take a nap afterward, the dogs having fits—really did actually occur on that same day. It seems now a mixed bag of memories has all gathered here for me, like marbles in Chinese checkers when you tilt the board, rolling up against the time barrier, the preschool timelessness about to let go into time.

Take it as you will: it was all there and real at one time or another. I'm no good in this particular instance at saying exactly when.

Anyhow, the bell has rung. It's time for school . . .

PART TWO

School

13

MISS JENNIE AND MISS WILLIE

In a small town that's been there for ages, some people look out and some look in. I now can see that the in-lookers far outnumbered the out-lookers. As for myself, I mainly just looked around me.

Photographs of those days powerfully back up my memories. From my birthday in late July onward, the sun became so dominant there was no way even to think about it. Grass parched, people squinted at the camera, everybody under twenty, it seems, went barefoot. This was before air-conditioning. Houses could offer wide hallways with doorways front and back, and some had breezeways, others screened porches, good for keeping out bugs (if not all mosquitoes), nice for naps, and a necessity for sleeping at night.

As children, we played incessantly—in trees, in the creek, on the tennis court. We sometimes must have talked about what those late summer days were moving toward, sure and steady as the sluggish drift of the creek.

The schoolhouse was a two-story redbrick building with cement steps up the front, set on a wide campus with swings and sliding boards to one side, basketball courts to the other. It was right up the street from our house, scarcely a five-minute walk.

Once there, you had Miss Jennie. She was Mrs. McBride,

really, a widow, but was always called Miss Jennie. As everybody, young and old, had always had her as their first teacher through grade three, she drew a large part of the tremulous awe out of entering the new state of being. She was gentle, firm, and quick, with eyes that twinkled at you from behind round glasses with black wire rims. Her hair, black and gray, was drawn back in a knot. Happy to be with children, she was often smiling. She wrote in a large, clear hand, dealt with ruled tablets and crayons of different colors and blackboards. Penmanship, numbers, the alphabet, with letters large and small. Next, reading aloud, memorizing, multiplying. Three grades in one room. How did she manage? She and God would know the answer, certainly not I. We sang. Everything was all right in our Father's house (pointing upward), and it was joy, joy, joy (circling hands) over there.

We came into the room (quietly, if you please) while she stood at the open door. We marched out in files, following a small flag. Mounting upstairs to chapel once a week, we would go in rows carefully stair-stepped by height, and all the older grades laughed as we paraded to our seats. Down in our classroom we also marched in and out for recess, and raised hands for "being excused."

Discipline? Stand in the corner with your face to the wall; write "I am sorry" ten times on the blackboard; stay in after school; or, coming up to the front, have your hand bent back, palm up, and get five slaps with a ruler. That last is the only one I remember catching; it didn't hurt the hand the way it hurt the pride. I sat through arithmetic trying not to cry.

Miss Jennie taught us the alphabet by Bible verses: "A good name is rather to be chosen . . ."; "Be ye kind one to another . . ."; "Create in me a clean heart . . ." Asked for Bible verses in other groups, some of the smart boys used regularly to quote "Jesus wept." Miss Jennie was ready for that one. Not even when we got to "J" did we get to say "Jesus wept." Her verse began with "Jesus," all right, but was longer.

Everybody's parents approved of Miss Jennie; every child respected Miss Jennie; Miss Jennie was beloved. Faced with her greatest test, a woman who wanted a crazy, obstreperous child to learn with the rest, she let the child in, gave her a seat, and tied her to it. I used to see her writhing out of the corner of my eye. She once ran berserk and pushed me down on a brick walkway, cutting my lip. Miss Jennie sent upstairs for my brother to take me home, bleeding and bawling. I still have the scar.

Retired from teaching, Miss Jennie lived quietly in her house up near the Presbyterian church, where she regularly taught the little children in Sunday school, right on to the end. She let out rooms, I understand, to difficult old ladies, who must have been worse than any first- or second- or third-grader, but could not be enjoined to stand in a corner, much less smacked with a ruler. A new primary school building was named, of course, for her; there was never any way for Carrollton, Mississippi, ever to let her go. There was no way to think of Carrollton without her. Even to let go of her at the end of the third grade was bad enough. I got scared all over during July and August. The only cold spot in the world was at the pit of my stomach. No longer to know precisely one's place in line, to get "Well done" for saying the memorized verse, to write correctly the names of Columbus's three ships, to march behind the little flag.

Who would teach us next? It was a real question because the Depression had struck and the school (I remember many worried conversations when my father returned from meetings of the school board) had hardly the money to operate.

During my last year in Miss Jennie's room, two new students entered late in the year. They had been living somewhere else. They were sisters named Meade Marian and Frances Keenan. Meade was always laughing, while Frances, quieter, had a good many thoughts of her own. They wore their dresses much shorter than we were allowed to do, rather like paper-doll children, skirts flaring up to the lace on their panties. In winter, when my mother would sometimes walk up to meet me after school, she would see them and say, "I don't see why those children's legs aren't freezing." Maybe they were. Their air said that style was more important than discomfort. They knew what they were doing. The Keenan girls.

Late in August of that year we heard that the school had employed their mother, Mrs. Keenan, to teach grades four and five. "Lucky to get her" was my mother's judgment. "All that family is smart and Willie especially." She had come back from somewhere else to live there; her husband, a man no one seemed to know much about, was employed elsewhere.

She was a member of a leading Carrollton family; her grandfather, or so I recall, had been a U.S. senator, and other relatives of a decidedly alert disposition could be met among us or heard about from elsewhere. One of her cousins, Mr. John M——, drove cows back and forth to pasture for his wife, Miss Annie, but if you stopped to speak to him, it was politics, current affairs, or history he'd read you a lesson on. All that sort of thing was going on in his mind (though not neglecting the cattle). He let his hair grow long and never went to church.

I first saw my new teacher on a street uptown, walking on one of those sidewalks that, owing to erosion and road-scraping, had got much higher through the years than the roadbed. I was riding in the family car. It was August—hot, blazing. She had on a bright blue dress with a flounce, almost to her ankles, and her long hair was caught up in a careless "bird's nest" way, puffed out over the brow. All this looked interesting. She walked with her head down, rapidly, the flounce swinging. "There goes Willie Keenan," my mother said. "I bet she's burning up in that dress."

In early September we got our new books from the druggist who always kept them. On the appointed day we entered our new room with caution, took seats, and waited. She had arranged her desk. No playthings, cutouts, colored stars, or maps. Books. And a few flowers. The hair was the same as I'd seen. The voice was nothing we were used to. It came from other places. For one thing, speaking to any one girl, it said "darling." We never used that word. Full of endearments—"honey," "sweetheart," "precious," "baby," "sugar," even "sugarfoot"—we had read "darling," maybe heard it in the picture show, but didn't say it. Mrs. Keenan did.

She was wearing glasses: horn-rimmed, they slid down to the tip of her nose and stayed there. Her hair, rich brown laced with gray, frothed over her brow. I think now she must have been pretty in a taken-for-granted way. She tapped the books, our texts. We would use them when we could, she said, but she had no use for much that was in them. (Astounding rejection.) "Take literature, for instance," she went on. She paused. I must have heard that word before, but didn't remember where. We had lots of books at home. We were always reading or being read to. But I don't remember hearing it called "literature" before. She said she had ordered another book for us. It would come.

From then on, awakened somehow by the words she had used, the sense of her return from far-off places, the climb up from young school to real school, the difference in her little girls' dresses (one was now across the aisle from me), I could not wait for that book. Never had a Sears, Roebuck order been so fervently expected. I remember it still. It was a narrow, tall volume, bound in pink paper: *One Hundred and One Best Poems.* It may be (I don't know) that she was never trained as a teacher. Laws about degrees in education came later. Mrs. Keenan would correct our arithmetic and give a passing hour to grammar and geography, but what she really liked was reading poetry. After lunch-hour recess was over, she saw us through some routine chore before she would open the pink book and read. I guess the poems were way over our heads. There were Shelley's "Ode to a Skylark" and "Ode to the West Wind," Kipling's "Recessional" and "Gunga Din," "Abou Ben Adhem" (I think she skipped that one), Browning's "Incident at a French Camp" and "How They Brought the Good News from Ghent to Aix," also Macaulay's "Horatius at the Bridge," even some Edgar Guest (skipped also). One began "I saw the spires of Oxford / As I was passing by / The cold grey spires of Oxford / Against a cold grey sky." This troubled me as I had been once or twice to Oxford, Mississippi, and knew there were not any spires there to speak of, certainly not cold grey ones. There were softer poems like "Annabel Lee" and "To Helen" by Poe, and Sidney Lanier's "Song of the Chattahoochee." She would explain things to us about these poems. Some odd phrases would have to be spelled out. "A kingdom by the sea" was not a real place, only where the poet imagined it, though he might have been, it was true, near the ocean. Then why couldn't it be a kingdom? Maybe it was, darling. There was also "Thanatopsis" by William Cullen Bryant. I couldn't make head nor tail of it when I first read it, but I had a cousin, older than I, who knew and quoted poetry, though he went to a larger school in another town. He would fill in if I started something. When I piped up that I'd read the one about "So live that when thy summons comes . . . ," he went right on with "to join the innumerable caravan which moves to that mysterious realm where each shall take his chamber . . ." I finally caught on. It was dying that was meant. "Approach thy grave," etc. Until then, the sound of the words, the stately march of the rhythm, were all I knew.

Each of these poems had a short preface of a few lines about the author, and a picture in a small oval of the poet's face. Tennyson had whiskers, Shelley looked scared, Byron wore a white collar, Poe had funny eyes, Elizabeth Barrett Browning a fancy hairdo. Mrs. Keenan (or "Miss Willie" as some of us dared to call her) liked to read us "The Bells" by Poe. When she read it, swaying from side to side, repeating "bells, bells, bells, bells, bells, bells, bells," hairpins used to fall out of the nest above and scatter over the desk. She didn't notice. Neither did I. I would feel uplifted, absorbed, not in that room at all.

She assigned us themes and let us write our own poems. This for me was easier than learning to swim or climb a tree. It continued and amplified my trance over the poems. The pink book, getting worn, was never far away. I had had stories read me constantly, since I could understand, but no one, I think, had read poems aloud to me before. Certainly not like that. Somebody in the family at home happened to remark that Rudyard Kipling had died. I took the news sorrowfully to Miss Willie. "Nonsense," she said. "He couldn't die without my hearing it." She was right. What world was this of hers, where you heard at once that Kipling had died? I turned in themes and poems.

It was still fall the first time she came down to talk to my mother. I knew she was coming, and I was naturally excited. It was an afternoon in November, after school. I sat down with them, minding my manners and not saying anything—listening to grown-ups was my specialty—when I was suddenly asked to leave the room. I understood at once that she meant to talk about me. I think I tried to eavesdrop, but failed. I went out back and talked to old Bill, our handyman. When I returned she was gone and my mother had a complex look on her face. I still don't know if she was glad of that visit or not. She had probably been completely happy with Miss Jennie. I later learned that I was to be thought of as "talented," "imaginative," and so on—all those superlatives Miss Willie had to give, and all the backing her old family name could bring to bear on them. To me, her opinion, right or wrong, simply flowed out from the poetry, the bells, bells, bells. It joined me more than ever to the poems, and along with them, to Miss Willie and that outer world she came from, saying "literature," and "darling," and knowing when writers died.

At a students' program in the evening before school let out that spring, I was asked to read a story I had written. Miss Willie read it for me, as I was too timid, and the cry of the small town audience was "Author, author!" I got up to be applauded, but what I felt about this, and the reason I couldn't read my story aloud, was by now a solitary thing, which frightened me because it was powerful and could not be shared. It had already separated me from my schoolfriends, and I became for a time an outcast, ostracized and mocked at, my blue tam stolen, my books and homework hidden, the road to school and back a miserable trek among cold mud puddles.

I was reading the pink book alone in the living room one day when my brother, seven years older, came in. He asked what I was doing. I told him just to listen and began to read aloud. He seized the book, tore it from my hands, and began to read the poem in a high voice, leaping around. When I reached for the book he hurled it across the room and danced out, waving his arms in some sort of triumph.

My father was worried about money. My mother, I think, was worried about me. In the summer, I kept writing stories. I used to go to secluded places among the woods and bluffs that were part of our property, ride my pony down to the creek, lock notebooks away in my room. One hears of the joyous discovery of new worlds, but to me this is glib. There is no denying that my newfound ways were causing me miseries of loneliness, pangs of feeling "different," evasiveness, and secret anxieties. I showed things I had written to my mother and sometimes to one of my jollier uncles, but it would be many years before I found any real community, or even knew that such a thing existed.

The Keenans moved away. Perhaps Mr. Keenan sent for them. Their going was not a real surprise, and I don't remember it as painful. Meade and Frances had sometimes come down to my house to play. I think I always understood that they belonged to the somewhere else they had come from, were among those few who looked outward. Yet even those who go away have ties they don't lose: the day a request came for me to write about some teacher—"some particular teacher who got you impressed with literature and writing"—I received a letter from California from someone I'd never heard of. Who was "Kay Keenan"? It was Miss Willie. This letter was the first I remember getting, though she'd left our little town in the early 1930s. Miss Willie, now eighty-nine years old, now known as Kay. She enclosed the last letter she had had from my mother, who died in 1974. Evidently they had kept in touch, my mother as fixed in place as Miss Jennie; Miss Willie, the wandering one, outward bound. Sure enough, she was leaving California for Virginia, and hoping I would write.

It was then I started remembering all the above.

How much she had let into my mind, simply by being herself! I do believe many things that have happened since are a working out of what she started.

Once I mentioned to my mother that Miss Willie had said the story of Adam and Eve in the Bible was "just a story." (She had actually said this rather casually, not in the manner of teaching anything or imparting some startling truth.) My mother, however, was terribly alarmed and told my father, who took a grave view of it. "With that kind of talk," one of them said, "she's leading those children astray." I guess she did.

14

GROWING PAINS

It came as an unhappy surprise to me that I was not popular at school. I had to learn how sheltered I had been (not to say spoiled?), and I had to encounter the meanness of other children. Nothing had prepared me for this, though my brother's bullying ways might have done so. I was full of innocent good will toward new people, which is not to say I could not sulk, wail, and act in a variety of ugly ways at home when things didn't go to suit me. I might risk refusal, scolding, and even spanking, but comforting love was always around the next corner at home. School was different. There are lessons waiting for everybody, of the kind not found in books.

First I had to learn snobbishness—to learn what it was, I mean; I was never to learn to *be* snobbish. I had always been told to be democratic: my father thought it would be bad for business to be otherwise; my mother believed that looking down on less privileged people was simply not right. My grandfather had told all his sons: "The measure of a true gentleman is his behavior around those he thinks are his inferiors. The important word," he would add, "is *thinks*." And so the scorn by town children for "country children" came home to me for the first time. I was a town child, but did this mean mocking at others? "If you like so-and-so, we won't play with you." Such threats were common.

Other problems multiplied. In no time I got labeled as

"smart." This was certain death. I had been a fragile child, frequently ill, and my mother, an excellent reader, had got me hooked on stories she would read aloud to me from marvelous books. I thought in school I would not only learn to read for myself, but also get to read more and more, and so in fact I did, but showing that I liked it was not at all the thing to do.

Of course, the teachers loved me, another source of social death. What was worse, I liked the teachers. I felt I could talk with them. That was unheard-of, a grave mistake.

I was "different" in other ways.

My mother had ordered some wonderful boots of fabric and leather I was to wear on wet days. They were hard to lace, and the teacher in an early grade would keep me there until we both worked out a way to fasten them so as to send me home looked after in the way my mother wished.

At first I was the littlest of students, condemned to the tail of the line when we played Pop the Whip. (This was a running game formed by a chain of players from tallest and strongest down to the tiniest. When a high speed was reached, the leader stopped dead and swung the line in a wide arc. The three or four unfortunates at the end would go tumbling and sprawling over the grass, trying to hold on, but failing.)

Like the beanstalk in the story, one night I grew. All at once, I was taller than anybody my age, as tall as girls in high school. My parents expressed alarm to think I might not stop growing, but when I had reached a certain line on the doorframe, my genes were satisfied. I was not. Though by today's standards I was not very tall—slightly under five-eight—to myself the height seemed ruinous.

To children's parties, once school began, I wore the pretty dresses my mother was proud to see me in, flowered challis in thin wool in winter, with a broad lace collar, but no one else dressed that way, and I often found myself in a corner alone. Perhaps being a skinny child with grown-up manners left me without a hope of belonging. It did not matter in the least that the whole town flocked down to our tennis court every summer. School was another game and I played it badly.

Added to my misery, a clear fact dawned: The boys shunned me. I didn't behave, didn't look, the way they felt right to be with? Was my family too strict by reputation (Presbyterian)? Had we such a special idea of ourselves (well-known relatives high in military circles) that I was to be set apart? Had I played at being tomboyish too long—riding horses, climbing trees, spending summers at Teoc—while all the time a crowd was forming here in town that did not include me? I didn't know, but suffered.

One Saturday I was walking home alone late after going downtown. I must have been about twelve or thirteen. I was going to take the shortcut up from the road to our house, the back way, which led up a steep path past the barn lot and stables. Along the road a carload of boys I'd never seen kept honking at me and following. They were piled into an old-fashioned open car, a four-seater. I walked on, but when I turned to climb the hill, at a point about halfway up, I heard the honking again. I looked back and there they were, waving gleefully. "Hey, baby, how ya doin'? We're coming up to find you tonight!" In a flash I thought: *I'm a girl.*

Even to think of books makes those of my childhood come trooping back. I can see them to their very bindings, the pictures and pages with the corners worn from turning. There was one called *The Wonder Book of Myths and Legends,* full of Greek gods, goddesses, and heroes. The picture on the front was of Chiron the centaur, who had trained the Argonauts, standing on a rocky shore, waving goodbye to the proud ship bearing Jason and the heroes as they sail out to find the Golden Fleece. Inside was also Bellerophon, mounted on Pegasus, about to spear the fearful Chimaera through the heart.

Perseus killing the Medusa was another favorite. As well as in the book, he could be seen nightly, having wound up among the stars. Years later I saw him again with glad recognition on the Piazza della Signoria in Florence, holding high the awful head crowned with snakes. Cellini, too, had heard his story.

Then Cupid and Psyche. I could hear it read dozens of times, never failing to grow breathless at the vow she made and broke when she took a lamp to see the face of her sleeping lover. I still have the book, pages yellow from use, binding held together with adhesive tape.

Another book was *A Boy's Life of Arthur.* The sword in the stone! How wonderful to read of that boy riding back to fetch a sword for his uncle, and how easily he drew it from the stone, thus learning of his kingship in this innocent way. Then we had *The Adventures of Robin Hood,* about that nice rowdy bunch, loyal to one another, living in a forest.

Foster's *Story of the Bible* was another book of wonders, not that I disbelieved it or dismissed it as "made up," but that I believed all the others too: they seemed to me actual accounts, and I fantasized stories of David the shepherd boy, right along with Robin Hood and Apollo. But much of the Bible was frightening. Illustrations for the stories showed fire falling from heaven, cities burning, the earth opening to swallow up sinful priests, bears eating children, floodwater drowning thousands of people, tortures and plagues and slaughters. It was good to have fairy stories, with their mainly happy endings, to fall back on.

Later we came to Peter Pan and Wendy, Lewis Carroll, and any number of others. The happenings, clearly visualized from the pages of these books, became as real to me as people and events I actually experienced.

Because I had such mythic worlds as company, the outer world, so often a strain to be in, could all but vanish. Running out of stories, I would invent them, tell them in a whisper to myself at night. And out ahead waiting for me when I learned to read and write was an important discovery, which happened this way:

The first time I wanted to write something down there was a fire burning in my grandfather's room. (One burned there regularly, as in the other rooms we used in winter—we had no central heating in that entire town that I ever heard of.) Watching in fascination how the light of the fire flickered, rising and falling, dwindling and returning, on the walls and ceiling, I felt I had to put this particular sight down on paper in some way. I was so urgently impelled to do so that I could not sleep for thinking of it.

The next day, I tried first to draw it, but thereupon discovered for good and all that no design or picture, inner or outer, would ever get from me onto another surface. So instead I wrote a poem about firelight. With this act I stumbled on an amazing truth, which came as a total surprise. A word, one or two or three or more, actually *connects* inner to outer. It joins what is seen to what is there within that sees it. It fixes what is felt.

Such an exaltation did I feel after this discovery that my mind became like a boiling pot—I couldn't wait to do it some more. Feelings so often squeezed up inside me could find a way outside. The stories I saw happening in my head could get out of there and onto an outer surface, a page!

I was half crazy with the discovery. I sat on the floor before the fire the next morning, holding in my lap what I had written down. I guess I must have shown it to somebody, because somehow or other the word got out this early on that I liked to write. Well, my aunt Katie Lou and my uncles when younger had written things as well. My uncle Joe teased me: Georgie, he called me, after George Eliot.

Now when I went walking by myself out in the woods on our property, I would take a notebook along and write down stories and poems I had invented. I used to hide these ruled tablets with a pencil inside, and go and find them to write more, a continuing story, dropped and picked up again. My inner world was coming out. But only by slow degrees. For one thing, what I wrote was imaginary; it was not about myself. Most of what I wrote I showed to no one, and I have forgotten nearly all of it.

Forgotten or not, it went on like an underground stream that came up at times, only to slide out of sight, but never not to be there, somewhere, able to surface again. Still, it seemed something not exactly myself, more like a contact I had made with another sort of life, which I now was carrying around with me. And this current was itself in touch with the noble qualities in what I read. It suffered by comparison, of course, but it was part of that world.

The teachers we had were underpaid, but we had good luck nonetheless, Carrollton being a known place where genteel families lived. One of the best teachers had come there because of marriage to one of the Arrington boys. Elizabeth Arrington was a graduate of Agnes Scott, an excellent college in Atlanta, and could teach Latin, highly prized by all the old families in our town. By grade eight I had finished the first- and second-year texts and was reading Caesar.

Another teacher was a friend of Elizabeth's, Virginia Peacock. Miss Peacock needed work and on Mrs. Arrington's recommendation was invited there from Crystal Springs, another Mississippi town.

Miss Peacock loved literature. She whirled right into teaching us all the authors she doted on—Hawthorne and Poe, Dickens and George Eliot. We slid right into reading adult works. (At that time, I had got stuck on Tarzan.) She raised a little money(!) and set up a school library (we never had one) in an old upright secretary. She kept the key herself and let us check out the books during lunch hour. Since our family had bookshelves stuffed with our own books, my impression until then was that "libraries" rightfully belonged at home, but now I learned better.

Miss Peacock even made us read Shakespeare aloud, taking different roles. Each semester she would choose another play—*As You Like It, Julius Caesar,* and *Romeo and Juliet.* She had studied Shakespeare from Walter Clyde Curry at Vanderbilt while attending teachers college at Peabody in Nashville. He was a special hero of hers and she loved telling us stories of his presentations. She was good at reading aloud, and a good talker. "I read you this because I wanted to," she would say, explaining some unassigned story.

She often came to our house in the afternoons, and I would sit in silent fascination while she talked of some book or other with my aunt and my mother. To think of people talking about books as if they made a common language with others outside the family! She was one of the first to read *Gone with the Wind,* which was published along about that time. She spoke of it once at some length while I eavesdropped. "I don't consider it the world's greatest," she said, agreeing to some observation someone had made, "but it is Southern, about us all, and I think we should honor it for that."

Through the years we had had other teachers, underpaid but devoted. It still seems to me especially significant that none of them (well, maybe one or two) had been trained in education courses, but they saw to it anyway that we studied basic subjects like mathematics, algebra, civics, geography, and history. The American history course ran full tilt into the Civil War. Our text was obviously written by a Southerner for young students. The heroic names of Robert E. Lee, Stonewall Jackson, "Jeb" Stuart, and Nathan Bedford Forrest were liberally evoked. At a certain point before Gettysburg, I remember, Christopher Bryan turned to me and said: "It looks like we're gonna win, dudn't it?"

I was finishing grade ten when Truth, like a warning ghost out of Shakespeare, appeared to the school board: there was no money even for upkeep. The school, a large two-story square brick structure, housed all twelve grades, the high school meeting upstairs, the grammar school distributed below. There were no funds for cleaning, or building fires. Neither was there money to pay the teachers.

Depression was all we heard about. In Miss Jennie McBride's primary room, so she told my mother, a small boy kept his overcoat on all day long. She told him twice to take it off and hang it with the others. When he refused, she had him come to the front of the room, and unbuttoned the coat. He wore nothing at all beneath it.

A family I remember from having seen them walking to and from school wore long black stockings and dark patched pants and jackets, all too small for them. For some reason I never understood they had wads of paper or perhaps cloth stuffed about under the tight clothes. They looked sallow, serious, and hungry, and spoke to no one.

One entire family came in from the country every school day in a buggy. I went home with them once and had to get up before daylight, as their chores included milking and feeding stock, as well as getting breakfast. One older girl rode her horse in each day. She wore a divided leather skirt, her dress tied up around her waist.

Country children brought their lunch with them, for we had no school lunches served. The contents of the little sacks or tin buckets were usually sausage and biscuit, sometimes a boiled egg or a slice of homemade cake. Town children went home for lunch. I walked the short distance down the hill, home to a hot meal.

One day I was given a lunch in a little flowered metal pail, put up in waxed paper—sandwiches, hardboiled egg, and teacakes—and told to eat at school. A new girl in our class told me that she lived in a house so large it took all day to walk around it. I couldn't believe such a thing, so I went there with her. We wound up at the old Bingham house, one of the town's Victorian mansions, which had recently been cut up into apartments. I saw that it would certainly not require a whole day to walk around it, and concluded she had exaggerated. We came back to afternoon classes.

I did not know until I got home why I was allowed to take a lunch that day. Now I found out. It was hog-slaughtering time. The little pigs I had seen grow up in their smelly, muddy pen far in the back of the property were now nothing but carcasses hanging upside down from their hind feet, pitifully split open from throat to tail, while strange black men I had never seen circulated around them. Nearby were huge black pots filled with water kept at the boil by fires burning under them. Of course, they had wanted me to miss the slaughter, the throat slitting, the screams, the bloodletting, the realities of meat and sustenance.

A strange, heavy odor filled the house. From inside our dining room I could hear riotous sounds, and the cook, going in and out the swinging door with full plates of hot bread and platters of something like meat, was happy as Christmas. It seemed like a celebration. Steam poured out from around the doors. I heard my grandfather's voice. He was in there!

At one door I waited for a glimpse and got it: a table full of old men, eating and talking, barely visible through the dense steam.

"Come here," my mother said, pulling me back to the other wing of the house. "It's all your grandfather's friends. They're eating chit'lings." Hog entrails, of course. Plenty to go around after the slaughter.

All in all, it was a strange day. I remember still that one glimpse through dense smoke, the talking heads of those old gentlemen above the plates and platters, a world they understood, with something like mystery and wildness in it, ancient.

The girl I had accompanied home to see if her tale was true I no longer remember. A transient; I suppose her family left soon after. I remember the day, though, as ceremonial, filled with the thought of killing and blood, kept from me, but actual nonetheless in my memory.

In those days I knew that people everywhere were hungry, though I think that in our town there was enough to eat. In addition to the pigs, we raised chickens, a staple of the Sunday dinner table. We had milk from our own cows.

Up on a town street, I sometimes visited a playmate, a girl named Eloise Lee. Here I was amazed to see what to her family was a common occurrence. A knock would come at the door, and someone strange would be standing there, asking for food. Her mother set a plate at a small table on the back porch and invited the person in to eat. Whatever was given, the wanderers would be grateful for, then would go on their way. I suppose this scene was repeated everywhere along main roads. Since our house was harder to reach, no one I can remember came there.

However, one winter Dad planted a whole acre of turnip greens in the field just beyond our drive. He put an ad in the town paper:

ALL YOU CAN EAT!
Anybody hungry can come down
to the Spencer place and pick a gunny sack full
of turnip greens!

Four or five times a day, people would wander down our road, gather greens in the field and leave with a full sack over one shoulder. Turnip greens with turnips attached are full of iron, and sustaining. In the South the habit was to put a slice of pork "side meat" in the pot with the greens, chop up the turnips, and serve the whole as a main dish, supported by potlikker and corn bread. One never outgrows the taste for it, but in those lean days it was a winter staple of life itself. Summers were easier. Anybody with the slightest initiative could plant tomatoes, corn, peas, beans, okra, squash, beets—anything at all would grow. And anybody could go fishing.

But summer was at hand and the school had no money to open in the fall.

Dad at this point pulled one of his greatest coups. North Carrollton—north town, we called it—was right across the creek from us. The attitude that prevailed was that it was never to be confused or mistaken for *us*. We were the county seat, the upper crust, the old families, the snobs. North Carrollton had grown up around the C. & G. railroad. Big Sand Creek, a willful stream that ran any way it wanted to, had so many curves in it that the railroad, in order to pass through Carrollton, would have had to build a number of bridges. It was also the case in Carrollton that the whole town sat, like Rome, on a number of hills. So the railroad took the easy route, and the train station was reached only by driving through North Carrollton.

North Carrollton had its own twelve-year school. It also had its own post office, mayor, and board of aldermen, and its own Methodist and Baptist churches. So much of contest and hostile feeling prevailed between the two towns, each with a population of scarcely five hundred souls, that annual basketball games might easily turn into fistfights. Carrollton families with school-age children swore that *their* children would never "cross the creek."

However, our school had no money.

My father knew the state superintendant of education and invited him home for dinner one day. The project he proposed in strict secrecy was simple. North town was not to be asked for anything. Proud Carrollton was not to appear as a supplicant. But if the schools could be consolidated, letting North Carrollton become the high school, Carrollton house the grammar school, side benefits from consolidation, such as school buses and state programs and "funding," could enhance the educational picture for both schools, and for the county in general, as so many children either attended one-room schools in small rural communities or came in from the country by any means they could find.

Both boards then met, and the state superintendant, carefully coached by my father in local history, grievances, grudges, and ill will, presented the case to each. A victory!

Several families carried out their vow and kept their children away from contamination by the common people in north town. They sent them away to high school in Greenwood, a Delta town eighteen miles away. I was expected to be democratic and remain.

I was fairly used to north town. There was, of course, the Chevrolet agency and the cotton gin. Gan had walked me "downtown" every afternoon throughout my childhood, stopping to talk with the men around the barbershop and the drugstore. Now, though the way to school was longer, I could usually catch a ride with Dad to come home for the midday meal.

The change for me turned out well. The children my age I met there and studied with were not a mean bunch, and I felt myself liked and accepted for the first time. "Our" teachers had been part of the deal. We considered them, quite rightly, to be a superior lot, Miss Peacock prime among them, and though a new superintendant for the combined schools was chosen to come in and oil troubled waters, I don't recall that any of the predicted conflicts took place.

It now seems to me, looking back, that maybe Carrollton, that haughty old town, had got tired not only of being stuck-up but of being anything at all. It still had its fine old names and its beautiful houses with their antiques, its family stories of a glorious past; but all was fading along with the upholstery and the damask draperies, gathering tarnish like the put-away sets of silver.

I don't think that "decadence" is a word to apply. I believe Carrollton was always Carrollton, and so it remained. As it resisted any progress, so it refused any change at all. Of course, like any other living thing, it grows older. However, it declines because of the declensions of mortality—and that is a different thing from decadence. Something there, bred in the bone, resists being anything at all except just what it was and is: Carrollton.

Through the years it stays fixed, shrinking up, season by season. Recently an apparent boom has come because of the all-white Carroll Academy, which hundreds of children are bused in from the Delta to attend. There are new homes on the hills near the interstate, and new bungalows among the old houses along the old streets. But all this is hardly Carrollton, which grows ever more ghostlike, more at one with the little family cemeteries behind the oldest homes than with anything new and thriving.

I felt uncommonly at home among the students in newly named J. Z. George High School. (Senator George was a harmonious choice, a U.S. senator from the county we could all claim.) Many students now came in on buses from the country.

We could afford a band director. So Mr. Wood came trumpeting in, friendly with all and sundry, loaded with instruments in worn leatherette cases, which we could borrow at first, then rent, or buy. He had a son named Billy I even "dated" for a time, another older one named Ross. I took up playing clarinet just to go along with the general excitement, and though I was prone to blow squawks as often as notes, I was more than covered by the first clarinet, Wilton Sanders, a north-town boy whose father owned a grocery store. We would pile into the back of a pickup and ride at night to play for games or occasions at other schools, buying hamburgers along the way and coming back sleepy but happy.

We had a football team!

The coach was a tall, handsome young man named Joe Stevens. All the girls were smitten instantly. He had played on the Ole Miss team, and in addition to coaching our new team, he was to teach typing. All of us signed up for typing. The class met in the afternoons in the typing lab. Before each of us was a typewriter and a manual with assigned exercises. Mr. Stevens would walk in, glance around long enough to check the roll, write "Do Exercise 4" on the blackboard and walk out to coach football. We would sit there typing "f f f space/g g g space" over and over. Mr. Stevens took one look, it seemed, at an attractive blond history teacher named Mary Ida Lee and was hooked for life. Their marriage was a long and happy one. I learned to type.

During those last two years in high school my life filled up in a way I had never before experienced. My cousin May, Uncle Tom's daughter, fresh out of college, had been hired for her first job, teaching in our grammar school. She was pretty, cheerful, well-read, and marvelous fun to talk to. All the young men around began to telephone her, though she was in love with a Winona man she later married. We talked interminably of books and movies and places we'd like to see. It was the start of a lifelong friendship.

I was enjoying a rich and mostly secret fantasy life, no longer based on Greek myths and King Arthur. Predictably (I now suppose), I got involved with movies. The picture show, we called it.

I know exactly when it started. I was riding my horse one wintry afternoon and stopped back by the Carrollton drugstore for something, when I saw a magazine called *Movie Mirror* with a picture of Jean Harlow on the cover. I bought it. The glamorous star was making headlines because she had changed her platinum hair for "brownette." I read avidly about this momentous alteration of an international image. I read everything else I could get hold of. I fell to dreaming of being "one of those" and having dates with Clark Gable, Ronald Colman, or Bing Crosby—an odd assortment of favorites. I never talked about all this, I suppose because I knew how silly it was.

Going to the picture show had always been a favored diversion, both for my aunt and uncle on Teoc and my mother in town, who would be persuaded to drive me to Greenwood if I schemed it right. She had an enduring childlike interest in plots and stories, and even in the stars, whom she took certain likes and dislikes to, remarking that somebody like "Jo-Ann" Crawford was "too coarse," or that "Old Bing" had big ears but could certainly sing. It may even be she had movie-star fantasies as well, though I doubt it.

Along with the movies, purveying scenes of emotional trauma amid plush decor, there was the radio, loaded with crooning about love (the eternal kind), parting, sorrow, laments of every variety. The sprightly tunes were many, as were Hollywood comedies, but the prevailing mood was torchy and very bad for young girls. I concluded that love was something you got heartache about. Maybe it was my early failure to feel anywhere near as attractive as I would have liked that made me know from the start I would never really fall for anybody around home. No, it would be somebody strange in a distant, romantic place. That would have been fine, but I wasn't in any such place and had no prospects of going to one.

I did learn something about myself when in school in north town that I never put in words but felt just the same. I was really a country girl. Teoc and McCarley, in my case, had prevailed over Carrollton. My strong roots were in them. I still look back with admiration to the names of our Presbyterian families who came "all the way in" to Sunday school and church—the Stanfords, the Willifords, the Shacklefords, the Wiltshires, the Brownings. There was even a family called Turnipseed. Good plain strong names of people who were not petty or derisive to others. If this is an Anglo-Saxon bias, then it has to be that, but who wants to reject or be ashamed of the rock they're hewn from?

During those last years in high school, a cousin named Lloyd Smith drove a pickup that had been licensed as a school bus for his neighborhood. The students who rode with him sat on wooden benches along either side in the back. Everyone, including Lloyd, had the look of wanting to get home before they had to milk cows in the dark. I used to hitch a ride with him to the back of our property, and go talking all the way. I liked him. I felt I might happily have been one of them all. Anytime I've made some foolish effort to be more "sophisticated" than I naturally am, or in any way scornful of people who might seem to be inferior, I feel shame for it and find it hard to forgive myself for what others have undoubtedly long since forgotten.

15

SOME SOCIAL NOTES

THERE were three families named Gee in Carrollton when I was growing up, all one family really, sons of "old Major Gee," who I suppose had been in the Civil War.

They all had money the old major had left them, and property around the town. They ran a store named for the major, O. K. Gee & Sons. The full name was Ormand Kimbrough Gee, but the pun was significant. The store was on the corner across from the courthouse. A mulberry tree stood there with benches beneath it. Known as "mulberry corner," it got to be famous in the state because so many passers-by would stand or sit there, talking politics.

Carroll County is said to be the only county in the entire United States to boast of two senators in the U.S. Senate at one and the same time. These were Senator Money and Senator George. It must be something to keep proud of through the centuries.

I never had the good fortune of knowing the original O. K. Gee, who died before my time, but all the Gees were, of course, part of the town's social picture. They lived in fine houses and had a great many things no one else could afford. Mr. Ormand was the oldest, a thin friendly man with a bit of a beard, married to Miss Recie, who had been a Gillespie, her younger sisters best friends of my mother as a girl. There were sons, two tall, good-looking young men, Joe and Pete. I was in awe of them, unnecessarily, for they were invariably friendly, even if they had the air of not quite knowing who I was. The Ormand Gee house, off on a side road, was quite beautiful, and beautifully kept, with a low, deep-set veranda and flowering yard behind a white fence.

The next in age I think was the Charlie Gee connection. Their house, like so many in Carrollton, was set in seclusion on a hill, the premises reached by a long flight of wooden steps up from the street, or if by car, through a wide, climbing drive. There were girls—the Charlie Gee girls—all attractive and popular, filled with small talk, wearing pretty clothes. They, too, had a tennis court down in back of their property, and interesting friends from their various colleges in Virginia or Missouri came to visit in the summer. Young men were powerfully in demand. My brother was often invited to glowing evenings. Once the occasion was to come up and see the night-blooming cereus, a mysterious plant that chose to open its wonderful white petals rarely, and then only at midnight. At other times there were lawn parties to celebrate a birthday or someone's departure to Europe.

The mother of the Charlie Gee tribe, Miss Nora Gee, a frail, taxed lady, was a Presbyterian (the Gees were all Episcopalians). She thus sometimes had the ladies' auxiliary meeting at her house. Once I accompanied my mother there for some reason I forget, and two of the daughters, Margaret and Josephine, came in as refreshments were served. They sat down on the floor before the ladies and began to strum their banjos and sing foolish songs. They were wearing short pleated skirts with striped blouses. Banjos were all the rage during the Depression times, and I remember this, with its Fitzgerald-like link to what was "going on" on the outside, charming, assured, and fun.

The third and youngest of the Gee brothers was Clint. His house was on one of the main streets. There were two older daughters, and two younger. Charlotte, the youngest, was a dark-headed little girl, rather popular in town for her friendly ways, though the family called her a "street angel," always implying the rest of the phrase, "home devil." They too used to have friends from out of town come to visit, and I remember the sight of their front porch on hot summer afternoons when I was driving by; invariably there were mysterious but interesting-looking strangers, a clutch of girls and young women, eternally drinking from iced glasses, talking and laughing, talking and laughing, through the endless hot afternoons back of the screens. They were great talkers, amusing, and never lacked for a story.

At a certain point every afternoon they would all rise and pile in the family car and drive around town. Perhaps they always had an errand, but mainly it just seemed they took a certain route without really wanting anything. They went uptown (Carrollton) and downtown (North Carrollton), then returned home. Maybe they stopped in one drugstore or another for a purchase or a Coke. One day, talking incessantly, they reached home, but missed Charlotte. Only on studied reflection and after much discussion did they realize what had happened. As they were circling the town well, which stood in the center of the north town business street, one of the rear doors had flown open and Charlotte must have fallen out. Nobody had stopped talking long enough to miss her. The summer heat in those pre-air-conditioned days was hypnotic, and life proceeded in ritual fashion, like slow-motion movies, or underwater swimming.

The Clint Gee daughter my age was named Cora Brown but called Coco. She later grew up to be a stunner with a fantastically beautiful figure and a languid, rather insolent manner. She inspired such lust among the young men far and wide that all sorts of stories about her were bandied about through the years.

The older sisters took personal credit for her fabled legs, saying that she had them only because, wanting to amuse themselves somehow (those long hot afternoons), they had made her climb up doorframes with her bare feet braced against either side.

She was sent off fairly early on to an Episcopal academy for young ladies in Vicksburg, but later went to Ole Miss, where things really got started. I knew her best, however, when we were all in the same age group in Carrollton, and she was only another of the growing-up crowd.

Once I was roller-skating uptown and started down the steep hill that sloped from the courthouse square toward the bridge. I saw Coco and a few other girls sitting at the foot of some wooden steps leading up to someone's front yard. About at that point, I got scared, for I was going faster and faster and could not stop. I was not even halfway down the hill, which was growing more precipitous every second, and I had nothing to catch on to.

I don't know if I cried out to them or not, but Coco rose, also on skates, and, coming straight into my path, caught me. We both fell sprawling on the concrete walk, stood up bruised and breathless but not really hurt.

It took nerve—even recklessness—to do such a thing, and I will always remember the sight of her getting up to help me, entering danger with a kind of careless air of not thinking about it twice. Years later, divorced, a working woman plagued for years by persistent back pain, which never left her and was apparently incurable, Coco took a pistol and shot herself through the head.

The Ormand Gee house is still standing, but the Clint Gee house is gone, either burned or pulled down. The Charlie Gee house, now sold, was occupied for years by an elderly aunt, who lived there alone, keeping it for any who wished to come there. Miss Edith Erskine's house is no more, though the wondrous yard now surrounds a new brick bungalow.

One of the Eggleston ladies (known throughout their lives as the Eggleston girls) once brought a friend home to visit Carrollton. She went driving about, saying to the friend, "That's where the So-and-so mansion was, but it's torn down . . . up there, was So-and-so's house but it burned . . ." After passing a long series of such nonexistent landmarks, Miss Eggleston concluded with a sigh, "I guess Carrollton is not really a place, it's a state of mind."

Yet enough of the old remains to put the town on the national list of historic places, and a mini-pilgrimage of the Natchez sort is now held each year to attract those who want to come and see. Streets that had names only on the town survey maps—we never put up names of streets in my day at all, since everybody knew where the Spencers, the Watsons, the Gillespies, and the Prices lived—now are labeled with signs, and houses have acquired patrician names: Tanglewood and Helm Home and Cedar Hill and the like.

A movie was made in Carrollton! One of William Faulkner's books, *The Reivers,* was filmed as a vehicle for Steve McQueen, who played Boon Hogganbeck. It was really quite a good movie. When the advance crews came down to find places in Oxford, Mississippi, for shooting the background scenes and much of the early action, it was a disappointment to see that Oxford had become too large and developed and did not have enough of a county-seat look anymore. So in wandering around and inquiring, they found Carrollton, came there, and judged it the perfect casting for Faulkner's Jefferson. The action of the book takes place in the early years of the century, and this is exactly when the clocks had stopped in Carrollton, forever.

There was high excitement. All the ladies of every age fell madly in love with McQueen, who flirted with them daily. Many people got to be extras. It was Carrollton's last big fling.

I am told there has been some precaution in recent years over tornadoes. One of those could wipe out the town. Drills have been held—what to do in case—for fierce storms can blow up, can look black and terrible, like an avenging demon, can actually strike. Hallie Eggleston, after her retirement, alone in a beautiful house full of antique treasures, used to meet these emergencies by sitting under her massive dining-room table holding tightly to the mahogany table legs. When I picture that diminutive aging lady alone and frightened beneath the massive table, I don't know whether it is funny or sad—perhaps both.

For if Carrollton has a spirit for me, it is probably centered in the Egglestons. They were the town's original Episcopalian family and lived next to the charming Grace Church. There were, in my earliest memory, only women in their house, for Mr. Sid Eggleston, a close friend of my grandfather's, had died, and I do not remember him. But the grandmother, a tiny, almost silent lady with observant eyes, I do remember, also the mother, a small, humped person, a quick thinker at bridge games, which we were often invited to play there. She was well-read and had her own opinion on everything going.

The Eggleston girls were three in number: Sara, Frances, and Hallie. All were appropriately courted but evidently hard to win, as only Sara married and lived away with a Delta planter.

Frances taught grammar school in Greenwood with considerable success, winning a national prize.

Hallie—known as Baby Hallie or simply Ballie—taught Latin in several small colleges but gave it up for a librarian's degree. She was a small, efficient presence in the Ole Miss library for many years. The boys praised her neat legs and charming smile. She retired home to Carrollton and was finally the only remaining Eggleston there.

Their humor and interest in life, their cultivated, reliable presence, their beautiful taste, made of them a sort of essence of all our town was meant to be. Others might scatter or go over to wild erratic behavior—drinking, adultery, murder, and madness were not unknown—but the quiet core life was being lived without questioning by the Egglestons.

Something surprising the Eggleston girls liked to tell about occurred during the Depression. Certain land speculators in Florida were advertising free trips to anyone interested in buying property in any one of a number of locales. The Eggleston girls volunteered as among those avidly interested in the area and got to travel all over Florida, stopping wherever they proposed to explore, looking for prospective homesites. They had no intention whatsoever of buying property, but thought nothing of saying so, daring fate that one time for the sake of a free trip.

16

THE POET

CARROLLTON should have had a great poet. It almost did.

Lawrence Olson was a distant cousin. He lived up the street from us in an antebellum house in the classic style, two-story with a portico and tall white columns. His father was often absent. His mother, Cousin Wanda, was there, and for a few years of my childhood, his grandmother, the formidable Cousin Frieda.

Frieda Liddell was from a German family, residents of New Orleans since the early nineteenth century. She had met young Dr. Liddell when he was studying medicine in that city. I remember an old lady with a strong opinionated voice, sitting in a corner with a spread over her knees. She was wearing a frilly white cap on her gray curls.

All summer long Lawrence came down to our house to play, and in winter when he was home from school in Greenwood (he was driven there daily by a family friend who worked there), he was often at our house. He was only four years older than I, and though we sometimes quarreled, I think I took him as almost a brother, at any rate, as someone always present. For many years it was no surprise to walk into the living room and find Lawrence seated there, reading or writing something, having come in without notice. He was known to be "smart," and he had to pay for every form of "difference" in Carrollton, just as I had. His mother, also a music teacher, was thought of as having an intellectual bent, a reader of various books, who "kept up" with outer things.

Because of being named for his father, he was at first called Junior Olson. I think he began to despise it early on. It was as if Carrollton had put a brand on him with that name before he could say anything about it. He took the stouthearted course of refusing to answer when called Junior. He finally won. But I think many in Carrollton probably still call him that, being every bit as stubborn as he, no matter to them that the name was his own.

Summer after summer, winter after winter, Lawrence was a constant presence, telling us about things we hadn't heard of. He was musical and used to bang out Verdi's "Anvil Chorus" on our old rosewood piano. He one night sat before the fire and recounted the entire story of Hugo's *Les Misérables*. It had recently been made into a movie we were all interested to see. He talked well, in a rich descriptive way. Stories should be told by firelight. He knew how to pronounce French names. He brought with him a window into a wider world, and I loved listening to him.

For several summers, J.J., Charles, and Leila (the Holman children), Eloise Lee, Lawrence, and I formed a stamp club. We all collected stamps and owned albums to paste them in with tiny glued hinges, careful not to tear. We had books that evaluated separate issues and catalogs for ordering. We swapped. "My two Camaroons for your seven-cent Washington. Is there a watermark?" These were the languid afternoons.

Another time, during an eclipse, we got up on the roof out the window of our attic and studied the majestic solar process through pieces of smoked glass. Up there we also had a chemistry set, ordered, I think, from Sears Roebuck. It would color litmus paper blue and pink according to what mixtures were used, and made angry concoctions in test tubes with drops of various acids. We could make salt.

Out in the swing one afternoon we told scary stories. Lawrence had culled a humdinger from a book of pieces collected by Alexander Woollcott. One was called "Moonlight

Sonata," about a man who as a guest in a spooky English country house saw by moonlight what looked to be someone playing a violin, but turned out instead to be a madman plucking the hairs from the head of the cook, whom he had murdered and decapitated. I was so frightened by this macabre image that I stayed awake at night shuddering to remember it.

Cursed (or blessed) with a visual imagination, I found it impossible to throw off an image anyone had powerfully evoked. Scary movies were a threat, boogeyman tales and lightning storms made me quake. At night I was afraid to venture into the yard with its long slopes and dense shadows of shrubs and trees that were friendly by day, but who knew what life they assumed as they turned black by moonlight?

Space, too, was frightening. I used to lie and look up at the infinite reach of the night sky full of stars, some looking near, others far. There was no end to it, *no end*! My very self seemed to be following my vision, outward, outward forever! This seemed so incredible as to be paralyzing, yet everybody lived calmly with that knowledge, day by day.

Lawrence's stories, related in the manner of a composed piece of writing, brought home to me, among other effects, the power of words to connect not only to the known and possible, but to the unknown, the improbable, the mysteries. Others of our club told stories too, I suppose, but I don't remember them as well.

But he had bad times. Other children tormented him by making him say that he was one-fourth German. Being German was a stigma, World War I having been too recent in the past. He was scarcely of a temperament to fight, but he would do it, only to lose and be held to the ground until he was made to say some foolish thing. He was high-strung, intelligent, and at times, in spite of his shyness, touchingly affectionate.

Most of all, he wrote poetry!

My aunt Katie Lou, home from teaching, expressed an interest, and he would bring long passages down for her to read. In her presence (and mine, of course) he would read aloud from his Swinburne-like verses: "The moon is a vessel of nectar / The stars are a cluster of pearls," and so forth.

An only child, often lonely, he needed our company. His father worked for the state extension service and was seldom at home. There were stories about drinking. His mother was pleased to have him play with other children, especially my brother and me, as we were kin and known to be "nice." She and my mother had been in the same crowd as girls. They both had been members of the Sans Souci Club.

Lawrence eventually went off to Ole Miss, where his poetry began to grow and find publication here and there. He went abroad one summer, having himself organized a small band to play in the third-class lounge of a liner. He told us very little about France, except that at one point in Paris his portfolio of music had been stolen and he had first to wheedle sheet music out of the French entertainers, then labor at translating the words into English. But he was leaving us by then, a handsome boy, brown-haired, with deep dimples and a charming smile.

It would have been a natural thing for him and me to grow closer, and though we went out to picture shows and over to Greenwood a number of times, we seemed, as we grew up, intolerably shy with each other. I was in awe of his intellect and found it difficult to think of anything to say he would not find hopelessly dumb. I remember one night he began to talk to me about William Faulkner. I had heard him mentioned before, but always as someone to be ashamed of, a writer who "raked up dirt." Lawrence told me my ideas were wrong and that Faulkner would be known someday as a great writer. He discussed Phil Stone, the lawyer in Oxford who was Faulkner's mentor in his younger days, and how Stone had been able to point Faulkner toward subject matter he could use in his writing.

Lawrence eventually left us entirely. I think he may have loved the family, certainly my mother, and I believe he had real affection for me. But he hated Carrollton attitudes. He would go to church with us: we were always to stop in the car and pick him up for Sunday school, a small boy running down the long steps to the street in plus fours and knee-length argyle socks—clothes no one else wore. Once we were on a program together at a young people's meeting. Lawrence read a short article cut from a church pamphlet, and on the way home he tore it over and over into confetti-size bits, which he tossed out the car window. That gesture said what he felt.

His stays at home grew briefer; his life elsewhere was, I know, a continuing story of restlessness and search. He sometimes wrote me. He always returned. However, he of course knew he had no real future among us, had possibly known it early on. Eventually, in 1947, he published a volume of his poems, *The Cranes on Dying River.* I have it still and read it over from time to time. Many of the lines I never forget. There are glimpses of the many places and times he had experienced.

How Frieda died and how the rain
Fell secretly in Oxford Street . . .

How Dorothea wept how quite
Impeccably at Havre the sun
Climbed the old wall and how the night
Came down the hills at Carrollton

He always said he loved the countryside around home, the natural beauty we grew up with.

I admire one poem called simply "1941," which speaks of our forebodings in that year:

And now the cities of the mind
Lie darkened and across the sky
Doubts move like searchlights and the blind
Achieve a novel certainty . . .

In World War II Lawrence was recruited for language training in Boulder, Colorado, and went there with his wife, Jeane. He had been in school in Wisconsin, where they met. They had married only weeks before. His exceptionally high IQ fated him: he was assigned to study Japanese. Many failed but Lawrence made it through.

Japan from then on was to be his life's work, in war and peace. He worked for years for the American Universities Field Staff in New York, spending two years in Japan for each one in the United States, writing long, informative reports on Japanese policies and culture, following with lecture tours in the States. He became a distinguished lecturer in Asian studies at Wesleyan

University in Connecticut, author of several books on Japan. The Japanese looked upon him favorably. They honored him in an elaborate ceremony, naming him to the Order of the Sacred Treasure.

Overtaken by cancer in retirement in Washington, he found that Carrollton came to mind again. He would telephone me, and was finally to say that though he never had a sister, he had thought of me as one. He knew I had recently been to Mississippi. "Did you go out to the cemetery?" "Not this time," I said. "Oh, you have to do that. You are more from Carrollton than I am, you know. It's all right for *me* not to go, but *you* must *always* go." (Of course, I had been right all along. No matter where I had traveled or lived, what books I'd written or awards I'd won, I was still his country cousin.) I promised that I would go to the cemetery. He went on: "You must see if our family plot is kept up. I send money for it, but I don't know if it is."

I made a special trip to Washington to see him, during his last days. I told him that to me he was always a brilliant boy, upstairs in that beautiful house, writing poetry. The thought came unprepared for, a spontaneous truth and occasion for tears.

As promised, I went out to the cemetery when next at home, and saw that the Liddell and Olson graves were tended. I wrote to tell him that they were, but before the letter arrived, he was gone. A brilliance like his should have been the town's pride. I never heard that it was.

Do we blame them? Do they blame us? The truth is that in Lawrence's case, despite his constant presence in our midst, the stamp club, the storytelling, and the music, there were never many points of meeting between the town and him, so nothing on either side really took place or was there for praise or blame.

Lawrence Olson was no longer among us, but in many ways he never was. He told me in one of our infrequent meetings that aside from my mother, the only person he valued in Carrollton was a fat old man named Milt Boone. Milt dressed in khaki shirt and trousers, and used to sit in a chair up at the courthouse. He was wonderfully friendly and conversant, but I never knew him very well. He doted on his niece, a girl I had been in school with named Janey Keys Ray. She was not often at home, having married someone from another town, but to him she was constantly present. He never married, I think, or had children. She was his family. He spoke at once of her. "Do you remember Janey Keys? She's the sweetest thing in the world." He would beam even to mention her. Lawrence praised him. "He was a human being," Lawrence said.

17

"THEM"

OF course they were always around us, fully half of "us" was "them." Jokes were told about them; their speech was imitated. Did we feel benevolence toward them, despite all this? Yes, and real affection, too; real friendships, though rare, were sometimes made. And hidden though such things might be, there were instances of real love.

The talk about them went on in lowered voices, so as not to "hurt their feelings." They would always be somewhere near enough to hear, cleaning or cooking or coming in to ask about what we wanted done. "Don't ever say 'nigger,' " my mother warned. "Even if other people do, you mustn't say it. Say 'colored people.' "

We had a cook named Laura Henley. My first playmate was her boy, whose name was J.C. He came with her every day to work because she had nowhere to leave him. Unable to pronounce my name, he did the best he could. I was "Woo-wee." We would stand together in the sun on the back steps, with the hot planks burning our bare feet. (Avoid the nailheads.) My mother said she could hear in her sleep what J.C. always said when we stood there: "La', La'. Ope de do'. Let me an' Woowee tum in."

Once J.C. and I built a playhouse up against the back wall of the house. We took out saucers and some tin knives and forks and made mud pies, getting filthy dirty. Once we got chewing gum in each other's hair and came in a total mess. My mother said to Laura: "You take yours and I'll take mine." The noise of our equal spankings and identical wails came from different parts of the house.

The greatest horror I can in all my life remember was because of Laura. Walking uptown she had been called to by a white woman passing in a car. Would she do some laundry? The woman later said that Laura had "sassed" her.

That night an unspeakable thing took place. We knew nothing of it, but just before bedtime, a voice called to us at the back door, out of the dark. It was Laura, some young black person with her, I don't remember who. She was hardly able to stand. She was covered with terrible purple blotches, seeping out blood everywhere. She had something white, like a pillowcase, wrapped around her head.

Her story came out in broken phrases. The white woman's husband had come to her house and dragged her out. The woman had held a lantern. Her husband gave the punishment. The instrument used was a board with nails in it. Laura could hardly stumble to our door.

Afraid for her, my father got Laura into a car and to the train station. He put her on the train that night with her companion. Where could she get medical help? Did we ever know? The fear was that she would be killed if she stayed in town. All my life I will remember her voice, the brown, home face of Laura, J.C.'s mother, contorted with her effort to get out any words at all, and the awful blue marks around the bloody nail holes.

Years later, when I came to write a novel that in the made-up terms of fiction brought in much that I knew by heart, I called it *The Voice at the Back Door.* Black people were expected to come to the back door. And many did come to ours, though not in such extremities as Laura's: to collect wages due, or ask for or pay back a loan, to beg time off from work, to sell plums or berries, or tell of someone sick. But it was Laura's voice I remember, halting and soaked with pain and shock, that sounds through all my days. "Didn' do nothin'! Lawd know I didn' say nothin' like she said!"

Before Laura and before I was born, my young parents' first cook was a remarkable woman named Aunt Lucy Breckinridge. She had been a slave Negro, owned, of course, by the Breckinridge family, though I never knew any of them and they must have left before my time. She lived out from town with her grandson David, whom she doted on, and after she grew too old to cook for anyone, she would come in to visit "her white folks."

Aunt Lucy came straight to the front door, a privilege she had simply taken for herself. She would tell all the news of herself and others to my mother, then go and get a plate of food for them both in the kitchen. She loved my brother, who was born during her time with us, and when his first child, Jim, was at our home during the war years, she expected visits and would sit the boy on her knee and talk with him. She had a fine cap of white hair by this time.

When her hundredth birthday came round—at least a hundred: not even she knew for sure—the Charlie Gee family gave a great reception for her out on their lawn. The whole town came and did her homage. She was forever one of us. She would make scuppernong wine and bring a jugful in each fall. It sat in our closet. If anyone had a fever, or was "running a low temperature," a small thumbprint glass of Aunt Lucy's wine was considered helpful.

After Laura, our cook was a daughter of hers, Mary Elizabeth, known as Snookums. Snookums was with us for many years. She never spoke a word that was not absolutely necessary. My mother once wanted to know from her what to do about mice. "Get a cat," said Snookums. There were other monosyllabic communications for us to repeat and laugh about.

And what can I tell also of Dora, black and docile, and Mayola, a light-skinned, pretty woman, full of pleasant talk; of Nellie, who saw us through to the end of the line?

We furnished our cooks with a house far in the back, out near the barn lot, along the shortcut route to north town. I had never been inside. No one went nearer than the porch, to call sometimes or ask for some additional work to be done, or to learn where something was. But once when we lacked for help and put an ad in the Greenwood paper, a young black girl came out from Greenwood with a girlfriend. We told them to go and look at the house she would be given to live in. They went, but came back laughing. "You call that a house?" one said, and they left, hightailed it out of there, as the saying went, not to be seen again.

I went there myself then and saw what all these years "they" had had to live in. One spare unornamented room, a few shabby chairs, a tiny room off to one side with a rack for a mattress, a shed of a kitchen area out the back. I was filled with shame for us. During the thirties Snookums had earned two dollars a week. Had it never been increased?

My father did make improvements to satisfy whoever came next. I think the true state of things had escaped his attention, too. Though we always lived well, one would have to say, with a large house and servants and plenty to eat, there was never much cash for anything during the Depression. Also my brother had to be put through university. Tuition, fraternity, dances . . . times were hard, so they said.

Dora's husband was a friendly black man named Robert. During the late forties, my father found a "place" in the Delta which was going for sale at a low price and bought it. It was thirty-five or so miles from Carrollton, set in Sunflower County, at a good distance as well from Greenwood. The land there was flat and rich. It had been regularly covered with floodwaters before levee systems were secure and only in recent times had the swamps been drained. It was muddy during the winter months, a peculiar heavy sort of mud called buckshot. Cattle mired in buckshot often died, unable to move out of it, simply trapped.

Mules in those days were necessary for plowing and planting the crops. Dad had some fine ones, sleek chocolate-brown animals with massive long heads, standing man-high at the withers, their hooves as large as iron skillets.

When cotton picking was done and the winter had started in earnest, Dad would send his foreman, Charles White, to the Delta place. He would load the mules in the truckbed and bring them to pasture on our property. Throughout the winter afternoons, lengthening toward spring, we could look out and see them grazing or walking in a herd from one part of the property to another, sometimes hidden altogether below one of the bush-covered banks that eased the property down toward the creek, but always emerging, a powerful band, peaceful.

One afternoon my mother (Mimi) and I drove in from Greenwood and found that someone had left the pasture gate open and all the mules were out. Dad was away on business; Charles, probably with him, was not in evidence either. There was no one to call.

At first, the mules didn't do anything. They milled around for a while in the side yard between the house and the tennis court and we thought little of it, deciding to wait until Dad appeared, or Charles, to take charge. My mother said she hoped they didn't get in the rose garden. We weren't afraid of them, though anyone would have hesitated to go too near them.

I was drinking coffee and looking out the window when they started to move. They moved with one impulse, as though they had planned it, as perhaps they had. They headed for the drive, walking with a powerful fluidity, as though one beast were on the march rather than numbers. Once in the open road they began to trot.

"The mules!" I yelled. "They're heading uptown!"

Mimi ran to the front door. "Oh, my goodness," she said.

We ran out and got in the car. It was a sky-blue Buick, and quite large. What did you do with eighteen head of mules?

Carrollton on that sunny quiet winter afternoon seemed to be asleep. Nobody at all was about on the town square, along the residential streets, anywhere. We drove slowly behind the mules, wondering what to do next. We thought we might nudge them along from behind, head them into some cul-de-sac where they might graze happily until we could get word to Charles or Dad. But the mules were annoyed when we came closer and began to trot faster. There was no telling where they might wind up. The only sound in Carrollton that afternoon was the clatter of those marvelous hooves.

They paraded round the courthouse, then trotted up into the Methodist churchyard. It was situated back of a brick wall and reached by some steps leading up from the sidewalk. The mules found this ascent easy. They milled among the cedars. One took bites from a shrub; others grazed. One got mad and kicked another.

They decided to leave. If we could only head them in the direction of home. I got out and waved before them, trying to turn them in the right direction. My mother edged in with the car. But the mules caught on, shied away, almost ran me down, warped around me, and entered the Presbyterian churchyard. Another move like that and they would pass the Episcopal church, and beyond that lay the country road to the far-off Littleton place, with the whole county to wander in beyond.

"Oh, my goodness," said my mother. "What are we going to do?" We were sitting in the car, totally helpless.

It was the moment for a hero to ride up. One did. A dusty pickup, carrying in the back the usual conglomeration of old ropes, old clothes, and a sack or two, banged up beside us. A voice called, "Is them y'all's mules?" It was Dora's husband, Robert, coming home from work.

"They certainly are," we said. Before we could say "Can you help us?" Robert was out, grabbing up a rope from the back of his truck. He went in among the mules.

They regarded him without alarm. He knew the head mule, how I don't know; he just knew. He walked straight up to it, noosed the rope about its head, and in a light bound, mounted. "Key's in the truck," he called and started off home, the whole herd jostling for position behind, finally stringing out at a trot, great hooves pounding, great ears flopping, great heads swinging to a contented rhythm, past the courthouse, down the street past the Baptist church, turning at Mrs. McBride's corner, proceeding past Miss Beauregard Somerville's, the schoolhouse, the Olson house—back to home pasture, where Robert brought them through the gap, then got off and closed it.

I was in the pickup behind, with Mimi in the Buick bringing up the rear. It must have seemed quite a procession for anyone up and watching, and though no soul appeared, of one thing we could be sure: Carrollton was *always* up and watching.

My mother, being plantation bred, thought she couldn't do without a cook. She never really learned to cook anything but cakes, especially fruitcakes, and goodies for Christmas. She made up the fruitcakes in large quantities, using enormous bowls the size of dishpans. When the batter grew too heavy with fruits and nuts for her to stir, she would call in the handyman, old Bill Burkhead, from the yard.

Bill did everything for us. He was thin and wiry, bent over from toil. He was helpful and kind and knew how to do whatever was asked. I used to follow him everywhere. I had a puppy

I loved, called Spud, a mud-colored mongrel. Dad did not want me seen with such a dog. Spud would follow me riding, trotting anywhere and everywhere behind my horse, but Dad thought for me to be seen uptown, trailed by such a common animal, was not a good thing. He made me give Spud away to Bill and got a purebred German shepherd puppy for me. This dog and I got along all right, but he wasn't Spud and I never felt the same about him.

When I went off to school, both dogs took up with Bill. He was not to be seen coming onto our property but that both dogs had met and greeted him and were trailing happily along behind him, mongrel and purebred alike.

Bill came in the early morning to make the fires. My waking up on school days was always because of Bill, who would be bringing in "fat pine" kindling and firewood from the cold outside, kneeling in front of the grate to shovel the last night's ashes out, lay the good-smelling wood, and light the blaze. I would go back to pleasant dozing for another hour while the fresh fire took hold, warming the room.

A more important person was Charles White. He worked many years for my father, almost like a partner. Truck driver, cattle herdsman, repair man, a grave, steady, and regular character. We were all a little in awe of Charles. He had a house to itself up on the hillside between us and the Liddell/Olson house, a wife, and a number of children. We seldom saw the wife or the children.

We were told later that Charles had had a long love affair with one of our cooks, but I forget which, and I don't suppose we would ever have found it out, as in the kitchen he behaved in the same decorous way toward them all, saying little and eating quietly. Charles was said to be important in the black community, especially in the church.

One year, unthinkably, my father fired Charles. He had not done anything wrong, and the only reason for letting him go was money. Dad thought he could not afford him. Charles got a job on the town roadworks. Once, passing in the car, my sister-in-law and I saw him working with the town crew to repair a water main on our street. "We miss you, Charles," I said.

Charles laughed. "Oh, I'll be back 'fo long, Miss 'Lizbet. He can't do without me." Sure enough, a week or so later, Charles returned.

At Christmas we all felt the obligation, also a pleasure, to find good presents for Bill and Charles and Snookums. We wrapped them carefully, and they were placed with all the others under the tree. At the tree ceremony on Christmas morning, they would come in with the rest of us and stand around, saying "Thank you, ma'am," or "Thank you, sir," and smiling. But they opened the packages only later, out of sight.

The small dining room where as a family we usually ate our daily meals, instead of setting up the large dining room beyond, was adjacent to the kitchen, and the life and talk of the kitchen were part of our meals. When we spoke among ourselves, those in the kitchen did not interrupt, and the same went for them. But there was considerable exchange. A death or an illness, an elopement, the effects of a storm, who was in town from the outside, "they" would have heard before we did.

The burden of the talk was almost invariably of the white community. Since the blacks worked throughout town in white homes, and since of course they talked with one another, it was easy to learn from them. But their tact was infinite. They knew when and how far to trust us, when to be frank, when to praise, when to be silent. In retrospect, I now read a lot into their silences. Who knew what life was going on among "them"?

Literally speaking, Carrollton did not have a Negro section. The houses for the blacks had simply grown up on or peripheral to the white properties. The large white houses of Carrollton were generally set on hillsides surrounded by enormous yards, full of flowering shrubs, the front walks lined with cedars, the fences fringed with jonquils, narcissus, and other bulbs. So as the town had taken shape in the old days, some of the houses for blacks wound up along the main residential roads of the town.

There was, however, one exclusively black section, located in the far rear of the Welch property, next door to ours. Many white houses were within calling distance of it, but it was visible neither from any house nor any road, and could be reached by climbing a steep path up a hillside from the town road that ran back of our property. That path was like a gash in the eroded red soil.

I had been to this section a time or two, I suppose, for I remember it. It was composed of a group of fairly large unpainted houses, with porches, all around a central area. As was done around most black dwellings at that time, the ground was scraped clean of every shred of grass. There may have been some plots for flowers, outlined with snuff bottles, planted with prince feathers, marigolds, or zinnias. There may have been marble holes for children to play in, or a swing made of an old rubber tire hanging from a tree limb.

This then, like a little African village within the town, carried on its own mysterious life. I was sternly enjoined never to go there unless sent on an errand, and then to go no farther than the edges. It was easy to forget it was even there. The name of it was Buzzard Roost. If any outsider asked about the colored section, my mother would tell them about it by name, but she would invariably add, "They named it themselves," which was true. But explaining was another sign of her making up for the gulf between us, the one there was no bridging.

Laura lived back in Buzzard Roost along with others of the Henley Negroes. They were said by some to be dangerous, "mean Negroes," I often heard, and part Indian. I can believe the latter, as they had brownish-red skin. But Laura was never mean that I can recall. She could sometimes get outdone and yell out the window to J.C. and me, "Y'all churren stop that!" "What are they doing, Laura?" "Chunkin' one 'nother. Lord have mercy, they's a sight!"

One of my happiest memories is of Laura and my mother. Many years after she stopped cooking for us, she would come at times to visit and exchange her news with ours. It was a mild spring day, warm and full of good odors, under a fair sky, new grass springing up, a fresh, vivid green. My father had a pile of new lumber in the field in front of our house, ready for Charles to build fencing, and down there Laura found my mother, who had gone to the field for some reason. I could see them from the house, how Mimi and Laura were talking, at times seriously, at times laughing, Mimi sitting on the woodpile, Laura wandering about nearby as they talked. This went on for a good long while, a pleasant sight.

I see their meeting and talk as being much like the daily aspect and mood of the conversations from small dining room to kitchen, not even yards of space between, and yet, as remarked on later, when things in the South came to the boil, that little agreed-upon space could not be closed. We could not ever go sit in the kitchen to eat with "them," nor could "they" sit at our dinner table, though we were eating precisely the same food. For one thing, there would have been no enjoyable small talk, nothing exchanged, nothing spontaneous to say. For another, if we had initiated such a move, we would have felt wrong about it. This is an odd thing to call wrong, but there isn't another word.

Once at an early age, I got excited about the Fourth of July. I can't remember why I was so stirred up; maybe an idea had simply arrived unannounced in my own head. Bill Burkhead was the subject. Why did Bill have to work every day? Even on Sundays, here he would come, walking in from a more distant group of Negro houses, back of the Charlie Gee property, a whole mile, to chop wood and build fires in the morning, then return in the late afternoon to milk and feed. Why did Bill never have a holiday? Why not let him have the Fourth of July?

Now, for one thing, the Fourth was never celebrated in Mississippi in my growing-up time because Vicksburg had fallen to General Grant on that day. The Fourth was a reminder of that, and of other tragic losses. So it was deemed a Yankee holiday. All this I knew very well, but thought it only appropriate, since Bill was not a slave because of the war, that he ought to have the day off. I pronounced what I thought at the table.

Dad and Mimi took it lightly. There was no direct answer. They often enjoyed me, I think, and thought I was "original" and in a childish way "funny." I kept it up. Why not? "Well," one of them finally said, "what would he do with it?" "Anything he wanted to," I said. But the argument was put to nothing. I was finally told to hush. "If Bill had a day off," my father declared, laying down his napkin with his familiar air of ending a discussion for good and all, "he wouldn't know what to do with it. He would come up here anyway. That's exactly what would happen." With this he rose and left the room.

Then there was the crime, the old crime, the one nobody ever talked about . . .

When did I first learn about it? I think out of bits of conversation, overheard, half-heard, not clearly understood. "In the courthouse wall," was a repeated phrase. But what was in the courthouse wall? At what age did I first actually see it—the shattered plaster, left just as it had been at the end of a fateful day, the gray lathes exposed beneath, pocked with countless bullet holes? "Well, there was a shooting." "Who did they shoot?" "These Negroes." "Why?" "Well, things had gotten out of hand." "What things?" "We never knew the straight of it." Or "We weren't mixed up in it." Or "It all happened long ago." "Then why leave the bullet holes?" "I don't know."

Then I would forget all about it. But in some context or other it would surface again, more fearful details would be told, others given as speculation on what might have happened, what was rumored to have caused it, what terrors had arisen out of what facts or dark suspicions, until finally I even learned that it had a name: the Carrollton massacre.*

So what exactly was it, this massacre? Once I had a name for it, I could make a search through old publications until real information appeared, and so eventually I did. It should be quickly told.

In 1886, two Negroes in the country out from Carrollton brought a charge against a white man and several of his friends. The charge was for assault with intent to murder. The trial was to be held in the courtroom upstairs in the courthouse. Though warned not to attend, a number of Negroes came anyway.

While the trial was in progress, fifty or more white men, armed with shotguns and rifles, rode into town, rushed into the courtroom, and began firing. Ten Negroes were killed at once; others tried to escape by jumping out of the windows, but many

* This account of the "Carrollton massacre" is taken from *The Negro in Mississippi: 1865–1890* by Vernon Lane Wharton, University of North Carolina Press, 1947.

were wounded and died later. It was declared that the Negroes were armed and intended to start a fight, but no proof of the claim has been offered, and no white was injured.

In a state just emerging from Reconstruction, where a lynching was accorded only a line or two in local papers, if any notice at all, an outcry of horror and shame against "the murderous mob at Carrollton" appeared everywhere in the press. There were demands for investigation and punishment. It was said that names should be known and perpetrators hunted down. But so far as I ever heard, nothing of the sort was ever done.

At last, however, my private jigsaw puzzle of the actual event was complete. But no explanation has ever been given for leaving the bullet holes left by that mob, never plastered or papered over, plainly evident in the walls of the courtroom, where cases are tried and justice is sought. As late as the fifties the scars were still there. Word has it that some "redecoration" was completed in the courtroom, as late as 1992. Why not before?

It is a primal mystery of Carrollton, haunting me still.

A memory (from age nine, or ten, or eleven?): To my mother: "Did they ever have a Ku Klux Klan around here?"

"They did, yes. Your father went to one meeting and came home and said he wouldn't join. He saw what they were doing, and he didn't like it."

To Uncle Joe (shortly after): "Did they ever have a Ku Klux Klan around here?"

"They did, yes. But when I heard about it, I said to Father, 'I'm not going to have anything to do with it.' He said, 'I don't blame you, Son. I wouldn't either.' "

When Hallie Eggleston retired from her librarian's position at Ole Miss, she came back to Carrollton, saw her sister Frances through a fatal illness, and lived alone in the Eggleston house. She was always the same, except that in her last years her memory was a little out of kilter.

Hallie hired and then made a companion of a black girl named Ida Bean. I think Ida Bean was one of the Buzzard Roost residents. She never worked for us, but I always knew about Ida Bean. My mother used to say that whenever you saw

Ida Bean, she was in the middle of a crowd and they were all laughing.

Ida Bean began to drive for Miss Hallie. They became the best of friends. Hallie loved to go on trips—she lived "with her foot in the road," as the saying went. Ida Bean would drive her. Here and there they went, inseparable. They brought flowers and produce in from country places; they searched out sites and towns to visit, and friends of long ago. When people worried about Hallie, the saying went, "But then she does have Ida Bean." I passed them both once, getting into Hallie's car together, Ida Bean loading some packages in. "Now you wants this one here, and this one over there." It is nice to think about a friendship like that.

The Negroes on the family plantation at Teoc were different from the town Negroes mainly because they believed in spooks. "Ha'nts," they called them. After supper in winter, I would sneak into the kitchen where the wage hands, who regularly ate their dinners at the kitchen table, would linger around the huge fireplace, still smoldering with a few unspent logs, and talk in low voices about what they had seen, perhaps that very day.

"Brer Meuks was out there standing by the garden gate. I seen him just as plain as day."

They were talking about Armistead Meuks, my aunt's ancient gardener, dead for several years.

Lucille, the cook, said that yesterday she saw where a white sheet drying on a line had fallen to the ground. It rose up and went away, a good ways off, then fell down flat again.

There were numbers of stories, not every night, but pretty often. I remember the strong black heads, round as cannonballs, in the darkening room—this was before electric power, and the main house was lighted with gas flares—how they seemed to float up in the fading firelight. I remember the soft slurred voices. Lucille would be seated at the table, telling her share of tales. I would be seated off in a corner, all ears, scared to go back through the passages to the dining room, from the dining room back into the house, though, sooner or later, I must. A ha'nt would march before me, sure as anything; a spook would grab me by the neck.

. . .

I went fishing in summers with a Negro woman named Alice. Alice talked almost continually with spirits. They were there along with us, evidently. We had our fishing poles, our bait in one bucket, another bucket with dried cow manure, burning, a smudge for mosquitoes.

Alice had one troubled and quarrelsome voice for the spirits, another high-pitched, affectionate voice for me. I often had to wait until she would wave a hand before her face, saying "Go 'way now, y'all go 'way," before she would listen to anything I said. They were evidently pressing her for attention.

No one ever seemed to think I was in danger going with Alice into the swamps to catch little catfish and crawfish ("crawdads"), but later on, after Aunt Esther died and Uncle Joe remarried, she was overheard loudly plotting the murder of his second wife while sweeping the porch.

18

COLLEGE

TIMES away from Carrollton and Teoc were few, but memorable. I was sent away to camp in the mountains; I was sent away to college. The camp was Presbyterian, and so was the college. In some important respects, I never left home at all. They might as well have picked up our house and the church and moved them first to Montreat, North Carolina, then to Jackson, Mississippi.

Yet pretty clothes had been liberally bought for me and large suitcases packed with some excitement. I was stowed away among all my possessions new and old, in the family car for transport a hundred miles south to Belhaven College in Jackson.

New worlds might be in store, even if the college president was married to my father's cousin. He was a Presbyterian minister named Guy Gillespie. So the same religion as I had at home was about to be drummed once again into girlish ears.

Belhaven was set in a spacious campus opening out from a white-pillared mansion that dated from the olden times. This building, enlarged and made into a dormitory, faced a twin edifice across a pond, where large goldfish lazed and waterlilies bloomed at twilight. The grounds were extensive, including a lake for boating and long afternoon walks. Pine trees towered up on the rolling land; meadows and playing fields provided the aspect of an estate. The rules were strict. One classmate of mine was "campused" for eighteen weeks when she was caught smoking a *cigarette.* Another little bunch caught *dancing* in the Christian Association parlor met the same fate.

But when it came to getting an education, there was nothing terribly wrong with Belhaven College. Dr. Gillespie (Cousin Guy) thought of all of the three hundred or so girls in the student body as his daughters, one could only suppose. Attendance to his chapel sermons twice a week was obligatory. Rolls were checked, and dozing or letter writing was spied out and reprimanded.

I was there to excel in my books, make new friends, and enjoy sports, and so on and so forth. I was there to get a degree that would help me in finding work after I graduated. The place itself was beautiful, and the faculty, though required to be practicing and believing Christians, did not have to be Presbyterian. Many were. Years later, a Catholic friend remarked that I might as well have been sent to a convent. He was right.

However, Jackson itself was there surrounding us. The Belhaven Conservatory was well known and had a fine reputation. Those in the Jackson musical community came and went, and many of our music faculty were part of their society. I never remember catching the bus to town but that I hear sounding after me: "Ah ah *Ah* AH ah ah ah" from the open windows of the conservatory.

Infrequently traveling companies of theater from New York arrived, and we went in chaperoned busloads. Gertrude Lawrence came in *Skylark.* That afternoon, on Capital Street, a critic for the local paper was hurrying up and down announcing to all he passed, "I had lunch with Gertude Lawrence! You may touch me!" Katharine Hepburn came in *The Philadelphia Story.* Joseph Cotton and Van Heflin appeared with her. Reporters at the airport must have said the wrong things to Hepburn. She said she would pose for a picture, then held a tennis racket up before her face. We had to interpret such behavior as connoting contempt for Jackson, perhaps for all of Mississippi: Who knew how "they" felt about us? Nothing good was the message we got.

There was also the local talent, represented by the Jackson Little Theatre. We were allowed to go, for supporting local efforts was judged a civic duty. Here I saw some good plays for the first time—*Street Scene, The Time of Your Life,* some naughty comedies of Noël Coward's. I remember vividly a receiving line of local people greeting us for an opening-night performance. Among them was a thin man with a distracted, sensitive face. I learned later that this was the painter William Hollingsworth. He was only months away from his death by suicide. Books on his scenes from Mississippi life have now been published; I own two of his paintings.

In literature classes—I would, of course, major in English—the emphasis was on the older works: Chaucer, Shakespeare, Spenser, with large helpings of the romantic poets. I continued to study Latin, taught by a buxom maiden lady, Miss Annie McBride.

Miss Annie gave Roman dinners for her Latin students once a year. We dressed in long tunics, and so astonishingly garbed trailed along in the late afternoon toward the dining hall. Here in one of the parlors, we reclined on couches, partaking of grapes, exotic fruits like kumquats, dried figs, and other treats thought to be Roman. No wine was offered—grape juice again—and we tried to speak in Latin phrases, addressing one another as "Domina Spencer," "Domina McBride," "Domina Murphy," etc.

Miss Annie taught us Virgil. She was mightily displeased with Deedoe's behavior with *Eye*-neas, though she did say right out what went on in that cave, as some couldn't make out the text and were puzzled. We all thought Miss Annie looked like Juno.

Our "sophomore lit," a traditional survey course in English literature, began with *Beowulf* and ended with Thomas Hardy. Newer writers were suspect and were hardly mentioned, much less taught. A certain suspicion crept rather darkly around the edges of literary study, namely, that real writing had ended with Robert Browning at the latest. Free verse was frowned on. The head of the department was an opinionated old lady with snow-white hair. She was much revered, and wrote poetry herself.

Miss Alice Wells, who taught us the survey course, however, was young, a fine, spirited enthusiast of good things. She made us memorize! Long, difficult passages had to be written out word for word, line by line. "Whanne that Aprille with his shoures sote . . ." "Shall I compare thee to a summer's day . . ." "Of man's first disobedience . . ." "Hearing often-times the still sad music of humanity . . ." I hated doing it, as anyone would, but loved having done it. For just as in the early days I lay awake, telling over the myths and stories my mother had read me, inventing others as I wished, so now I could find Shakespeare and Wordsworth and Keats and Spenser treading through my mind in sleepy rhythms.

Alice Wells came from a distinguished Jackson family. She was a redhead like her father, Major Wells, who was president of the Belhaven board of trustees and would come out once a year and make a speech to us, always terminating with the same advice, "Don't study too hard!" The Wells mansion on North State Street was a grand brick structure; a hitching post stood before it for many years—the statue of a small black boy holding out an arm for the bridle. "Old-fashioned Jackson" was what it said to all who passed.

Jackson had been burned by the Yankees during the Civil War. General Sherman had requisitioned the governor's mansion on Capital Street. The story went that the Yankees had stabled their horses there. It was one of the few surviving residences, as Sherman had reduced Jackson by fire until it was called Chimneyville. Jackson in my time at Belhaven had a population of only about sixty thousand. We always said that Mississippi had no cities at all, and referred to Memphis and New Orleans as the "real" cities of our state.

For teaching our classes, Alice Wells drove into the campus from town. She came from an outside world, and I welcomed the feeling this fact gave me. Belhaven had no walls in the literal sense; anybody could walk right off the campus and be on a town street. In the daytime this was permissable, though a book was kept in the main office for signing out. At night, departures were forbidden, but rules were made to be broken, and those who dared to slip out were probably more numerous than anyone knew.

There are walls of every kind, but the worst are the walls of the mind. The problem is, well-meaning people put them up without knowing what they are doing. Brick at a time, they wall you in. They think it is "all for the best."

A short time before I entered Belhaven a literary meeting for college students throughout the Southwest had been inaugurated.

Member institutions were to rotate as hosts. Robert Penn Warren, the famed novelist, poet, and critic, then teaching at Southwestern in Memphis, spoke at the first meeting. Called the Southern Literary Festival, it was the first of many such gatherings. Nowadays they have broken out everywhere; since the South has discovered that living writers are of some importance, there is a regular epidemic. But then the meeting was the only one of its kind that I can recall.

When I was a freshman, Belhaven's turn came round. Writers, critics, and students from all the various member colleges and universities were to be upon us, along with any of the public who wished to attend.

It was then discovered that here in 1939 the Belhaven library held not a single book by Mississippi's best-known writer. No, there was no entry whatsoever for William Faulkner in the card catalogue. Yet an exhibit of Southern—especially Mississippi—writing was obligatory. What to do?

Now, it is true that Dr. Gillespie had his problems with literature in general. He was heard to speculate that Shakespeare probably should not be taught to "his girls," because he personally couldn't tell what Shakespeare's theology was. Milton was all right, but he had trouble with Miss Wells's adored romantic poets. Wordsworth appeared to be a pantheist, Coleridge undoubtedly took drugs, Byron was a libertine, Shelley a declared atheist, and Keats an unabashed pagan.

Throughout Mississippi the name of William Faulkner was well known. By the genteel readership, he was thought to be "not on the right track," mainly, I think, because they knew little as yet about modern writing. He was also known for having written all that awful stuff about sex in *Sanctuary*. It was talked about in whispers, and I could never overhear exactly what had gone on. Yet word of his importance was getting through chinks in the wall. What was Belhaven to do?

Fortunately, Faulkner himself had innocently furnished Dr. Gillespie with a solution, as some up-to-date person on our committee must have realized. He had recently published *The Unvanquished*, his most gentle and loving book, relating the trials of the Sartoris family during the Civil War and Reconstruction. I remember seeing this book on the display table in the library and thinking vaguely that I must someday read something by the author.

The following year this festival was held at Ole Miss (the University of Mississippi at Oxford). I had submitted a story and so was allowed to go there. One of the speakers had an odd name: Cleanth Brooks. I was not to learn for a while yet that here stood one of the mightiest voices in the so-called New Criticism. I observed a dark-haired, small, sturdy man, who spoke in a quiet, clear way on a sonnet of Wordworth's, "Upon Westminster Bridge." He said that most people thought the work was "simple" or "charmingly simple." He then proceeded to show, line by line, even word by word, that it was nothing of the kind, but was rich in philosophic meaning. It took a solid absorbing hour for all the lines in that short poem to be skillfully, patiently, turned inside out. This mild-mannered gentleman was full of hidden fire. I was hearing the New Criticism for the first time.

Also at that meeting I heard Faulkner praised and appraised; the early perceptions of his scope and purpose were beginning to come in. Faulkner himself actually lived in Oxford, but had refused to show up. "Not my cup of tea," he was said to have responded. I don't think he ever came to anything of this kind. But I went back to school with a prize for my story, and my head buzzing with all I had heard, all I had before me to learn about.

During my last two years at Belhaven two events of great significance for me occurred. One was the coming of Joseph Moody McDill as head of the English department. Dr. McDill's credentials included his having been trained for the Presbyterian ministry before he changed course and took a doctorate in literature at Vanderbilt University.

I remember the first time we met. He was talking to our dean, Miss Purnell Wilson, in her office, and she called me in from the hall outside to meet him. He must have been still in his thirties then, a stocky, intense man, with thinning reddish hair and blue eyes. His brow was broad and there was obviously a lot behind it. His voice was resonant. I liked him at once.

Of course, we got along well, developed an "in step" relationship in class, in thinking, in meetings of our student writing group, which he sponsored, in talks of every sort outside class.

He was eager to encourage creative students; he was excited to find some of those among us. I soon took him things I had written. He had the good sense to tell me I was mostly on the wrong track. But some of it he liked. Instead of praise, I had to get used to the word "promising."

Behind Dr. McDill stood the authority of Vanderbilt University, where my admired high school teacher Virginia Peacock had studied with Walter Clyde Curry. Dr. McDill was wonderful at teaching Shakespeare. He knew dramatic technique and could read lines from *Hamlet, Othello,* and the rest to bring out the emotion, the ring of the language, the tensions of conflict and passion. We had some exciting class sessions, over, it would seem, before they had time to begin.

But the major thrill he brought us was one day when he came to another teacher's class in modern poetry to introduce us to the work of T. S. Eliot. I had heard the name but inquiries had produced little enlightenment. We had been studying Vachel Lindsay, Edna St. Vincent Millay, and Sara Teasdale. It must have been Dr. McDill's enthusiasm for Eliot in some social conversation that led to his being invited to old Miss Newman's class, she with her reverence for Edgar Allan Poe (she was from Virginia and thought that Poe was too) and Alfred, Lord Tennyson.

After speaking for a time on Eliot's life, his thinking, beliefs, and career up to the present, Dr. McDill began to read *The Waste Land.* It sounded like the words of a divinity speaking in an unknown tongue. Yet it was powerful; we knew that. It seemed to steamroll right over us. Finishing, he then began to talk of the poem, to go back over the lines and show us the fluidity of the technique, the syncopation of the rhythms, the wide range of allusions and shifting frames of reference. He remarked on each of the various sections, then proposed ways of seeing the whole as one poem. We had no copies of the text as yet. I made sure to go and find one. I felt I had turned a corner and found the modern era. I had been living in it all the time, but no one had told me so.

By the time I had become a senior, Dr. McDill was talking seriously to me about where to apply for graduate study. He thought that I should go further, and he was eager to recommend me wherever I wished to go, but he strongly favored Vanderbilt. Most graduate departments in universities were not so good for a creative person, he thought; in fact, they might be deadly, burying creativity in laborious research projects. Vanderbilt still retained the creative glow from such spirits as Donald Davidson, John Crowe Ransom, and others who had flourished there. He loved speaking of them all, describing them to me in advance. One could tell that being there had been a high point in his life and that of his wife, Margaret. She also spoke happily of their time there.

The other significant Belhaven event was the chance to meet Eudora Welty. Her first book, *A Curtain of Green,* had come out in 1941. We saw it noted in reviews. Well, she had been there all the time, born in Jackson; her father had been president of a well-known insurance company. She was, in fact, living right across the street!

Our little writing group began to squirm. The local lady poets who would come read their work to us had been generously sampled, but here was something else again, a young writer whose work was being nationally recognized. Yet we were unusually nervous about approaching her.

I wonder now why we were so apprehensive. I think it was William Faulkner's eccentric ways that gave us pause. Maybe all writers were like that, hostile to invitations, cold toward admirers. Often, if the tales had any truth to them, insulting.

Yet we were going to ask her, come what may, and somehow it fell to my lot to ring her up. I remember shaking in the dormitory phone booth. I had seen her, after all, from time to time—once in her front yard in a pair of slacks, pushing a wheelbarrow full of leaves, gardening, and again, riding the same bus as we rode to town, wearing an exotic suit of pale green suede. Still, to her I would be nothing but a frail little schoolgirl voice.

It was a very soft voice that answered my ring—her own. Somehow I got my message out. Would she come and talk to us? Well, no, she didn't make speeches. (My heart sank.) *But* . . . could she come simply as our guest? (Gleeful response: "Oh, yes!") The way she had put it, it seemed I was the one to grant the favor.

She appeared for us by walking across the street on a lovely spring day. Everything was blooming, and everybody had a glow from simply seeing her appear. We brought her to the McDill apartment, where we usually met. We read some things we had written and she listened with care. It seemed an enchanted afternoon.

Later, we walked with her across the campus toward Pinehurst Street. She seemed to have taken an interest in me from the story I had read, and we talked in an informal way about writers she had known—Katherine Anne Porter, I remember, among them—and what plans I had. I mentioned hoping to go to Vanderbilt. She told me of some friends I should meet.

Eudora herself has written of this occasion and the afternoon she spent with us. For me it was the beginning of a long friendship, which continues to this day. A young first-book writer then, she is now in her mid-eighties, celebrated everywhere for her achievements; a Jackson library is named for her, and an impressive collection of her "papers" is the stellar attraction of the Mississippi archives. Innumerable honorary degrees and awards and unending tributes have poured down on her.

One of the last times I was in Jackson I took a cab out to Pinehurst Street to see her. The cabdriver said, "Lady, unless you got some reason to go there, you ain't got a prayer to get in." To get him in motion at all, I had to tell him I was expected.

An amazing aspect of Eudora's life is how personal, despite her fame, she is able to keep all her relationships. It never seems to enter her mind to be anything but her own Jackson, Mississippi, self. This intimate quality enters into her writing and gives it much of its appeal; when we compare it with the work of others of considerable note, it seems all the more singular, a gift.

The bad thing about being at Belhaven, for me, was the absence of social life. The things I had been told by then about "boys" and how to attract them, how to please them, how to hold on to them, were so many and various that to believe any of them served one purpose only: to make for silly ideas about what they were like, as though the male of the species inhabited another planet. I listened to such talk but none of it was suited to me, and growing up, as a result, began to seem a never-ending pain, not eased at all by seeing other students whose room buzzers constantly summoned them to dates and phone calls.

I felt that where boys were concerned I must be the plainest and dullest of girls. I didn't see then that any kind of supervision made my spirits fade away. Permission for dates, restrictions about leaving the campus, monitors who went about checking to see that everybody stayed out of the dark—who could feel that life was tracking along in a natural way?

Following advice (so liberally dished out by my mother, my aunts, my cousins, and my ever-flirting friends), trying to be "like everybody else," resembled trying to waltz while tap-dancing. Trip-ups and spills were right ahead every time. Did I really care to be Miss Pickle Queen of Wiggins, Mississippi? Miss Watermelon Festival of Crystal Springs? Of course not. The ways of "cute girls" and "Southern belles" were a blind alley for me. But what else did any girl in that place and time have to wish for?

I became terribly shy. I could remind myself that in summers, in Charleston, S.C., where my brother was an intern in Roper Hospital, or off visiting friends, I had times of real blossoming. I met "cute boys," or better still "interesting guys," and got my share of calls and gifts and dates, like anyone else. But in school I felt hopelessly isolated from all this.

How to explain it? To myself I became at times an intriguing mystery, but mostly I was someone I had rather not think about.

I had to learn that becoming a self for better or worse is the only way, but sometimes yet I feel the shy streak creeping in, and wonder how anyone could possibly accept me as I am.

Then the years had passed and I was packing for another reason: graduate school. With Dr. McDill to recommend me in glowing terms, I had gotten a scholarship, and would be coming to Vanderbilt as a favored student.

PART THREE

Widening Orbits

19

VANDERBILT DAYS

It was 1942, during World War II, an odd time to be getting a master's degree in literature.

Vanderbilt University, where I had been granted a scholarship, is in Nashville, Tennessee, a city in a valley surrounded by the low Cumberland Mountains. During the winter, coal smoke could not escape and made a smog so thick it was possible to see only a few feet ahead. It soiled white blouses and shirts, and medical students reported cadavers in the labs with lungs stained black as tar. Nevertheless, the university rose proudly on what was then the city's southern reach, and a few blocks away, Centennial Park, with its replica of the Parthenon, confirmed that here indeed was the "Athens of the South."

What I had come for was something less visible but in literary circles more famed. The Vanderbilt Fugitives, later known as the Agrarians, had had their beginnings here, and their word seemed nothing less than *the* Word. Spreading outward, it had become law in the world of modern letters. The great names—John Crowe Ransom, Allen Tate, Robert Penn Warren, Andrew Lytle, Donald Davidson—cast a shadow that had nothing in common with coal smoke. Here one entered an ambience rather like that of a sacred grove.

It is hard to imagine now, when all sorts of literary voices are shouting together, none phenomenally heard above the rest, what centrality of judgment this group commanded. When one looks back into recent critical history, it is interesting to recall that a remark from T. S. Eliot kept a whole generation of eager young students from reading Milton. Word went out far and wide when Eliot declared that it was all right to read Kipling! The Vanderbilt group, in touch with British and French literary figures principally through Allen Tate, were accorded that same awed regard everywhere. What did they praise? One must hurry to have it in hand. What did they condemn? Admitting an admiration for Somerset Maugham, to give one instance, was a bid for scorn and censure. Just as *The Waste Land* was endlessly unraveled as to nuance, source, and meaning in hundreds of student papers, so the latest poem of Warren or Ransom was to be pondered and dissected, the latest critical article passed around.

I had heard about them all at Belhaven from Dr. McDill, and from the first it was Davidson—the only one of the illustrious tribe remaining on the faculty—who attracted me. I was determined to write my thesis, a requirement for the degree, with Davidson as my director. With this end in mind, I enrolled in his course in modern literature.

There was something about Donald Davidson that scared students to death. I used actually to shake when I had to go into his office, stand in his presence, and stumble through whatever I had to say. I have heard strong men relate how as students they felt exactly the same. Feature for feature, nothing suggested the effect of his presence. He was scarcely above medium height, neither fat nor thin. He dressed in a mild, gentlemanly way. But he had steely gray eyes that seemed to look straight to the inside of your thoughts, a kindly tone of voice (until something angered him), brown hair growing thin, the small beginning of what looked like a smile. It suggested many things: a willingness to listen? to sympathize? to laugh? to reject? You couldn't know which, but felt its quality was mainly one of waiting. When seated, he appeared taller than he actually was, a figure so erect behind a desk he might have been on horseback. What he had was *authority.*

His lectures would start low-key. He was informative but never spewed out an overload of facts. It was one of his tenets (in this he followed the New Criticism, though he never classed himself as one of them) that knowledge of a writer's life was no substitute for the writer's writing. The history and social habits of the writer's times might be helpful but were not of primary importance. Neither did it matter so much—in many cases not at all—what emotions a piece of writing might (or might not) waken in the reader. What mattered was THE TEXT. What was it saying? Pay close attention. Read. Let it speak from the page. Form mattered. Structure mattered. Style mattered. Davidson liked to say that excellence in a novelist—Thomas Hardy, for instance; William Faulkner, for instance—had come from a "careful study of Greek tragedy." Who could doubt he was right? Certainly no listener in his classroom dared to do so.

I came into his office one day, a shy, frail, dark-haired student, to ask timidly if I could request his direction for a thesis on William Butler Yeats. As we were talking, a slim, sensitive-looking man entered from the hallway through the open door of the office. He was wearing a checkered vest and a black velvet jacket. He had an extraordinary face, not at all handsome but arresting, his brow being so high that his features seemed rather minimal beneath it. Mr. Davidson introduced us: "Miss Spencer, this is Allen Tate."

I must have said hello. A woman did not offer a hand to a gentleman in those days (I wonder when this practice started). Mr. Davidson continued: "Miss Spencer has just announced she would like to write a thesis on William Butler Yeats."

Tate moved to the window and stood there, profiled in thought. "One should note the influence of the French poets on Yeats. Some of his early work comes straight from French lyrics. 'When you are old and gray and full of sleep,' for instance. It's pure Ronsard." He quoted others, mentioning names which my ignorance of them did not permit me to remember. I felt he knew a lot. His voice was sensual, softly slurred, a quality he never lost. I sat paralyzed, wondering if I would be able to tackle my chosen subject at all, until Davidson changed the subject. "Yes . . . well . . ." he said and turned to me. "To begin you must go and read all of Yeats. Read everything he wrote." "*All* of it?" I asked. "All of it," he said. He smiled. There was nothing so nice as an approving smile from that formidable man. "Then come back to me," he said.

I went out more shaken than when I came in. But at least, I thought, he had got me out of the mysteries of France, which I, with my two years' study of French at Belhaven, was in no way fitted to deal with. Perceptive to all I was feeling at that moment, Davidson had stepped in to give me something I could *do*.

Davidson's thinking and feeling were most passionately concerned with the South. The old, much maligned, backward, impoverished, tobacco-chewing, front-porch-rocking, cotton-picking, Latin-and-Greek-revering, racially segregated, agrarian South. Even then it was whispered that he was obsessed. He dwelt on events of the Civil War, tales of past military glories, on Southern writing, and on the thoughts and character of men like Jackson and Lee. Not that he necessarily scorned all that was Yankee. He would have said he loved America—the older, rooted America as it was meant to be—divided regionally, but despite differences in culture and climate, compatible and in many diverse ways one people.

What Mr. Davidson hated—and when he hated he grew enraged, eyes flashing, voice harshly polemical—was Leviathan. He saw it as monstrous, the great standardizing commercial machine that was rolling over and plowing under home-grown cultures that had flourished earlier. He loathed mass culture. He was staunch in his beliefs, immovable, unchanging. Disagreement from a student on some issue basic to his thinking—socialism, for example, or racial equality, or "progress"—brought a response as if to blasphemy. He was vehemently opposed to President Roosevelt and the New Deal.

Much later when I was myself working on a novel in Nashville, I had a period of helping him grade papers. I also met with some of his classes. A student from a Northern state had written on John Steinbeck's *Grapes of Wrath*. "Look," said Davidson, observing the title. "He couldn't stay away from it to save his life." He laid aside the paper as though it smelled bad. Yet Steinbeck was on his reading list in modern literature. Novels by Tate, Andrew Lytle, and Caroline Gordon were obviously approved, and William Faulkner, whom I was myself just discovering, was the subject of Davidson's keenest thought and presentation.

As his student I once chose a novel of Faulkner's for a critical paper. Davidson read it aloud in class, then launched into a voluble attack on my point of view. My criticism took some note of Faulkner's contemptuous behavior, as it was always being talked about in Mississippi. We had all assumed he was showing scorn for the society we, like him, had been reared in. I next related this attitude to his writing and found many evidences of it, and I felt I was being loyal to my own people to criticize it. But Davidson pointed out that Faulkner's intention as a writer was quite otherwise; I had not found the true meaning of the text. Furthermore, what did a writer's behavior have to do with what he chose to write? Nothing . . . at least nothing that a critic could properly present. Down on my small head came the whole weight of the New Criticism. I went to his desk at the end of the class. "I'd like to have it back," I said, "that is, if there is anything left of it." Again, the smile. "A very fine paper, Miss Spencer. I thank you for it."

What contradictions there were in that man's makeup! Now it seems clear that he had seen my mind at work, even if going off on the wrong track, and thought me of enough value to want to haul me back and set me down to start over again, think things through onto firmer ground.

For it was clear that I had ventured into sacred territory: he believed that I must not mistake what was there. Reasoning on subjects so important had to be both careful and precise. His own caring gave him the motive for taking me to task. Another lecturer might have said, "Well, this is one approach to Faulkner. But I wonder if you have considered . . . ," etc. Not Donald Davidson.

Davidson once published a monograph called "To the Warders of the Gate." It was about the role of the teacher. The metaphor is revealing. A battle is indicated—attack and defense. The matter is that crucial, of maximum importance. What is taught reaches through to minds that, once set right, have a chance of staying right.

Davidson was wonderfully perceptive when it came to novelists outside the Southern frame. Theodore Dreiser came through on the winning side. Willa Cather stood up strongly and cast her individual shadow. She believed passionately in traditional cultures; she doted on seeing them survive when transplanted to the

New World. But Davidson's lecture on Sinclair Lewis left a trail of shredded paper. I remember laughing aloud. Davidson thought that Lewis was naturally a comic writer. "How can he do a serious subject when he can't keep a straight face?"

Novelists all but forgotten, like Frank Harris, sometimes are "rediscovered," and I find myself remembering Davidson's comments, seeing again the fine penetration he brought to bear. He was a bit too derisive at times. He valued Thomas Wolfe but with so many reservations that Wolfe had a rough ride. "What does he mean that he's lost, he's . . . *lost* . . . ? Where exactly are the 'ramparts of his soul'?"

His Jamesian lectures focused on *The Ambassadors*. He was scarcely at home talking of Parisian manners; at an elegant soirée he might have felt a little gauche, certainly not in his native element, though he had courtly, old-fashioned manners. Many years later, however, he wrote me with enthusiasm about *The Bostonians*—a fine novel, he reported, with Basil Ransom, a Mississippian, among all those New England doctrinaire "do-gooders." "He showed them all up," he rejoiced to say.

In his class, we also studied the British novelists, beginning with Hardy. Hardy's ties to the soil, the English farming country, led straight to Davidson's high esteem. Then there was the spirit of Greek drama, which Hardy called to mind. Davidson denied that Hardy was a pessimist. He had no more responsibility for the tragic outcome of events than did the singer of a harsh old ballad.

Conrad he admired so much he could find no fault to proclaim. I, too, made the Conrad discovery during that course. I would never like to be without him. He gave no easy answers, and led the reader's mind out naturally into the wider world that he knew firsthand. I see his long shadow everywhere to this day, extending to Graham Greene, to Robert Stone, to V. S. Naipaul. Back then both Faulkner and Hemingway were easier for me after I read Conrad.

But there were other aspects of being "modern," and these opened up increased complexities. Davidson taught Joyce's *Ulysses* as a gigantic satire on life in a modern city. I remember writing one of our required papers on Joyce's *Portrait of the Artist as a Young Man*. Davidson had remarked that it seemed symptomatic of the modern era that a writer must stand up and identify the "I" (Stephen Dedalus), that it seemed necessary to establish a unique separate experience, an enabling act for writing at all. Writers of other times, he believed, had felt no such necessity.

"Stream of consciousness" brought Virginia Woolf to the fore. She was not dismissed, but his reservations were many. "Compare her to Joyce," he proposed. "She is like a little flute player confronting his grand orchestration."

On one of these absorbing days, Allen Tate once more wandered in. Tate was living at Sewanee, Tennessee, at the time, and the trip to Nashville was an easy drive down from the mountain. At Davidson's request he came into our lecture hall while we were still on Joyce. Our eager faces were expectant. Tate, a born dramatist, knew how to make the most of an unplanned appearance like this one. He began to talk, first about *Ulysses*. In no time he had led us into a fascinating tangle of ideas—all suggested, lightly indicated, alluring. Vividly he reminisced on the first time he had actually read the book. An early copy had compelled his attention so much that he walked about reading it, and waking without it, recalled he had been interrupted and forced to put it aside out on a summer lawn. He went out on a rainy night to find it.

Tate remarked that he considered *Finnegans Wake* one of "the great tragedies of literature." Someone was timidly puzzled as to his meaning. Not that it was itself a tragedy, he explained; he thought its failure as a work was tragic. Once again, Davidson was skillful in bringing his bedazzled flock back into the fold.

College courses may be of some cumulative benefit, but few are absolutely defining, continuing through life as a means of judgment—in this case a way of perceiving literature. This was what Davidson's course meant to me. What he personally meant is easier to see now than then. At the time I felt myself a humble worshiper, resentful a little that anyone should assume such a large degree of authority. Now I can see how much his perceptions of me were of benefit. For *he* could see me as a well-brought-up but totally unsophisticated small-town girl of a farming family, and he could approve of that; and furthermore only he could positively rejoice in my being able to excel not in spite of but *because of* this upbringing. He himself, sensitive and bedeviled by a load of work no gifted poet should have had to bear, had begun to share a great many personal matters with me, as a favored student. And in the end, I suppose, like many others, I was a disappointment, unable to accept his dogmas—which as time went on grew more and more strict, especially in matters of race—finally straying off for good.

As for Allen Tate, he was often discussed among the graduate crowd I socialized with. Some knew him; everyone had stories about him to repeat. His poetry was read and quoted. Word of his sexual affairs, his marital crises, perhaps exaggerated, reached our ears.

I puzzled as best I might over Tate's poetry. Its brilliance was obvious, its meaning not easily discovered. I found some lines opaque. Whatever did "one peeled aster drenched with wind all day" have to do with the tragic matter in "The Death of Little Boys"? Well, maybe the aster was a plant in the windowsill in the room where the child died. But a few lines on, suddenly "delirium assails the cliff in Norway where you ponder." Norway! My literal brain was something of a handicap for taking such extravagant leaps. I got on better with the famous poem "Ode to the Confederate Dead," where by a cemetery wall the poet sees the charging leaves in an autumn wind as a reminder of charging armies. But when I reached the lines on how to think of the sacrifice the dead have made and find we must resort to

> *. . . mute speculation, the patient curse*
> *That stones the eyes, or like the jaguar leaps*
> *For his own image in a jungle pool, his victim.*

I wonder what a jaguar is doing in this Southern scene. Many a young brain worked hard to discover the meaning of such difficult images. Yet there were wonderful, accessible and justly famous lines, like "What shall we say who have knowledge/Carried to the heart?" and ". . . the salt of their blood/Stiffens the saltier oblivion of the sea." Here was brilliance at work.

This studious attention went side by side with the textual study of Eliot, Ezra Pound, Gerard Manley Hopkins. Few others were so thoroughly approved. Tennyson was out, Browning was a maybe. Besides, who studied Victorian literature anymore? You had better go straight back to John Donne.

Then there was poetry by John Crowe Ransom, the pride of Vanderbilt, recently hired away "up north," to Kenyon College. To my reading, Ransom was so deep buried in the Southern myth of people, landscape, history, that his marvelous lyric gifts seemed always to be wandering around there. The speaker of his poem "Old Mansion" is wandering, too, thinking about one of those old Southern houses, an icon, so easily read as a model of how we all lived once, or thought we did or should have:

> *Each time of seeing I absorbed some other feature*
> *Of a house whose annals in no wise could be brief*
> *Nor ignoble; for it expired as sweetly as Nature*
> *With her tinge of oxidation on autumn leaf.*

Settings are pleasant, sunlit and warmly Southern. "Blue Girls" stroll across a "finishing school" lawn. Little "Janet Waking" weeps over her pet hen, stung to death by a bee. In the twilight, a "gentleman in a dust coat" tries talking to a pretty girl. It flows so beautifully into things long known, bred in the bone.

What was wrong with that? I used to wonder. I, too, had been brought up on these myths. Someone needed to speak out in celebration of it, to invent litanies to their beauty and melancholy, their persistence. But when I read poems like "Judith of Bethulia" and "The Equilibrists," I got glimpses of a wider landscape. Chills go up my spine when I read of Judith: "Beautiful as the flying legend of some leopard . . ." Or when one hears spelled out the plight of two lovers kept apart by honor:

> *Leave me now, and never let us meet,*
> *Eternal distance now command thy feet.*

There was a passionate spirit here, not ever perhaps released from what someone has called "the Southern obligation."

Ransom was something of an elder statesman of the onetime close-knit group, who had begun back in the twenties to come together to read their poems and excite their minds during what must have been great evenings of exchange. Tate had brought in an exceptional discovery, a red-haired undergraduate named Robert Penn Warren. And Davidson was present, along with others, like Merrill Moore, whose names have dropped from sight. Ransom, courtly and charming, was ready to gather them and others into a widening orbit. Then he left.

At that time there were stories circulating as to why this departure. The Agrarians were controversial, it was true. They delighted to kick the stuffing out of soft Victorian optimism, to show how cherished poems, like Joyce Kilmer's "Trees," were weak efforts. If audiences were shocked, it was good for them. Let them see what literature was actually saying, something neither simple nor sweet. Rumor asserted that conflict with the administration had forced Ransom out. All this has found its recorders elsewhere. I knew little but that they all were measurelessly gifted, had stimulated one another, had been in glad accord for one brief, shining moment which changed forever the way we read literature.

They still revered one another, and seemed to think of themselves as still present, still united. Learning later how bitter literary quarrels can become, I marvel at how loyal a band they remained. They might cast aspersions in private conversation, but no outsider was allowed to do so unchallenged. We heard that Ransom and Tate had dismissed Davidson's poetry, but Davidson, though perhaps resentful of the slight, still taught Ransom's lyrics and Tate's highbrow stanzas with care and pride. Scandal about the Tates might rock the mountain at Sewanee, but Davidson, who was singularly upright, could be seen lunching at a local restaurant with Allen and his wife, Caroline Gordon.

Carrollton, Mississippi, seemed a greater and greater distance away from me during those heady years. But once, when I was walking the short distance from my rooming house to the campus, a surprising encounter took place. I found myself overtaken along by an energetic, brisk gentleman, who was one of the Vanderbilt professors, Frank Owsley.

Professor Owsley was a historian, noted for his work on Southern subjects. He asked where I came from. "Mississippi," I said, but he wanted more. What town? When I said "Carrollton," he paused and we walked on a few steps in silence. "Then you know about the Carrollton massacre?" he said. It was half a question. "Yes, I do," I answered. That was all.

Robert Penn Warren's departure to go up north to Minnesota was the subject of grand lament. He had been teaching at Louisiana State University in Baton Rouge at the time. With Cleanth Brooks, that other pioneer of the New Criticism, Warren had founded the influential *Southern Review* at Louisiana State University. There was evidently some hostility to them within the LSU administration. The fears ran that Warren might never come home again. How could he do it? his Southern admirers wondered. It seemed he had done something to all of *us*. But Brooks, too, had left for Yale, where Warren as well would eventually take a position. Still, their group never regarded him or Cleanth except as one of them, in some mystical way still living below the Mason-Dixon line. They never quite gave one another up.

Who else could be put beside them? They reached out with high selectivity, and drew in whom they would. Faulkner was never part of their group or any other, but they did much to advance Faulkner criticism, which was only in the forties beginning to make sense of his achievement. George Marion O'Donnell from Mississippi, a student of Davidson's, had done groundwork on Faulkner criticism which was to be basic to all future critical exploration. Peter Taylor gravitated to them and when the war ended swung easily into their orbit.

Up north, working with undiminished energy, Warren encouraged the young Saul Bellow. His friend Albert Erskine, at Random House, edited and promoted Ralph Ellison's *Invisible Man*. They were unanimous in noting and praising Eudora Welty, just as before her Katherine Anne Porter had won their high esteem. William Styron, inevitably, became an accepted friend. Among the poets, Robert Lowell had sought out the Tates, and spent time in Baton Rouge with his wife of that time, the gifted Jean Stafford.

Eventual differences within the group seemed to me (entirely from the periphery) not so much based in literary theory; instead, they tended to spring from the "Southern way of life." A basic idea of the old South's true nature would always be held by them as common knowledge and a common bond. Thus when the Agrarians put together *I'll Take My Stand,* a collection of essays to set forth their position, they sought out others who held that knowledge too—Stark Young from Mississippi, for example, and John Gould Fletcher of Arkansas, and several more.

But a joker was hiding in the deck. It was black and it was bound to show up sooner or later and it raised a question.

In his later years, I was told, and have every reason to believe, Davidson grew more and more reactionary. His scorn for those who questioned the segregation of races in the South was evident even back in the forties, when I was a student. He regarded those blacks highly who were able, always as individuals, to "find a place for themselves," in terms of the prevailing white culture. He remarked once in class that a plantation owner he knew had said that when a black worker misbehaved he had to do something about it, so he gave him a whipping. "They're just children, after all." Davidson admired a Disney movie that came out about that time, *Song of the South.* It celebrated the Uncle Remus stories of Joel Chandler Harris. It glorified, said Davidson, "the old-fashioned Negro." He seemed to fear, even back then, that Warren's more generous attitudes toward race, as expressed in his essay in *I'll Take My Stand,* foretold defection.

I never heard from Davidson again after the publication of my own novel on a racial subject, *The Voice at the Back Door.* He must have had to recognize that I had jumped the fence. I don't doubt that in his view outer darkness was my lot, and I believe there would never have been any chance of my getting back in. Perhaps I behaved too timidly in the matter, but I know I would have had to survive his wrath, and this I had no inclination to risk. I saw once or twice in memoirs of the group that Tate had admired my novel. I was surprised and gratified, especially as I knew Tate had remained in touch with Davidson. There is also the fact that after the novel appeared, I was awarded a Kenyon Review Fiction Fellowship, and Kenyon called Ransom to mind at once. Warren was generous in his praise of the book. Enough said.

I like to think of them, despite differences of whatever nature, all remaining eternally in touch. One thinks of some Valhalla reserved for them, of meetings still going on—the lengthy discussions, the ideas advanced for talk to turn on, the new poems brought in fresh to read aloud, frequent laughter at genuine wit, the rise and fall of excited voices. A large fireplace burns companionable logs in the somewhat rundown, pleasantly shabby Southern parlor, windows reaching to the floor, dogs snuffling out on the front porch in the night. Their joyousness in one another, the pure zest of the intellect they shared—all this should never die.

Davidson has celebrated them in a poem written long after the group dispersed. The writers are dominant, but Frank Owsley is thought of as one of them also:

> *. . . remember the firelight blessing*
> *Owsley's uplifted head, Ransom's gray eye,*
> *The Kentucky voice of Warren, until that household's*
> *Oaken being spoke like a plucked lyre.*

I take to heart more personally—not to say it was so meant, for I knew Davidson long after it was written—a poem called "Spoken at a Castle Gate," dating from his earlier days. It seems to breathe out the spirit he gave to his students, the prophecy of what might lie ahead for stubbornly creative spirits:

> *Before you touch the bolt that locks this gate*
> *Be warned. There's no return where you are going.*
> *A sword is tinder at the touch of fate*
> *And crumbles in a way beyond your knowing. . . .*
>
> *A voice that follows you past endless night . . .*
> *Even as you touch the bolt that locks this gate. . . .*
> *. . . Ah, yes, what you create*
> *Perhaps you'll find,—but never come back again.*

20

VANDERBILT AND BEYOND

MORE even than the Agrarian movement, for all its dazzlement, the one overwhelming fact about my time at Vanderbilt was World War II. Social life was either minimal, or conducted in odd ways. The girls I knew from our classes all had boyfriends in the service. I, like the rest, got my share of V-mail with APO numbers for return addresses. Paragraphs were cut out, messages absurdly reduced to fragments. I remember a girl who received one of these missives with all but the salutation blotted out, no text left. "You suppose he said he loves me?" she wanted to know, waving the sheet in the air.

Sometimes, for the lark, we piled up together to go to soldiers' dances. Other times, servicemen on leave came in to visit. Nightclubs, floor shows, dancing, whiskey and beer. Letters from lonely men who would fall in love with you if you'd only write back.

Of the men around school who were still not in service because of 4F status, or who were soon to be called up, not many were of more than intellectual interest, though I found their talk of things I had little knowledge about was stimulating, and we developed friendships that seemed "meaningful" at the time. I learned to do wicked things like smoke cigarettes and drink beer. There was a gathering place across the street from the university called Butch Petrone's. It was where we went to laugh and drink after the library closed, and it was fun. I used to feel daring, and I liked the free talk and the company. They say that college trains you for life. Much later, when I made it to Paris, I found people who sat around the sidewalk tables at the Deux Magots were doing what we did in Butch Petrone's.

But even with all the loving thoughts of men in uniform, the war put life on hold. Everything one saw ahead seemed dependent upon it. A cloud had to lift before the sun could shine. We followed the papers and broadcasts and talked about men, as girls do in any time or place, but it was all a waiting game. We were young and lively. We read the war news, and answered our V-letters, and felt that for us the times had not been fair.

I continued to write. I showed fragments of a novel I had started to Donald Davidson, but had to see that it was only "promising." I wrote my thesis on William Butler Yeats, graduated, and was offered a job teaching English in a junior college at Senatobia, Mississippi, a town south of Memphis, Tennessee.

In Senatobia I met a young woman whose interests were similar to mine, Carolyn Pugh, daughter of the college president. We became fast friends. Carolyn was also at work in a first job, teaching high school in the Delta. But she, more than I, was leaning outward. The war was on; jobs were available that usually would have been filled by young men. She revealed in confidence that though she valued family ties, she was acquiring a real dislike for Mississippi, its narrow outlook, its ignorant disdain of a larger world, the poverty of cultural interest. Many people were charming, many were endlessly laughable, but to her it was not the world she wanted to live in. Predictably, she left a year later, having found secretarial work in Washington. Like me, she had broken off early romantic interests when it seemed they were going nowhere.

For myself, I had at that time no notion of leaving the South. I think after Vanderbilt I was more attached to tradition than ever. I had thought all along of trying for some branch of the service, but had to give up the idea because I had never been very strong physically and had been subject to any number of ailments and frequent stress from overwork. I did dare to hope for publication of my work, to win through to a writing life. I clearly saw that reaching my goal would take an excessive amount of luck.

But to leave the South, my home and native land, seemed a sort of betrayal. With his great skill as a teacher, Davidson had led me to see modern literature as a profound experience. But he also sought to imbue his students with a sense of what Southernness meant, a quality that was more than just American. To him the South was still a nationality, an allegiance, a continuing cause, a land to take a stand in, to live and die for. If I was to write, then sticking with my heritage would be the only route possible.

So I reasoned, though I had to note that "sticking with the South" at the moment meant living in an ill-heated dormitory room, eating greasy food in a noisy dining hall, getting up at six for breakfast, or trudging across the highway to eat at a filling station, teaching four classes a day, and doing all the chores regularly assigned to the English teacher. These included: assisting with the school paper and the annual, teaching a Sunday School class at the Presbyterian church, going in a pickup truck on cold, sometimes rainy, nights to see the basketball team play in a drafty gym in some town even smaller than Senatobia, one of them named Independence but known as Bucksnort. One end of the Bucksnort gym had a small iron stove, burning red-hot and doing little good beyond ten feet. A white-haired man sitting near it looked me over and heaved up out of a cane-bottom chair. "Gal," he said, "you need this worse'n me." I was also asked to direct the school play, but refused. "There are some things the English teacher always does," they said. I said I couldn't. The typing and shorthand teacher, an attractive girl who smoked a corncob pipe, agreed to the chore but didn't like it much.

I had no car and every afternoon I walked uptown. The family of a man I had known at Vanderbilt lived there, and their enveloping hospitality was a big help. Once I came down with flu just as the school was closing for a holiday. They came without a second thought and took me in.

This junior college was one of a number run by the state. It offered two years of college, tacked on to a four-year high school. There was a big emphasis on vocational training, such as agriculture and secretarial skills. The students in the college were well-mannered enough to teach with some pleasure, but the entire football team seemed to have landed in the twelfth-year English class. Keeping them halfway quiet took most of my time, and furthermore was not really possible. If I turned my back to the blackboard, paper airplanes whizzed across the room, loud noises exploded, rickety desks squeaked and clanged. I taught grammar and composition as best I might; I graded innumerable half-literate papers; I even taught Shakespeare. One student wrote some pages dealing with "Macbeth and Miz Macbeth," how they had ganged up on this old king.

Nearby Camp McCain (named for "Uncle Pink") was the scene of soldiers' dances. I was inevitably asked to chaperone, but wound up with not one but two boyfriends myself. I shared them with Carolyn on weekends, and we found ourselves dating polite but awkward Yankee servicemen who had not the faintest idea of the wondrous things we talked about and wished to have as part of life.

Girls and women everywhere in civilian life were restless. A society at whatever level stumbles along in wartime. The college girls dated high-school boys who had scarcely begun to shave. "Nursemaids wanted for our escorts," ran one headline in the school paper.

Hard times, a daily fact of life during my childhood, and part of the Depression, now said to have ended with the war, still persisted. I was earning less than one hundred and fifty dollars a month, plus the room (no private bath), and meals.

After one year of teaching in Mississippi, I was offered a job in a finishing school, Ward-Belmont, in Nashville. A return to Nashville, where warmth and encouragement for my writing, not to mention intellectual stimulation, had been found before and might well be again, seemed the best and only course. Carolyn was gone from Mississippi. She would visit, as I would also, we would exchange voluminous confidential letters, but we would never live in the same place again. I had no sister, and think at that time she filled my need for one.

At any rate, the friendship had occurred between us at a crucial moment and had been rewarding; we were two young women different from our social group in our intense interest in reading, our family backgrounds, our sensitivities. She was attractive, questioning, both venturesome and vulnerable, but no bluestocking, not brash or overly bold. Senatobia was near enough to Memphis for us to go see traveling New York theater together (*Life with Father,* Tallulah Bankhead in *The Little Foxes*), or to shop and see a movie. These were happy times, discussing, laughing, comparing ideas.

And so, back to Nashville. I expected things I craved most to open up again for me there. Eventually, they did. But not at first.

At Ward-Belmont I found myself in something of a Belhaven situation. There was not much emphasis on religion, but manners and deportment were up for their accustomed workout. The war rolled on monotonously; the heavy news rolled in.

At the school, the girls I had to teach were smart and eager, but once more a sense of confinement closed in, and I knew I would not be there long.

Who told me about it, I don't remember, but I began going by bus to downtown Nashville to a night school called Watkins Institute, which specialized in vocational-training courses and had, tucked away in its curriculum, a "workshop group" in fiction writing. I was shy, but did it anyway. It was conducted by a mystery-story writer named Raymond Goldman. He was crippled in both legs by polio. He taught to supplement his income, and also sold men's shoes in a local department store. A kinder, more receptive and earnest character than Raymond Goldman was never born. He took to my writing with a delight that all but stunned me. He was a natural enthusiast anyway, born to chuckle, encourage, and understand. He not only limped but wore thick glasses and a hearing aid. He thought that life was glorious.

His approach to writing was odd. He listed a number of possible plots—I think there were fifteen in all: "The biter bit" . . . "Nothing ever happens here" . . . "Aint love grand?" . . . "Grandeur in unexpected places," etc. If a story that didn't fit turned up, he would sometimes add another one. Being from an old Nashville family, he knew, or knew of, all the famous names clustered around Vanderbilt.

My attention shifted from teaching to writing stories to read before the rather mixed group he had nurtured for years, to seeking out the works of published writers we discussed, to finding my way once more. I think that no one really writes just for himself. An audience is what we have to have. We will find it someway. I once had a friend from a Tennessee farm who could find no one to listen to what he wrote. He would ask the black farm laborers to listen for a while in the evenings while he read aloud out on the porch. They would laugh when he laughed, and cry when he said it was sad. It wasn't much of a help, but it was something.

Mr. Goldman took the time to talk with me often. He thought teaching at Ward-Belmont was not the thing for me, and wondered about newspaper work. One thing led to another: I found myself angling for a job on the Nashville *Tennessean.* With Goldman's and Davidson's help, I got it, though Davidson scarcely approved of the move. "Why on earth anybody wants to work on a newspaper . . . !" he raged. I slunk away feeling permanently dashed, but then found he had done one of his amazing turnarounds and had called the managing editor on my behalf. I think I would never have landed anything there except for the war. As reporters, men were definitely preferred. But now they were scattered far and wide—Europe, the Pacific, the Middle East. And so the knowing faces in the city rooms were often those of young girls like myself, observant of a world laced with rough talk and cynicism, hard-boiled, more than a little relentless, often out to trip us up.

Still, it was another start.

On assignment from the city desk I wrote up minor stories, like meetings of Rotary or the Optimists Club, obituaries, and rewrites. Once the newspaper, a strong supporter of the New Deal and the Tennessee Valley Authority, sponsored a farm-produce contest for the TVA area. Reports poured in and prizes were to be awarded. I went daily to a central office distant from the paper, to read about community achievements and put them into feature stories. It was winter and there was even snowfall to go through. One of the city-desk chieftains nicknamed me Little Nell, the Farm Girl. He seemed to enjoy this.

I got some hard knocks, but on the whole the experience was a good one. For one thing, newspaper writing gets right to the point, with no frills, no browsing about for descriptive glimpses or eloquent meditation. We reporters who worked in the city room had as boss a growling city editor who seemed right out of plays or movies about a city room with a growling city editor. Maybe he had seen some. He was said to sometimes have fist-fights out on the pavement with rebellious reporters. He volubly resented having so many women around; he lived for the day when the "real" reporters would come home.

It was while I was at work in the city room one day that news came through of Germany's surrender. It seemed we had lived so long with war—war feared, war coming, war not coming, war come anyway, piles of censored mail, news of killing and dying, soldiers everywhere, headlines and radio announcements, speeches and disasters, more speeches and tides turning—that war was part of the air we breathed, that life without it would not even be life. The European theater was to be silenced. But the war with Japan went fiercely on. My uncle Sidney, now Admiral McCain, was in the thick of it, commanding an aircraft carrier in a group under Admiral Halsey. I followed the intense action in the Pacific.

I was again in the city room, checking rewrites, when the news about Hiroshima broke. The European war's ending had been breathtaking—dizziness, wonder, and general rejoicing were part of everybody's shared feelings. But this was different. We looked at the great black headlines pouring from the Teletype machines, heard their relentless clashing from the Associated Press rooms, read news so shocking the print, which kept pouring out a flood of detail, seemed to rise up off the page.

A strange thing occurred. Two of the young women who worked as reporters—especially well-dressed, chic, and knowledgeable types—became charged-up, elated, voluble. You would have thought some bacchanal was in progress, mounting to heights of sexual excitement. They thought it was wonderful, that nothing so marvelous had ever occurred, it was the world's greatest event! One might say, of course, that they rejoiced at the war's ending, soon to follow. But, no, that was not what it meant. It meant something else: the consummation of power.

This little scene being near, before my eyes, continuing through the stunned feelings of the afternoon, frightened me almost as much as the news of the bomb. You needed no imagination to see them as mad revelers, dancing around a blood-drenched god of war.

Come home from work to my rooming house, I found Melba Sherman, a Vanderbilt graduate student from Mississippi, who had a room down the hall from me. She was in a state like mine, benumbed with awe, and we sat down together with the Bible and read chapter after chapter from *Revelation.* Were "vials of wrath" being poured out upon the earth? We agreed that the world would be different now, and that a frightening era had dawned. Having been brought up in religion-centered homes, we both had fearful thoughts. The Second Coming might really be at hand.

In those days my lodgings were in a widow's house near Vanderbilt, owned by Mrs. Susan Souby, who taught at Ward-Belmont. It was on Dixie Place, a street long since swallowed up by the massive extensions of Vanderbilt Hospital. The long bus ride from the newspaper office home was trying, as I had to work until midnight. But two days off a week left me time to write. I was writing more and more. Stories I could finally begin to believe in had begun to form around characters much like those I had grown up with in the small towns of Mississippi. The distance from Tennessee to Mississippi helped me frame scenes I had lived among, to make whatever was extraneous drop away and leave important outlines clear to view and thus able to be described.

I kept up acquaintance by one means or another with students at Vanderbilt. I went in to see Donald Davidson and others there from time to time. The important threads in life are the major veins in experience, and must have the bloodstream flowing through them to be kept active and alive. Losing contact is like losing life. I felt Vanderbilt as a source for me and I did what I could to maintain its power. My stories, which went out to magazines such as *Accent, Story, Kenyon Review,* and others, did not place but often stirred editors to return them with personal notes. I began to find a recurrent phrase in these notes. It said, "Have you ever tried a novel?" "Why not try a novel?" "You should try a novel." Finally I thought, Well, why not?

Specific encouragement to break loose from jobs entirely and concentrate solely on writing came from a young Alabama man, just back from the war. This was Edward McGehee (pronounced McGhee). He was aiming for a writing future himself, having done a good many poems in the modern complex manner, and was now deep into a novel. He had been given the Vanderbilt writing fellowship under Donald Davidson's supervision.

This coveted residency paid only five hundred dollars a year, and it is amazing to note that at that long-ago time a single person could live a year on such a meager sum. You could not, of course, own and run a car, take taxis, afford the best seats at the theater, have your own bathroom and telephone, or eat many good dinners at downtown restaurants. But you could go drink beer at Butch Petrone's, or walk with your date over to Al's Tavern out near Centennial Park. You could go to the picture show. I reflected that I had, because of a tightfisted Scottish streak, or perhaps because of being brought up during the Depression, saved up a bank account of about five hundred dollars. It wasn't much, I had to measure and weigh, but I decided to risk it.

My father objected strenuously to my decision. His view was that I had held three good jobs and given them up one after another, that the road ahead for writing was too chancy and difficult, that I would have immense trouble getting anyone to hire me should I fail. I couldn't think like that. I knew he had wanted me to accept the first marriage proposal that had come my way, at age seventeen or thereabouts. I thought for a long time that he was considering my happiness when he favored the match, though both Mimi and I told him I was not in love with that eager young man. "What does he want to do?" Dad demanded. "He wants to write," I said. "That boy's got too much sense to *write*." Dad's judgments were always ready.

I was still at Mrs. Souby's when he telephoned one evening. The denunciation was long and severe. Melba Sherman overheard some of this dialogue. Confidences we had shared let her guess what had transpired. She heard me crying. Melba searched out a passage in *Julius Caesar* and came in to read it to me. "There is a tide in the affairs of men / Which, taken at the flood, leads on to fortune . . ." She said she believed I had come to that point. I always thanked her for that encouragement—two Mississippi girls, clinging at crucial moments to the King James Bible and William Shakespeare.

I moved from Mrs. Souby's to an apartment in a shabby rundown rooming house on neighboring Highland Avenue. Someone I knew had lived in this family home and recommended me as a lodger. The apartment consisted of a large bedroom with one window and no view at all. There was a bed, a dresser, and a wardrobe for hanging up clothes. Part of the plastered ceiling was dislodged and hung dangerously over the bed. The bath was shared by three other apartments. A rickety outside stairway led up from the back yard into a small back porch, private for myself, where I had an old-fashioned wooden icebox. Twice a week the iceman came and left a large cube of ice fitted into its zinc-lined top compartment. I kept a small trunk out there, and what with chairs from the kitchen, where I worked each day at a table, I could seat whoever came by to call.

I had some considerable acquaintance by now among the students at Vanderbilt. There was not only Edward, who since I had met him had been cheering me on, but others, who were finishing up degrees and were in touch with the events and characters in and around the department.

I found now more than ever the real joy of a writing life.

The formula is simple: Get up. Eat breakfast. Sit down to write. Spend a long morning writing. Feel the stops and starts, the flow, which often will be meager and hesitant but on some magical days will run freely, never wanting to stop. Pause and look up to realize the clock says three o'clock and you are hungry. But now you are something else: You are *happy.*

I also had guys calling up for dates. Mostly the interest was friendly, not intense, though one was special enough to feel strongly about for many years. Except for the first few wonderful months, it was an unfortunate relationship with a man doomed by recurrent neurosis and other unhappy symptoms I was ill equipped to judge. What with meetings and partings, it came and went through the years, as we each strove to recapture something of that first marvelous time.

But nothing could really cancel or weaken the delight I found when writing is emptying itself out, onto the waiting page. This is the way to live, I thought, glad to be aware of it.

So I continued through the summer of 1946. One day I got a call from Donald Davidson.

He knew of my decision to write. Previously, before I left the paper, I had come over to his office to speak to him about it. He was like a second father, one I feared but also by now felt I could talk to, as I could never talk with my own. He knew that through the years of my studies and my return to Nashville, I had kept on trying to write fiction. But other than a draft of an early novel I had started at Belhaven and then abandoned, I had not showed him my efforts. When I confided my plans, he thought things over in his own way. "You would do better to get married," he said sternly. But then he smiled. "I'm glad you're taking the plunge." It was enough of a blessing, and what I had come for.

The morning he telephoned and said someone was in his office he wanted me to meet, I dropped everything without question and hastened there. The man in Davidson's office, waiting to meet me, was David Clay.

David Clay was exceptionally handsome, a brown-haired, solidly built, youthful-looking man. He was exceedingly polite, wonderfully attentive to every chance remark. He had studied at Vanderbilt and was now an editor at Dodd, Mead, a New York publishing house. After introducing us, Davidson picked up some books and left for class.

"Don says you are working on a novel," Clay said. "May I see it?" I said I hadn't brought it with me, and anyway it wasn't finished. He persisted, so we walked together back to Highland Avenue and I handed over to him about two hundred typed pages. I felt nervous about doing this. I had planned the novel carefully, and thought I had foreseen everything that was going to go into it, but as the characters had taken hold, unplanned events had occurred, while others might as well have fallen in the creek. At that point I had only the sketchiest idea about how the book would end. Suppose I couldn't bring it off at all? Still, a New York editor was waiting down in Miss Gerring's shabby parlor, so after taking a long breath at the head of the stairs, I descended with my typescript and gave it to him.

Then he was gone, brown envelope tucked beneath his arm. It seemed he was walking away, an all but total stranger, with a good part of my life. I am now astonished to remember that it was *my only copy!* I disliked using carbon paper, and worked from drafts, each typed out with revisions to make it better than the previous one. I did have the version just preceding the one I gave up, but photocopying in those days was not easy, and would have caused delay. Something told me the moment was now, and I gave him the copy.

Before a month was out, I had good news. Dodd, Mead would offer a contract. I was invited to New York, to talk over the manuscript and discuss the closing chapters.

NEW YORK??!!

I telephoned home. The news did not excite them. They had thought I might be engaged.

In those days travel by Pullman was the way to go, and friends came down to put me on the train. We were a seedy bunch, having sat up till late hours on my tiny back porch, drinking beer and celebrating, but I had got myself a new dress and suit, and hoped to revive on the train. Raymond Goldman had reserved a room for me at a hotel he knew. An appointment at the publisher's offices had been set up. Good wishes were flying over me like flags.

I reached old Pennsylvania Station, and immediately one thing I had never thought about occurred: Nobody in New York could understand a word I said. I think that now, in the media age, television has ironed many oddments out of Deep South accents. But in those days, mine was so thick I couldn't even make the hotel clerk understand that I was reserved there. Sometimes I had to write down what I was saying. Some made a joke of it; others, brusque and hurried, were merely annoyed. "What kinda lankidge is *that*!" Strangers teased: "Don't tell me where *you* came from!"

At the publishing offices on what was then Fourth Avenue I was presented to the head of the firm, a pleasant man named Edward Dodd, and a few of his assistants. It seemed they liked the book and thought that I could finish it ably. David Clay was to be my helpful editor. I little foresaw that I was beginning a relationship that would take primal importance in my life.

David was from Athens, Alabama, a town I have never seen, but that he spoke of as being much like my hometown; and actually towns in the Deep South are remarkably similar, especially in architecture, in attitudes toward family and relatives, and in the predominantly Anglo-Saxon origin of the white population. He had moved to New York some years before, and I often thought that I was calling back to his memory how life was in the place he had left. He was, of course, for that reason an excellent sounding board for my own characters and impressions as they surfaced in my writing. What might have been mysterious or wildly eccentric to a Yankee editor was clear as day to him.

David's important relationship at that time, and throughout his life, was with Robert Penn Warren. They had become friends as students at Vanderbilt, and since Warren now lived out of the South and was frequently in New York, their friendship continued. They were part of an inner circle, mainly Southern, who were fully conscious of the great effect of Vanderbilt on American writing, and who were involved in writing and publishing.

David had worked with Warren on his most successful novel, *All the King's Men.* This triumphant book, always to be regarded as a classic of our literature, had come blazing out a year or so earlier, just as I had begun to write my own novel. Everyone talked of it; everyone bought it and read it. Warren's name was golden everywhere. Blessed were they who could talk about "Red."

The novel had been dedicated to David and his wife, Justine. He had had an important part in its editing.

Though David looked the part of the sophisticated New York editor, his character was so excessively upright he seemed an anomaly. Even back then I found him puzzling. Many of his remarks struck me as deriving from ideas that seemed far afield from anything familiar. I had to learn later that he and his wife and mother-in-law were devout Christian Scientists, the mother-in-law being a practitioner in that faith.

However, at the time I didn't know this. New York in itself was exciting, new, untried. It filled me with eagerness to know more about it. If David was trying to change many of my attitudes, I judged he was only giving helpful hints to someone who must obviously seem like a country girl, awkward and unsure of what was right to do and say. The novel was the main thing for me anyway, and he gave me to understand this was true of him as well.

I returned to Nashville and finished the manuscript without too much difficulty, meeting my contract deadline and taking my modest five-hundred-dollar advance with pride. There was a publication date ahead, there was the check in hand (the kind of proof my father would recognize), and there was beautiful old Carrollton, always the same, waiting. I returned home with the sense of a job done, and thought of myself as having worked hard and now wanting a much needed break.

Little did I dream what I would encounter.

I had always been able to discuss favored books or movies with my mother, at least, and so without much trepidation I showed her my manuscript. It was not to my total surprise, but certainly I was disappointed when both my parents became terribly upset. Before I knew it I was the center of a major family crisis.

The book was called *Fire in the Morning*. The title now seems to me a very youthful choice, overblown and poetic, but back then I thought it was fine. It dealt with a conflict between two families in a small Southern town. Who would think, I argued, that anyone we knew was actually in it? But, they asked, didn't everyone in it resemble somebody we knew? Who in Carrollton, I inquired, would even bother to read it? Well, of course, they said, everyone would.

Furthermore, how did a well-brought-up girl from a strict Presbyterian household get to know words like "damn" and "hell," and others even less proper, including dreadful phrases like "God damn" and "Go to hell"? And how did this same proper girl learn anything at all about sex? To my parents my small triumph was ashes of shame poured on their heads. Years later, my cousin Jamie said that my father stayed at home from work for weeks, ashamed to show his face in public. (Jamie exaggerates.)

My brother and his wife were supportive, and my uncle Joe did his usual work for tolerance and open-mindedness, admirably mixed in with understanding of different attitudes and affection for all concerned. Still, I believe the book made a rift in my parents' thinking about me that was never entirely mended, though what with the encouraging talk of those close enough to her to speak about it, my mother gradually got her equilibrium back; and that was about all, I saw, that I could hope for.

My parents' reaction showed me for the first time in what ideal terms they had viewed me. It was true that teachers and friends had spoken well of me, perhaps with an aim of pleasing them; that I did go to church; that I had made a good record at Belhaven and had done fairly well at Vanderbilt. But I had never seemed to myself such a marvel. Shouldn't parents' view of their children be based on what the children are actually like?

I could also reflect that as my mother well knew, her brothers could swear a blue streak with the best of them and indulged in drinking and gambling whenever they liked. A good many of her lifelong women friends were the same. She had heard all the local scandals and could see I had scrupulously used none of them in my book, preferring to invent others. Still, the shock registered high on her Richter scale. She was more than a little mystical, more than a little childlike in her views of life. If she had dreams about her children, her feeling was that her dreams, being right, *ought* to be true. I was sorry not to live to please her.

Years later, I read a story by Henry James called "The Jolly Corner." It's the tale of the man who came back after a lifetime of absence to his proper family residence and met the pale ghost of what he might have turned into if he had stayed put. I was never cut out for the life I was supposed to live.

The family spent that winter of 1946–47 in a kind of limbo, dreading publication of "that book." I continued to hear regularly from David Clay and worked on a number of cuts and editorial suggestions. Beginning writers need the sort of detailed

attention he was able to give me. But writers with twenty books behind them, still need the encouragement, advice, stimulation, and line-by-line attention of a good editor. Editors are the invisible heroes of the book trade. One can confidently say that behind every good book stands a good editor. And behind every great book, a great one? Such as those do exist.

. . .

That winter I took a brief substitute teaching job at Belhaven, at the suggestion of Ellene Ransom, whom I had known at Vanderbilt. She was the sister of the poet John Crowe Ransom, and was now head of the English department. She wrote to ask me to come to Jackson and help her. Here I once again got to see Eudora Welty, and found her overjoyed to hear of the forthcoming novel. Her visit that memorable spring had led to a friendship that continued, though I often still have to regard it as sheer luck.

Eudora's loyalty to the friends she chooses to make is a wonder. When I think back to our meeting at Belhaven, I also must note the time: 1942! The last time I saw her was in December 1996. A number of my friendships have lasted, but some, unhappily, have dwindled or vanished into quarrels or simply disappeared. One that has gone on for over fifty years is a treasure to rejoice in.

The many good times I had in Eudora's company occurred at far-apart intervals. I had always more to learn about her, there being a brush of unexpected magic in what happens when she is present. Once, in Jackson, we had driven out to dinner in her car, a Plymouth, of a model that was so good it had had to be discontinued. Eudora told me that because the front seats were built exceptionally high, boys often wanted to buy the car from her to go fishing. I took this as one of her inventions, but on the way back, we stopped at a service station for gas. Out of the night, a young man in rough clothes and a pulled-down cap showed up at the window. "What you want for yo' car?" he asked. Eudora said she didn't want to sell it. "I need it for fishing," he said.

For Eudora life is lived close to the everyday detail of it, but it isn't boring. Nothing is too small to be noticed, and once noticed, there is nothing that can't also be extraordinary. The best way to catch her quality is to be in her company, but next best is to read her. Those who know her can see how her fiction joins seamlessly to the actual. Are many writers like what they write? I don't think so, but she is.

I recall numerous samples of Mississippi lore that she has either invented or brought to light: the girl so dumb she would sit for hours wondering how the tail of the C got through the L in the Coca-Cola sign; the woman who caught her husband's dying breath in a balloon; the fire ball that rolled through the room when Uncle Daniel Ponder was tickling his wife during a thunderstorm. Are all these actual stories? It's a strange state. In the story "Moon Lake," two little girls are walking through a swamp, golden light filtering down through the lofty treetops, beneath myriad vines looping downward. She writes that it was like being on the inside of "something that breathed." Couldn't any writer think of that? But only Eudora could have written the rest: ". . . something that breathed and might turn over." That last is pure Welty.

Once when I was in Jackson she asked me to go on a picnic with her and her lifelong friend John Robinson. We were getting toward fall, and everything seemed golden. She had made up a box of tomato sandwiches and cold fried chicken. We sat on the banks of the Pearl River looking down at the water and talked—of what? Who can ever recall really charmed exchanges word for word? A dazzling dragonfly sat down on the lunch box. "He looks as proud of his colors," said Eudora, "as if he got up and put them on every morning. Maybe he does," she added.

From her chance remarks I occasionally learn surprising things about her fiction. One story that has always puzzled me is "Music from Spain." Laid in San Francisco, it concerns the day-long wandering of a Morgana, Mississippi, man with a mysterious guitarist, who had given a concert the evening before. I told her I had never understood the story. She offered no explanation for it whatsoever, but of the guitarist she said, "That was Segovia." Had the great Spanish musician played in San Francisco during her visit? How did he wander into a Welty story? So, too, did I learn that much of *Delta Wedding* was drawn from somebody's diary. Whose? And where is it? There are no end of strange origins for anyone's fiction, but Eudora's might be a box full of wonders. She once said she liked to start a story with some conversation she overheard between people she didn't know and couldn't be sure what they were talking about.

One could follow a good many false leads in knowing Eudora. So gentle and charming? Watch out! A temper fierce as a buzz saw is something to pray to avoid. When she feels some matter of conviction is being coarsened, mistaken, or set aside, she will blaze up. A sharp remark will jerk the rug from under confident feet.

A prime example that reached public attention was her response to an adverse review in *The New Yorker* by Edmund Wil-

son of Faulkner's *Intruder in the Dust.* Her letter of reprimand was a polemic. The magazine did publish it, but Wilson's meek reply to her, which she showed me, was never printed, so far as I know. To our astonishment, Wilson said he'd never read Faulkner (besides the book in question), though he "had been intending to" for some time. One thinks eternally less of a major critic after an admission like this.

Each time I see her, a different story will spring up. On my last visit, December 1996, I entered the long-familiar living room on Pinehurst. She now sits in a chair with multiple levers to adjust her position and help her rise. Someone has made a beautiful walking cane for her, and she never fails to mention the carver by name. We go slowly to the car, get her inside, and, more slowly still, out of it at a favored restaurant.

We settle down to her regular bourbon, brought by a knowing waiter, and order bowls of fresh seafood gumbo. This time the story that comes out is about, of all things, Hershey bars!

She has been reading a book on the great flood of 1927, an event we both remembered. She was a student at Mississippi State College for Women in Columbus at the time of the flood.

As a prank, she wrote a letter to the president of Hershey's chocolates in Pennsylvania, saying that the students at her college were starving because of the flood. Columbus is in the far eastern part of the state, near the Alabama line, nowhere near the flooded area in the west, where broken levees along the Mississippi had made the entire Delta a still sea of flat gray water. However, her letter evoked a response she had scarcely foreseen, and a huge box of Hershey's chocolate bars arrived from the company president, hoping to prevent starvation.

During the short period I taught at Belhaven, I became closer to a remarkable family, the Blissards. I had known them all before, in Jackson and Nashville, but now they were in walking distance of Belhaven, and I made full use of calling privileges. We had good talk of books and politics and people, played interminable games of bridge on the front porch, and enjoyed lots of laughter. The three sisters—Thomasina, Frances, and Jo Anne—and their mother became like kin, and the sister I always wanted to have was multiplied by three. Their father, often out on business, was widely known as "Breezy" Blissard.

While I was in Jackson, David Clay came down from New York with news that I was to head Dodd, Mead's 1948 fall list. I had thought publication would be sooner, but trusted him that fall was the best season to launch a book. (David was becoming my oracle.)

Together we telephoned and went over to see Eudora. She received us in the memorable living room where through the years she could always be found, with its friendly disorder of mail and stacked-up books, its comfortable armchairs and view of trees and shrubs out the front windows, with Pinehurst Street and the white buildings of Belhaven beyond. She and David knew many people in common in New York, and the conversation went well. He told me later that he had never heard a more beautiful voice than Eudora's. Later she gave a wonderful "quote" for the book jacket. Robert Penn Warren was approached for a similar favor. I perceived that I was being "launched." Regret for my family's attitude continued, but how not to become excited after so many years of fruitless trying?

. . .

Fire in the Morning had not yet appeared when I knew I would have to find work outside Carrollton. My love of Mississippi was such a constant with me that though I did write to Louisiana State University at Baton Rouge, and one or two other schools, I had the strongest hopes for going to Ole Miss. I had actually wanted to go to that university when the family had decided on Belhaven. My brother had gone there, and my mother's brothers. It was less than fifty miles away, and driving home would be easy. I got an immediate response, the interviews went well, and my course was set for the next few years, teaching as an instructor in freshman English and "sophomore lit."

My novel came out during my first year at Ole Miss. It was widely and well reviewed, with considerable excitement from the national press at finding a "new Southern talent." David Clay's able work had paid off, though he thought the advertising Dodd, Mead was willing to commit to the book was too scanty, and soon after, to my surprise, he left the firm. I was given to understand from various sources that he had done this in protest for the lack of support given my book. This created for me a feeling of indebtedness to David, and I determined to pay him back for his support whenever I could.

Ole Miss that first year was full of interest. It sprang up everywhere.

Ella Somerville appeared, that cousin of the redoubtable Miss Beauregard, familiar with the Carrollton terrain. Her mother's people, the Vassars, had come from Carrollton. In fact, the old Vassar property, its cedars everywhere encroaching, its fallen porches and wasted walls, was the "haunted house" of my childhood, where on Halloween the most daring would venture to locate spooks.

Ella was the Oxford lady to reckon with, known everywhere, a portly agreeable well-dressed woman with reddish hair, unmarried but scarcely old-maidish. She held the social reins of Oxford, as Cousin Beaurie, sitting straight in her chair, had ruled Carrollton.

Her main genius was for entertaining. She often did it, and she did it right. Her home was a white Victorian structure on South

Fifth Street, and as was common in a hill town, it was reached by steep concrete steps up to the front lawn, thence to the deep porch, with its swing and porch furniture. The position of the house made it seem larger and more imposing than it would have seemed on a level terrain. Within, a curving stairway led to the upper floor, and two parlors, one formal, flanked the hall. Her maid, Willie Mae, wore black with a white apron; her silver was flawlessly polished, and highballs were crisp and amber in her tall glasses.

But the best of Ella was her talk. She had the Southern lady's gift for telling a story, and you knew when she told it that she had told it right, with all the social nuance brought to surround every person who figured in it. The tone of her voice when she mentioned a name could let you know how they figured. "Of course, I never knew the little man," I can remember her saying of some slight acquaintance then being discussed. What did she mean? At least three things: (1) He was unimpressive and not worthy of her interest. (2) His family were not anyone important. (3) His masculinity was dubious. No doubt the subject in question deserved all this.

But those she chose to love were always to be held dear.

I had no sooner got to Oxford than some news of my writing had reached her, and she knew already of my background. She called. An invitation came. I found myself, in no time, standing in a receiving line in the formal parlor with a bunch of flowers stuck on my shoulder. It was the amazing start of a long friendship. I admired her, I liked her—no, let's be clear about it. I loved her.

I've not even to close my eyes to see her vividly still, sitting across the room from me, for she took to ringing me at times to come alone to what she called "a funny little Sunday-night supper." Her rich voice, her drink in one hand, the huge square-cut emerald she wore on the other flashing with her gestures.

Others in Oxford came to the fore. Again, the Carrollton connection. Elizabeth Hamilton Willis was living there with her husband, William Willis, who was head of the classics department. She was from a Carrollton family who had moved away to Meridian, Mississippi, the year I was born, but my mother's affection for them never wavered. To be asked to the Willis home was then, as it remains, a treasured experience.

To know a man more learned than William Willis would not be possible, neither to find courtesy and right judgments in such a degree as his. His father, a gentleman like himself, had worked at a modest job in Meridian all his life, but had somehow managed a life of the widest cultural interest. He collected first editions of works by Conrad, James, Yeats, the Rossettis, and others, and corresponded with many of them. He owned a copy of William Morris's Kelmscott Chaucer: it was fascinating to be allowed to turn its pages. He had a collection of classical recordings, among them Brahms himself playing one of his own compositions, and for amusement also collected gemstones, which his daughter-in-law loved to be given for setting.

Elizabeth Willis was stunning to look at. Her talk ran on without effort, in a friendly, interested way. When William spoke in easy reference to Greek literature, philosophy, or culture, or for that matter to anything at all, she gave him the setting of sober respect, but she had a racy, girlish side as well and loved parties, going to them and giving them. William's convivial side was easy to awaken. With them we all enjoyed high moments.

Within a week or two at Oxford, I must have realized I had landed on my feet.

Oxford was constantly aware of Faulkner. Whether absent in California or resident at Rowan Oak, he was a felt presence, a subject of endless gossip and speculation. (Ella, of course, knew him well. She accorded every respect to his gifts.)

But the ways in which Oxford at large viewed William Faulkner were a strange and wonderful carload. For one thing, the town seemed full of derision and dislike. The stories of his contemptuous behavior were widely circulated, with whatever truth in them being constantly questionable: Southerners exaggerate. The "Count No 'Count" label was freely applied. His arrogant incompetence as university postmaster was fully noted. His tendency to drink limitless quantities of whiskey, his long absences in Hollywood, his scandalous way of dress and shocking attitude toward— But the list grows longer, and once the premises were established, it all became repetitious, a bore.

Faulkner's lifelong friend Phil Stone and Phil's wife, Emily, also lived in Oxford. Emily's one ambition was to be a published writer, a goal that eluded her all her life. She and Phil soon sought me out. They invited me for an evening of sipping whiskey and talking. Their stories about "Bill" were many. But these were of a different quality than the town stories and mainly concerned the writing itself. Phil, a lawyer, had a lifelong interest in literature and was widely known as having been the young Faulkner's mentor and encourager.

One wonders at the effect of such a friendship when the protégé role slowly reverses itself and the mentor seems left flailing about, isolated more and more on the lonely rock of an outgrown relationship; yet talking of it, talking critically, talking affectionately, talking in a superior way, talking, talking compulsively, on and on.

The Southern Literary Festival was still meeting annually, and the turn of Ole Miss to host it came round that very spring.

It was April, one of Mississippi's most ravishing spring times, a riot of bloom and fresh green and soft nights laced with scent. Ella Somerville would figure largely in this university occasion, for her old friend Stark Young was invited to speak.

Mr. Stark, as I later came to call him, was originally from Como, Mississippi. He was, in fact, a distant cousin, deriving from another branch of the same Young family that my grandmother came from. He had gone to New York many years before, bent on a literary career, and had built a strong reputation as America's leading drama critic. But he was also a novelist, author of *So Red the Rose,* which to my mind still ranks as a fine novel. Others now consider it a romanticized version of Mississippi society; I prefer to think he wrote from established facts, out of genuine admiration for some fine characters, the likes of whom he had personally known. His translations from Chekhov, which were performed in New York and elsewhere for many years, perhaps still have a place. He had done the first English translation of Machiavelli's comedy *La Mandragola.* He had traveled extensively, especially in Italy, and had known Eleanora Duse, as well as Eugene O'Neill and a host of other names of note in the theater.

Stark Young's speech was beyond a doubt the high point of the festival that year or any other. He titled it "Oil from Strange

Lamps." He wished to encourage young writers to read literature in the original languages, to find a second language (at least one) and come to know what its writers were actually saying in their own tongue. To illustrate he chose, among others, the Greek inscription at Thermopylae: "Go tell the Lacaedonians that we lie here still obeying the commands of the fathers"; also Francesca di Rimini's speech from Dante: "The book was to us a Galahad. In it we read no more that day." There were others from Virgil, from St. John of the Cross, from the French dramatists—I quite lose my way trying to remember them all. Like the whole audience, I sat enthralled. It was approaching noon of a fine April day, the windows open, the soft air entering. I even remember the dress I wore: it was lavender.

Also among us was John Crowe Ransom, whom I had heard once lecturing at Ward-Belmont. I was delighted that someone had sent him my novel, and that he had read it and sought me out to compliment me on it.

Ransom was formidable in a way one was liable to miss, it was so quiet and understated. To look at him, a well-brushed man of medium height, you would have thought him a high school principal, or some longtime academic dean in a minor college. Flying high in those days as a great poet and a commanding voice among American critics, he showed nothing of the arrogant manner he might have acquired. His lecture, though hardly enthralling, came with the starch of real authority, while Stark Young, though scarcely arrogant either, had a theatrical bent, and his came over to us as a thrilling performance.

That afternoon Ella gave her reception. It was in especial honor of Stark Young, but the other festival guests were invited, and so was I.

Such an afternoon could never come again. We came in small groups up the steps to her white two-story Victorian house on Fifth Street. We were swept at once into the greetings, the good feelings, the murmurous talk.

William Faulkner, while he had declined to attend any of the program, had accepted his old friend's invitation and had actually appeared. Dressed in a tweed jacket with leather patches at the elbows, he stood in one corner silently throughout, smoking a pipe, holding a glass, but drinking nothing. He was a small, handsome man, his graying hair youthfully thick, his mustache a becoming touch. What he most resembled was a portrait, an introspective study of himself.

That day he neither moved nor spoke to anyone, and most everybody was wise enough not to try speaking to him. I have always wondered at the irony of it—a man so taciturn, so devoid of the gregarious nature native to Southerners, moving onto the world stage. Was he ever mistaken as typical of what we normally are? Stark Young remarked on his behavior later. "He hides behind a wall of silence," he said. "I hide behind a wall of words."

Hiding or not, Mr. Stark that day was everywhere, glorying in his success at reaching an audience in such high style, loving the occasion to find old Oxford acquaintances and discover new ones. He was a drinker, too, but a good talker, and moved through various groups as if on a well-orchestrated stage. He singled me out more than once. Ella always spoke later of the many references to our meeting in his letters to her. And I had every reason to rejoice that he liked me.

He wrote; he kept in touch with all I did. Once when I was in New York, he came into the city from his home outside to take me to lunch. He chose the Gripsholm, a Swedish restaurant on the East Side. He did all this much in the Jamesian manner of cultivating a "young person of talent," a distant relative, a "young woman of good family," a fellow Mississippian, a friend of Ella Somerville's. But more than all this, I felt his genuine interest in me, his admiration for my writing, his feeling that I was a discovery of his. (Good luck again.) I welcomed his feelings with all the warmth I knew how to show.

It was Stark Young who, as a young man in London, had told a close friend of Henry James that he would like to read James's work but did not know how to begin. As Mr. Stark himself remarked in his memoir *The Pavillion,* any Southerner would have known his real meaning: that he had no notion at the time of beginning at all. But the lady appealed to H.J. himself, who wrote in some detail to the "young man from Texas." (Stark Young was only briefly in Texas.) James wrote out a list of his favored novels and the order in which they should be read. He promised "the dear young man from Texas" another list of the shorter works. "You shall have your little tarts when you have eaten your roast beef and potatoes." All this was done with typical Jamesian kindness and real affection for a questioning youth. They both understood courtesy, and I think of courtesy when I remember Mr. Stark.

In the afterglow of favorable attention to my novel, I was ready to find an even more expanding world. I never dreamed of leaving my roots, and the world that Oxford had generously made accessible to me was something to cherish and return to.

Still, my feelings nagged. They whispered that the South drew one continually inward toward its motherly bosom. This inwardness of regard has been for Eudora Welty and many others a wondrous source. But for me it just didn't work that way. I did not want to deny, discard, leave behind, or denigrate any of my upbringing. But I had to recognize that I had a seeking nature, something that related me to others of my kin—to my mother's brothers far-flung in military service, not the least to my father's brother, the long-lost Willie, who had set out to discover—what?

Two years before, my dear friend Carolyn Pugh, who wrote me steadily, had gotten an appointment to go to Europe to work in the American team at the Nuremberg trials. She had been employed in Washington and had learned of the chance to apply for secretarial work in the cadres who were needed as assistants in that process. Also a seeker, more courageous than I, she had prepared herself as best she might, and set out by boat with others who were to work for the American team in Germany. Her letters were filled with details of her adventures. She not only experienced Germany with all its postwar difficulties but also had visited Paris, Switzerland, and Italy.

My friend Edward McGehee was now in Paris, working on a novel and meeting many of the writers and others who felt Europe was opening up to them once more. It was certainly cheap, with the dollar at advantage against foreign currencies.

I had made a little money on my book, which had gone into a second printing, and I had, as usual, saved up a little from my teaching. It seemed the moment for a real leap across the ocean was at hand. I searched out ways and means. As summer came nearer my head was full of plans.

21

THE MAGIC SUMMER

BACK then you crossed the ocean by boat. I booked to leave from New Orleans in June 1949 on a French Line freighter, a lend-lease boat. These were prewar ships, still in use in the postwar era. This one was named the *Wisconsin,* ludicrously pronounced in the French manner, "*Le Vis-cõ-sĩ.*" It had come from Tampico, sailed the hundred miles or so upriver to New Orleans to take on cargo and passengers, and was headed, we were told, to Le Havre, via Havana.

Certainly by the time it had reached New Orleans it had accumulated a few assorted characters, one a burly red-faced man, named Charbonneau, big as a bear, who walked with a limp and leered at all the women. Another outstanding specimen was an Italian, Fulco, who got on in New Orleans, along with the main lot of passengers, including me.

Fulco at once wanted to scoop me up and go into New Orleans while the boat took on cargo. But I elected to spend a hideous night on deck with the others, for the cabins were hot as ovens. The deck, though cooler, caught a slow rain of black flakes of soot. When we finally began to move, late the next afternoon, we all took a bath, scrubbed off, and got to look at each other for the first time.

There were teachers on sabbatical, a threesome of a Nashville mother and two sons bound to see Europe, a young man returning home to Paris after studying international law at Tulane, an American woman and her son, she titled La Marchesa, her husband being the Italian consul in New Orleans. Many other wisps and shreds of humanity were among us, a total of perhaps thirty or forty, with others about to join us in Havana.

Fulco, not one to give up easily, could be counted on to follow me down corridors, lurk around corners, pop up for every stroll around the deck.

Years later, the marchesa, who resumed my acquaintance at intervals through the years, told me I should have written *Ship of Fools.* Certainly Katherine Anne Porter's novel held many parallels of that time at sea.

In Havana sightseeing was permitted, but perspiring taxi drivers, whom we employed to drive us to "places of historic interest," went lurching through streets crammed with other Cubans, who all seemed to be yelling at once, and took us where they were supposed to—the palatial rum factories. Here we were led through the various smelly distilling processes, tunneled among rows of molasses-colored barrels, and wound up in a cool dusky basement at a long wooden table. We were served small glasses of sweet liqueurs, flavored variously with pineapple, banana, coconut, and mango. The next step—ho, ho, ho—was to sell us lots and lots of rum. We came staggering out into the broiling sun, laden with bottles, sweating from the syrupy drinks, and wanting nothing but ice water in the shade.

From Havana harbor, leaning over the ship's rail, we watched the boys who swam in the oily waters, calling up to us for money. They dove for the coins we flipped, coming up with the gleam of dimes and quarters, sometimes in their teeth. They wore G-strings, had rags tied around their heads and were sleek as seals. Within the boat lounges, the French officers in their starched white uniforms were sharing wine and socializing with the Cuban officers, also dazzling in white. A good many Cubans piled on as passengers that afternoon, carrying stacks of rumba records, which they immediately put on the loudspeakers. I remember the rest of the voyage for the taste of rum and the beat of rumba music.

The Cubans kept pretty much to themselves. One dour couple

sat constantly on deck without speaking to each other. The story went that each was married to someone else but had lusted after the other for years; finally they made their dash for freedom and true love. The look on their faces was one not of guilt or even regret but of pure sullen boredom.

It was a long voyage, taking eighteen days from the time we left New Orleans until we would dock, not at Le Havre, neither at Antwerp, as we were later told, but at Bordeaux. The wireless office had to send one message after another for us as plans changed, but to go in the office was chancy, as the proper French teacher from Newcomb had found a handsome Spaniard and they were often there together, locked in strenuous embrace.

Meanwhile, gossip abounded. Charbonneau, the shady bear from Tampico, was now supposed to be a murderer, certain to be "put in irons" the minute we reached France. Fulco was going back not to see about property confiscated during the war but to a rendezvous with Lucky Luciano. I was supposed to be sexually involved with a mild little French professor from Tennessee. The marchesa got drunk on rum at one of the evening parties and tangoed about the deck with a broom. We all got tired of everything.

An American woman named Amber who had got on in Havana on impulse—she had been at the beach with her husband and friends when someone mentioned a boat had docked—was not to be restrained one minute longer from going ashore. She was from New York, an example of what she called "the nightclub set," and had come aboard wearing an orange beach robe over a bathing suit. She also had thrown one or two things in a small valise—a low-cut black evening dress and one evening slipper (she said she must have dropped its mate while packing). She was not unfriendly and told us a good deal about her debut, her various face-lifts, her three or four husbands, interspersed with lovers, her favorite late-night clubs.

But we finally reached port and now were leaning over the deck watching the river flow past the Bordeaux harbor, red sunset streaming on the water, the city lying low beyond, and all the mysteries of a new land waiting our discovery. Orders were to stay aboard and disembark the next morning, but we soon learned that Amber had slipped off the boat with Charbonneau.

We were all astounded at the pairing, never guessing they knew each other. The marchesa remarked that there was a shoe for every sock. She said it was a French expression. They were both caught, detained, and hustled back to the ship.

When Fulco got word the next morning that the French had come aboard, he immediately ran to the deck with his arms out, crying "Couchez avec moi!" Whether they would have slept with him or not, when he found he was running toward a number of astonished French customs officers instead of welcoming girls, he came to a dead halt and slunk away.

In Paris I at once found Edward McGehee, who had reserved a room for me in his Left Bank hotel. Most things seemed rundown from the war years, and the hotel no less, but it was friendly and comfortable and had a silky gray cat, who visited all the guests' rooms.

I was invited at once with Edward to Sunday brunch with Saul Bellow and his wife, Anita, and their little son. I liked them. Saul was living that year on a Guggenheim Fellowship; he had been encouraged by Red Warren, who had admired his little-known early novels. *Augie March* was yet to come, along with *Henderson* and *Herzog,* and the fine string of others that followed.

Saul seemed very much at ease with himself and his talent and in charge of his European experience. He knew what he was looking for, what he wanted Europe to provide. Caring and observant, and certainly attractive, he had a strange quality of both being present, participating in the moment, and standing aside to observe, not only those present and what was happening, but himself as well. He had the writer's habit, to be both watcher and participant at the same time, to a marked degree. Later, I felt the same gift—and it must be a gift—emerge in his work. *This is me, Augie (or Herzog, or Henderson). Come, let's look at me. Let's see what I'm up to.*

Anita deferred to him. His place at the head of the table set him in command without debate. He had already been in Paris a good while. He confided on another occasion that he was thinking of leaving France for a more colorful society, which he felt Italy might provide.

If I had been given to thinking in such terms, I might have foreseen that though Southern writing had been ascendant in American literature for several decades, the Jewish writers were going to take precedence soon. The Bellows had several literary Jewish friends there in Paris and spoke of others. But I could never make much of groupings; to do so seems to obscure the real question, whether the work—Russian, Greek, or Mexican; found in a bottle or composed by space aliens—has real merit.

At any rate, Saul was no longer bowled over by Paris and perhaps had never been. But I was ready to be impressed and enchanted. The next day Edward and I took a city bus together. Whizzing past the Étoile, the Place de la Concorde, the Tuileries, the Louvre, left me stunned with excitement. When the Arc de Triomphe loomed before us down the Champs-Élysées I burst into tears. Were these things actually there?

I insisted on going up the Tour Eiffel. As we waited for an elevator to the second stage, a stocky workman was being led down gently by two officers. His face was swollen, purplish in color; he was groping along as though blind. Someone explained that he had been working very high up, but his safety belt had slipped. He had fallen only to the next balcony, but the close call had terrorized him. I was half-sick to think of that chunky little laborer, way up high, letting go to fall toward the city below. I thought maybe people after torture might look a little like that.

Why so long in Paris when my goal was Germany, where my friend Carolyn was awaiting my visit? That country was still being governed by its conquerors, and special permits were needed, allowing visits for a specified time. True, I was not especially panting to get on the road, and at the embassy, which I visited immediately, I was not terribly disappointed to learn that though they had my papers, I would have a few days' wait. Why? I didn't ask. Nobody in her right mind would have objected to lingering in Paris. I went out and bought an elegant umbrella with a curved handle in amber-colored Lucite. I kept it proudly for years.

Signs of the recent occupation were everywhere, in the strange wooden shoes the poorer women wore, and the bizarre wood-burning cars chugging past. Many people rode bicycles. Paper tablecloths were common in small restaurants. The day's menu, like the bill, was scribbled out between the plates. Things were cheap until it came to the real fashion items like my umbrella. I also bought paperback copies of Henry Miller, banned in the United States, from bookshops along the Seine, and a bottle of Femme.

Notre Dame . . . Versailles . . . Chartres. I can't remember if Edward was always with me. While not the kind, as they said in those days, to have girlfriends, he was a good companion nonetheless. He seemed to take real pleasure in seeing these many sights once more. I think, more than anything else, he was homesick. The accent the Bellows found amusing filled up his thirsty ears. He introduced me to artichokes and onion soup, rosé and Pernod. We talked about Vanderbilt people, though not so much about writing, and I judged his was not going well.

My permit was cleared, but not before the Bellows organized a Sunday picnic in the Bois de Fontainebleau. Edward and I were along, also their little boy, and a couple named Kaplan, perhaps others, I forget. We bought sausage, wine, cheese, and pastries at the various shops, and spread everything out on the wonderfully spacious boulders among the little twisted trees. After lunch Saul and Kaplan, wearing French berets, put up music stands, took out recorders, and opened their sheet music. Bach fugues, piped softly, filled the air.

In the twilight we drove back into Paris. I had the reassuring feel of a return home after any Sunday picnic at some nearby lake or sandbar down home—a little weary, scratching an insect bite, thinking ahead to bath and bed, noting the evening sky, while a tired little boy slept pressed against one arm. But here were the great Parisian boulevards swinging us toward the heart of the city, and along a path in the Bois de Boulogne a young woman, erect in a black riding habit, was trotting a glossy chestnut mare.

Germany lay ahead, reached by night train to Frankfurt. Carolyn had been employed in Nuremberg until the trials finished and now was working in another office in Bad Nauheim, a well-known German spa in the prewar days, now the seat of government for the American sector of Germany. Tom Brown, whom she had met since coming and was now seeing, had also been moved from Nuremberg. He had been a translator at the trials, and had been reassigned to work with American radio broadcasts following the transition period from military rule to rule by the State Department.

The Nauheim living quarters were more luxurious than one might have expected, and as far as I could see the town had not been bombed. Americans had taken over everything they wanted. The golf course, where the two of them played every spare afternoon, the swimming pools, and tennis courts—all now were for the Americans.

The Germans themselves were subdued, but their presence was something like a sullen background music, discordant and muffled. They went about on foot or by bicycle, mainly without looking to one side or the other. One heard no laughter and saw no smiles. The vibrations all said hatred and loss, loss and hatred. One of the favorite American sports was driving so close to a German bicyclist he had to get off the pavement or be knocked down.

We went to a piano concert in another town. The auditorium was only a shell—a stage with a piano, rubble cleared back to the sides, and benches ranked out in the open. But the rapt audience, largely German, were caught up into another world by the music, which I remember as passionate, full of bravura and flourish. Beethoven, Schumann, Brahms. The applause was loud and long. This was the world they still could enter, could feel was their own.

Socially, the Americans largely grouped together. Fraternizing was frowned on; you could never know what the past record might have been. Attending parties, one felt as if among colonists on an island full of distant natives, who must be off somewhere, saying and doing things we could never know, but who we could be sure held no love for us. Jokes and laughter were strictly American in pitch, but the resonance was lacking.

The twilights, usually following cloudy cool days, were long but scarcely languorous. There was something monotonous about dusks which night seemed impotent to close. Nerves felt the strain of them.

Naturally my friends had to work. I was often lonely and took up horseback riding at a local stable, placed, oddly, in the middle of the town. It was run by a friendly, active couple, whose English was fairly good, and a number of people of various sorts went out on the rides. We would pass in file through the town center and soon be into open country laced with trails. It was cloudy and cool most of the time, and the trees seemed everywhere dark. One thought of the Black Forest, and stories from Grimm.

On one of these rides I met a young Viennese who was at loose ends in Bad Nauheim, waiting for a work visa, as I recall. We talked a good bit and he began to ask me out. He was pleasant and presentable, and I felt fortunate to have found him. In the afternoons we could either ride or go swimming together. He even met me for church services.

My friends reacted strangely. It said something, not so much about them, I now realize, as about the general atmosphere, still bruised from conflict, not yet ready for healing, charged with suspicion of everything and everyone. "What does he want?" Does he have to "want" something? I wondered. Perhaps he wanted my company. Perhaps he liked me. To them it seemed any such innocent notion as that was ridiculous. Cynicism had grown up like weeds.

Carolyn and Tom kindly drove me on trips. Once we went up the Rhine, another time into Switzerland. We stayed once at Starnberg, where I felt the essence of what "Bavarian" must always have meant. Its woods and lake had some wordless mystery to tell. The chateau of the "mad king" could be seen across the lake, crowning a promontory. Hadn't Eliot written of it, too?

> *Summer surprised us, coming over the Starnbergersee*
> *With a shower of rain . . .*

I found a stable there, too. To my surprise, the horses had luxurious tiled stalls, left over from prewar days, and the stablemaster, doting on them, could still be polished and military in his demeanor around them. I liked the trail riding but when it came to jumping practice in a large enclosed barn, I regularly fell off, not being used to the walls.

On the trails I rode several times beside a small plump Frenchman, whose reason for being there was not revealed. He rode well. One day he gestured with his crop into some woods along the trail and exclaimed, "*Écureuils!*" "*Quoi?*" In broken English he explained: "In the air, *bat.* On the ground, *mouse.* Under the ground, *mole.* In the tree, *écureuil.*" There are worse ways to learn new words, especially as I soon saw squirrels too, racing about among the branches.

I also met a little blond boy named Peter, whose bright face and blue excited eyes are vivid to me yet. He loved riding, but he also wanted to practice his English. He was the friendliest of all the Germans I remember, and I got a spark of hope for the future from his face and eager talk. "And when, please, Meez Leez, does one say 'Okay'?"

Many pleasant things occurred, but on the whole, the visit was not a success. Something about the traditional American viewpoint, which typically comes on smiling with helpful friendliness, had hardened. It had encountered realities so cold nothing could warm them. Americans knew now that human decency not only could vanish in theory, but had vanished in fact.

It was in this atmosphere, too, that I came to realize an unpleasant truth. What I had hoped still to find in my friendship with Carolyn was no longer there. Perhaps we both tried, but could not bring it to life. Her involvement with Tom, some doubts that were in her mind about it, may have entered more strongly than I knew into her behavior. But I think primarily it was Germany itself, the attitudes one had to acquire in the simple daily course of living there. The person who did not change under these conditions must be extremely rare. Try as my old friend and I might, the past never revived.

The experience was a lesson in how things are in our present world. It was whispering to me: *Relationships do not last. If the same person is in one's life for many years, that person will have been several other people during those years. It is in the changes that most people find it necessary to drop away, fade, and become a memory. The trick is to know when the time has come either to go or to let go. The person who learns that and acts on it is the one who knows best.*

But I have a heart like a small town, of minimal but treasured population. It was hard for me to learn that *friends are not permanent residents. Friendships serve for a time: the time passes.*

This is also true of family relationships. It is true of marriages. I recently heard a man of this new world, Norman Mailer, speaking on television of his six marriages. He said that marriages were like sojourns in foreign countries—so many years in Egypt, so many in Paris, and so on. The experiences were cultural, he said; one eventually moves on. I would hate to catch myself believing such a thing.

So out with all the above! I think of the wondrous presence, continuous through the years, of different spirits, who dance to a different measure. They may never get to run the planet, but they make living on it worthwhile.

Though I always felt warmly toward him, I seldom heard from Edward after that summer, but I knew that he had left off writing for work in New York City, and that in later years he went back to Montgomery, Alabama, his place of birth, where he died. I also learned that Carolyn discovered a late-blooming love of Mississippi and often returns to see what cousins and remnants of family she can find and enjoy.

The time of my State Department pass to visit in Germany was limited to a month. During the Bad Nauheim stay, I often heard references to Italy, and how wonderful it was to visit, if only simply to see the sun. Why did people speak so warmly of another Axis enemy, surely full of the same feelings remarked in Germany? No, it was different, they said. For one thing, it was not as heavily bombed, except in certain areas; for another, the people had an entirely different character. And furthermore, it was beautiful.

I found ways of saying goodbye to the Viennese. He wrote and sent photographs. I was a bit sorry for him, as I felt he had been unjustly shunted off.

Almost, I decided to go back to Paris. But I still had all of August, I had enough money left, and there was an overnight train from Munich to Milan. Thus, unexpectedly, I came to the heart of my summer.

Arriving in Milan in the wee hours, I took a cab through dimly lighted streets. The hotel was so new, the smell of fresh cement was everywhere in the corridors and the room was sparsely furnished, but I was glad to sleep. Borders and passport checks had left little time for that on the train.

When I woke sunlight was piercing the cracks in the blinds. I opened the shutters and was instantly drenched in sun from head to foot. I picked up the telephone, but scarcely knew what to say. "Café" is pretty nearly universal, so I said it. I got a "*subito*" in reply, and soon had not only coffee—rich, smooth, and hot—but also croissants with gobs of butter and jam. I opened a window. Singing came up from the streets. What world was this? An illusion, doubtless, soon to vanish. Horrors had happened here, a short time before. The ride from the station had shown me bombed-out buildings—shattered walls, gaping thresholds. Bitterness must lie below the surface.

Still unbelieving, I went out, found my way to the cathedral, bought a guidebook, wandered, fed pigeons at a café in a piazza. I smiled and talked to beautiful, smiling people without knowing a word they said.

"Americana?" "Si."

Before me stood three young men, one with a camera. They were taking my photograph. I realized they would want to sell me the pictures. "But I'm leaving soon." "*Va via,*" one explained to the others. "We bring to your hotel." I gave them some money and scribbled the address, thinking never to see them again, but at the hotel that evening, the pictures were waiting. I ran across them again the other day. A thin, dark-haired girl in a skirt and checkered blouse, the cathedral of Milano behind, pigeons and passers-by all in place, as we all were together, that sunny day in August 1949.

I wandered all day without very well knowing where I was bound. I climbed to the cathedral roof and found a Coca-Cola machine among its myriad statues of saints and angels. The refectory of the former monastery attached to the church of Santa Maria delle Grazie had been just put back together; a bomb had trashed the walls. But—by a miracle, it was strongly suggested—Leonardo's *Last Supper* had been left intact. It has faded more than ever now, but perhaps one can still see how much of its enormous quality lies in the perspective—the wall it covers at the end of the oblong room is simply made to vanish, and the viewer feels ready to enter and sit with others at that long-ago table, come to life again. A breathless step into the eternal.

I also walked to the church of Sant'Ambrogio, and found one of the loveliest and holiest places on earth. Forty-five years later I saw it again and was swept by memory as well as by the sight of it.

I was leaving it that first time when a car pulled up beside the sidewalk and an elderly man in shorts and an open shirt leaped out, crying "Signorina! Signorina!" Obviously English, he was dripping maps and guides, wanted directions, and had thought me an Italian. I've no idea why I remember this except for the curious realization that I did not at all mind being taken for Italian.

A whole month lay ahead.

If my friends had been stationed in Italy, I wondered, would things have been different? So pondering, I walked around till a

certain truth dawned. I could think whatever I liked about whatever I liked, but everywhere around me, Italy was making its first great statement. Germany had been only a preface to Italy: if it had opened my eyes, it had also bruised my feelings, leaving me, though I was hardly conscious of it, with a heart ready for Italy to impress. And the measure of what Italy can do is infinite, never to be taken.

From Milan I went to Verona, to another hotel, breakfast, and guidebook—but this time, as I went about the streets of that softly lyrical town, I became at every step more aware of what beauty was being cast up at me, regular and almost as rhythmic as the waves of the sea, on every side, at every turning. And all out in the open! Anyone raised in the Deep South is not apt to be ignorant of architecture, but I had never before thought of statues and fountains as the accepted ornaments of life—its daily dress—to be enjoyed by everyone from moment to moment, mingling with the talk and bargaining and breath of life, with sunshine.

If you try, even after many years, you can reconstruct a good deal of everything that has happened. (The look of my room in Milan, the smell of recent cement work, the pastry and jam, sunshine and song.) But I cannot reconstruct anything from my first day in Verona except my own dazed feelings. I recall my wanderings of that day as a kind of drunkenness, all this on perhaps one glass of wine at a lunch I cannot remember eating.

I do know that under orders from my old Baedeker, I trudged to the outskirts of the town to see that (starred and not to be missed) Church of San Zeno Maggiore. I walked across the harsh stones of the old square before the church with its bare upcurving sweep of Romanesque façade, tawny in the fall of the strong afternoon sun, and as anyone would, I felt its nobility. I saw then that what had been kept from me by a too strict Protestant upbringing was true—that art can express religious emotion more truly than any sermon. Years later I saw this very church used as setting for the fatal burial crypt in a fine English film version of *Romeo and Juliet.* If that story happened at all it would have happened in this place.

And then . . . Venice . . . Florence . . . Siena . . . Rome . . . Memories grow jammed with impressions, and not only of galleries, piazzas, mosaics, and frescoes, but also with people, a montage of remembered faces.

Florence especially had (in addition to Michelangelo, Botticelli, and all the rest) a free and lively feeling about it that year, an airiness that was all ease and rightness. In recent times when I have returned, tourists seem about to carry it off, like trooping multitudes of ants methodically lifting whole the carcass of a wonderful beast. But not so in that early postwar year. Italians were glad to be alive in a life that was possible to live, and their gladness filled the air and reached out to all comers.

All the easily made friendships, the dancing and romancing, parties, dates and dinners, meetings by chance, partings forever, may seem frivolous to talk about—though not so much is wrong with frivolity, God knows—but one felt more in the air in France and Italy that summer. These countries had come up out of the inferno; sun, moon, and stars were looking down on a resurrection. The news might never reach Germany. But it had taken up residence in Italy.

One of my discoveries was opera. The first evening after I reached Florence, I was strolling back along the Arno to the Hotel Berchielli (still there, but infinitely more expensive) when a young American couple stopped me and after some chatter invited me to come with them to the opera.

To me opera meant dressing up and suffering. I had gone during Belhaven days to a performance of *La Traviata,* given by a traveling company. Grand opera, they called it back then. I had heard performances from New York on the Saturday-afternoon radio broadcasts, and along with the whole town, had gone up to the Carrollton schoolhouse to see local talent in a production of *The Mikado,* this being something like opera, though not "grand." Habitually, when exhausted with summer heat and outdoor play, I with others used to sit around the side porch listening to Lawrence, my poet cousin, bang out some rousing chorus of Verdi on my mother's old rosewood upright piano with yellow keys, some ivories missing.

The Jackson *La Traviata* was supposed to bring us at last to the real thing. A portly Alfredo bellowed his passion, a heavyset Violetta warbled hers also. At the end, the dying lady collapsed, still full of enough energy for prodigious song, into the arms of her lover, singing lustily as well, and the heavy curtain, trying to close, struck both such a blow they all but fell off the stage into the audience.

When they said to me in Florence, "Come with us to the opera," I quickly said, "Oh, I'm not dressed." But neither were they, and I thought they must be joking. The girl was in a skirt and blouse, much like my own, the young man wore neither jacket nor tie. "You don't have to *dress,*" the girl said. "Half the auditorium isn't even repaired. We can buy tickets at the door. Come on—it's *Rigoletto!*" Well, why not, I thought, and we trooped off together.

The auditorium was makeshift, having stood in the part of central Florence along the river that had been badly hit by the retreating Germans. There were boards for seats. Could we have come to the right place? The loud chatter of the Italian crowd, the rustling sense of excitement, the boys who passed with programs to sell and little bags of candy, cigarettes, and the like, put me in mind of a school play at home rather than anything resembling a Verdi masterpiece.

"*Noccioline americane! Noccioline americane!*" I'd no Italian to interpret that cry, but looking in the tray that was passing, saw peanuts. We were not even at the schoolhouse; we were practically at the baseball game!

The curtain swung open to loud, irreverent cheers from a crowd that wanted it, needed it, had come to savor it, enjoy it like sex, consume it like pasta. *Ecco Mantua!* We were in Italy, where we ought to be. There was the lustful duke, here the mocking hunchback, and soon the clear voice of Gilda. Things began for the first time to be understandable, not only in fact but in feeling. Couldn't anyone know what they were saying about love—"*E il sol dell'anima,*" of course—with a little Latin, what's hard about that? "*Caro nome*" is certainly "dear name"; a line of cosmetics was called that. And who had not heard the jaunty singing of "*La donna è mobile*"?

Cheers at the end of the arias, loud bravos. Some stood and shouted; others threw flowers on the stage.

It is just as well to discover opera along with Italy. What I had heard before had not been any discovery at all.

From Florence, I came eventually to Rome, where it seemed

natural enough to hear once again, "Would you like to go to the opera?"

I was eating in a restaurant in the Via Bocca di Leone, talking with a young Canadian. We had struck up an acquaintance some nights before while trying to figure out the menu. This time I saw nothing odd in the invitation and scarcely bothered to think twice. I just said, "Can we get tickets?" He said he thought we could.

Summer opera in Rome is held under the skies in the gigantic ruins of the Baths of Caracalla. Acoustics are terrible, the singers shriek to carry their top notes outward to the stars, the mosquitoes bite, but the thrill of the scene, the dramatic lighting, the mass of the crowd, all carry enchantment. That night the production was Berlioz's *The Damnation of Faust.* How impressive was the solemnity of the final scene, torchlit, with gravely mounting staircases and choral effects of great majesty.

The applause faded. The crowd separated, scattered, murmuring, voices spreading out far among the towering ruins. We decided to walk home. The way was the Via Appia, and it was certainly long and lingering. Like so much else, it lingers yet.

Time to *go*? Oh, NO!!!

Back I went to Paris, where the former bases were waiting to be touched. Adventures to tell, friends from *Le Vis-cõ-sĩ* appearing, evenings at the Deux Magots. On one such night with the Bellows, an American girl they all knew, who worked in Paris, came by. Everyone called to her and when she turned Saul leaped to his feet and ran toward her. It was impetuous, a momentary impulse, but I was caught by the out-going, on-going look of the way he did it, not so much toward that girl herself, but a look of moving on, on . . . so eagerly, so charmingly, so dashingly . . . on.

Germany was almost forgotten except for the countryside, fairylike, with some shadowy magic about it that seemed not to have heard of the war. Italy was not forgotten, nor would be.

. . .

My Mississippi travel agent had booked my return on the *Île de France*. The marchesa and her son were also returning to the United States on that passage, and so were the Nashville woman, Mrs. Nixon, and her boys. We reached Cherbourg by boat train, and had to face the stunning sight of that giant liner, arcing up lofty above us at dock, dwarfing all memory of *Le Vis-cõ-sĩ,* waiting to draw the whole summer into its wake.

The song of the year—and everyone who visited Europe that summer will remember it—was "*La Vie en Rose.*" Edith Piaf's throaty voice blared from the loudspeakers. We stood at the railings and listened, thinking our private thoughts, and saw the land receding, slipping from our grasp. Everybody had fallen in love. Everybody was leaving a time, along with whoever or whatever had caused it to happen. I thought of France and Italy and felt that I had fallen in love with the whole of it—every person, every thing.

22

THE GULF COAST

IF I could have one part of the world back the way it used to be, I would not choose Dresden before the firebombing, Rome before Nero, or London before the Blitz. I would not resurrect Babylon, Carthage, or San Francisco. Let the Leaning Tower lean and the Hanging Gardens hang. I want the Mississippi Gulf Coast back as it was before Hurricane Camille, that wicked killer which struck in August 1969.

All through my childhood and youth, north of Jackson, up in the hills, one happy phrase comes down intact: "the coast." *They've just been to the coast . . . They're going to the coast next week . . . They're fishing at the coast . . . They own a house at the coast . . . Let's go to the coast . . . When? For spring holidays? Next week? . . . Now!*

What was magical about it? In the days I speak of, it did not have a decent beach. Strictly speaking, it was not even a seacoast. The islands that stood out in the Gulf of Mexico—Horn Island, Ship Island, Cat Island, and the rest—took the Gulf surf on their sandy shores; what we called the coast was left with a tide you could measure in inches, and a gradual silted, sloping sea bottom, shallow enough to wade out in for half a mile without getting wet above the waist. A concrete seawall extended for miles along the beach drive, shielding the road and houses and towns it ran past from high water that storms might bring, also keeping the shoreline regular.

Compared with the real beaches of Southern California or Florida or the Caribbean islands, all this might seem not much to brag about: what was there beside the seawall, the drive along it, the palms and old lighthouses, the spacious mansions looking out on the water, with their deep porches and outdoor stairways, their green latticework, their moss-hung oaks and sheltered gardens, the crunch of oyster shells graveling side roads and parking lots . . . why was this so grand?

Well, it wasn't "grand," let that be admitted. Natchez was grand. New Orleans had its seductive charms securely placed in a rich Creole history. Still, nothing gave Mississippians quite the same feeling as our own Gulf Coast.

We would come down to it driving through plain little towns, some pretty, some not, south of Jackson through Hattiesburg. The names come back: Mendenhall, Magee, Mount Olive, Collins, Wiggins, Perkinston. Somewhere along the way was D'Lo, curiously pronounced Dee-Lo. In all of these, people of an Anglo-Saxon sameness in admirable (and not so admirable) qualities were pursuing life patterns thought out so long ago they could never be questioned. A day or two to piece the relationships together, learn a few names of Scottish or English origin, discover a cousin or two, and anyone from Carrollton or Winona or Pickens or Vaiden could pick up the same routine of life there as in the ancestral home.

But soon the thrilling smell of salt was on the breeze, increasing until suddenly we were in Gulfport and straight ahead lay the harbor with its big ships at rest, and to either side the long arms of the beach drive stretching east to Biloxi, west to Pass Christian and Bay St. Louis. Here were people with names foreign to our ears; and the mystery of these almost foreign places, easy in their openness, leaning toward the flat blue water, seemed serene beneath the huge floating clouds. That first thin breath of sea air had spread to a whole atmosphere.

What to do in a car crowded with friends on holiday from

school but drive straight to the water's edge and sit breathless, not knowing which way to go first, but ready to discover.

I must have come first with girls from around home, or friends from college in Jackson. Someone would have borrowed the family car. Occasions blur into one long sighing memory of live oaks green the year round, and the pillared white houses the trees sheltered, set along the sweep of beach drive, boxes of salt-water taffy to chew on, and little screened restaurants advertising SHRIMP! ALL YOU CAN EAT FOR $1. Gumbo, too, "made fresh every day." Jax beer.

Prohibition lingered for a long time inland, but the coast never paid it much attention. Names alone would tell you they wouldn't. French and Spanish were here from the first, but Poles and Yugoslavs and Czechs had come long ago to work in the fishing industries, while the French traded and the Spanish built ships. But we wouldn't have thought of looking up their history. It was the feeling those names breathed that stirred us: Ladnier, Saucier, Legendre, Christovich, Benachi, Lameuse, Lopez, Toledano.

Religion here was foreign to us too: churches like Our Lady of the Gulf stood proclaiming it, with a statue of the Virgin in the wide paved entrance court, and a bare but graceful façade, facing boldly out to sea. Those who ran the restaurants, and went out in the shrimp boats, worshiped here, as did no doubt the men who waded the shallow water at night with flambeaux blazing, spears ready for flounder, and the women, too, who sat talking through the long afternoons on latticed porches.

We learned that annually at Biloxi, before the shrimp boats go out to their deep-sea fishing grounds, an outdoor mass is held to bless the fleet. It is a fine occasion and one of general rejoicing. These were ancient ways. Above, the white clouds mounted high, the gulls on broad white wings soared and tacked, tilting into the wind. The pelicans stroked toward land in flawless formation. Midafternoon in spring. Intense heat had not yet taken over, but a stillness came on, a sense of absolute suspension. The camellias were long finished, the azaleas, lingering, but past their height. Magnolia blooms starred green branches. Jasmine breathed in the back gardens. The moss hung breezeless. Time stood still.

We were used to staying at the Edgewater Gulf, a wonderful hotel between Gulfport and Biloxi. Its grounds were ample. I remember a cool lobby of gently turning ceiling fans, plants in white recesses, and rooms designed each facing on the sea but with a long entrance passage to draw a constant breeze through latticed doors.

Parting admonitions—"Don't talk to strangers," "Be careful where you swim," "Be sure to call Sally the minute you get there"—may have sounded in our girlish ears for a while on the way down, but vanished after Gulfport. Yet I cannot recall any serious mischief we ever got ourselves into.

Grown beyond all that and long out of school I was to return to the coast many times over. A nagging sense began to persist that the coast was withholding something; I'd something yet to solve. Then I took the boat one summer and went out to Ship Island.

Ship Island is the largest and best known of the coastal islands, and the only one that excursion boats go out to. It takes these little tourist ferries well over an hour to make the twelve miles or so to the island. But who is in a hurry? Someone in the pilothouse will be playing a harmonica. Cold drinks and snacks are sold in the galley. The island is low and white, like a sandbar with dunes. Once we are ashore, the dunes seem higher: they mount up before the visitor, low hills fringed with sea oats, which blow in the steady breeze. Wooden walkways climb among them. There are signs to an old fort to the west, dating from Civil War days. History will be related on the dutiful markers. An old weathered lighthouse, wooden, four-sided, gray, stands guard.

The first visit I made to this spot was during the summer of 1951. Already it seemed part of my own personal geography. Everyone had been to Ship Island. Picnics were talked of, summer days recalled.

On that first time for me, I walked ahead of friends (a man I went with, two friends of his) straight south, taking the walk through the dunes. Then, cresting, I saw before me what I'd come for without knowing it: the true Gulf, no horizon to curb its expanse, spread out infinite and free, restless with tossing whitecaps, rushing in to foam up the beach, retreating, returning, roaring. Out there, I thought, astonished, is Mexico, the Caribbean, South America. We are leaning outward to them. Everybody back on land, all along the coast, feels this presence, whether they consciously know it or not. What was it but distance, the leaning outward, the opening toward far-off, unlikely worlds? The beyond.

Here at the Mississippian's southernmost point of native soil, one had to recall what inland Mississippi was like, how people in its small towns (or even in larger towns like Meridian and Jackson and Columbus) related inward, to family life, kinfolks, old friendships and hatreds. How hospitably newcomers were welcomed, but how slowly accepted. Once I heard this remark: "The H——s haven't lived here but thirty years, but look how everybody likes them!" In talk of the outside world, not much was to be accepted, nothing could be trusted to be "like us." There were Yankees "up there," we said to ourselves, looking north; the other Southern states, like neighboring counties, offered names that could be traced in and out among one's connection and might prove acceptable.

In such towns people lived on stories of one another's sayings and doings, repeating and checking for the facts, speculating and measuring and fitting together the present to the past, the known to the suspected, weaving numberless patterns. It was a complex and at times beautiful society; much fine literature has been created to do it justice; but the smell of salt air did not reach it, and none can deny that it was confined and confining.

So one from those places comes to stand, in memory fixed forever like a monument or a snapshot, on a Ship Island dune staring out to sea.

I wrote a story named for the island. In it a young girl comes to it with her summer lover, and in the sight and feel of the sea discovers her own true nature—good or bad, she finds it there, like a wonderful shell dug out of the sand. In Walker Percy's book *The Moviegoer,* we read: "You come over the hillock and your heart lifts up; your old sad music comes into the major." That's another way of saying it. But it may be that the only way of knowing it is to go there.

. . .

The year that I speak of now was 1951–52. I had taken a break from teaching in order to write, and had chosen to live in an old town named Pass Christian. It was during that year that the long affair that started in Nashville reached a point of no return.

How do they come about, these primal feelings of love and future promise? Everybody has different story. Call him what you will—Bob or Will or Ted. There is no use now in disinterring either the feelings or the man. When we first met it was in a postwar glow of every sort of possibility. He was back from the war, having made a good enough record, and was resuming study for a doctorate in Vanderbilt. In prewar days he had studied at LSU with the distinguished faculty there, Warren, Brooks, and others. We were first drawn into talking about them as they seemed to him, and to comparing notes on Vanderbilt; soon we began to discuss my own hopes for finishing a novel. He said at first he thought I was too young to consider writing a novel, but when I ventured to show him samples, he had a change of heart. Meetings grew more frequent and attraction grew stronger. Before long we were being thought of as a couple. Beyond the radiance of falling in love, I sensed, in knowing him, a continuance I had always looked for—continuing in Southern terms all that I had experienced of literature and life so far.

But a strange sort of emotional distance began to make mysterious breaks in our fine good times. How to explain this? Sudden alienations, a complete change of mood, followed by heavy drinking, absence, self-reproach. Then, like the sun after a rainy day, he would return, all lively fun and good times again, as though nothing had happened.

But the breaks had grown longer and more severe, and at times irrational. When I finished my novel and returned home to Carrollton, contract in hand, and some hopes at least fulfillable, I came to the tearful but necessary decision to let go.

If I had a daughter, I would certainly tell her this: Once a love relationship has slipped and slid, gone wrong, never try to mend it. Don't look back, don't go back. I doubt if she would pay any attention, but this is what I would say.

Through the years that followed, he kept returning. Only let me make a fine healthy start with someone new, and here he would appear, bringing his wit, his fine intelligence, his undoubted intellectual scope, his good times. Where had I ever found better?

The time I had set for working at the coast, there he was, teaching at a college not far away, showing up every weekend. Once again, I was beguiled and heartened. But the shadow was waiting, and throughout that year it was to grow, disappearing only to get stronger. By the time I learned that the name of the shadow was schizophrenia—rather like learning about the "massacre" in Carrollton—I had firsthand experience of it, and had lived through all its opening stages. I must say for him that he did not learn the name of it either until it had gathered such speed and power that no amount of loving response or good hopes or goodwill could do more than distract it for a short while.

One last good time had passed, and I was in Carrollton for a visit, when the letter came that finished everything. It was full of blackness and gloom, a diatribe of despair. Friends of both of us told me that this too would pass, as other moods had done, but I sensed this time that the trend was not reversible, and I knew I would never try again.

I went back to clear up my possessions in Pass Christian. I remember burning love letters in the back yard of the house where I lived. I put the stack in a wire frame that the landlady used for burning her own trash, and set them afire, remarking to myself, with the sort of bitter irony the writer of them was especially good at, that the smoke was at least good for keeping the mosquitoes off.

What to do now? I resolved to preserve carefully my memories of "the coast." What it meant to all of us in general, to me particularly, was an opening to the sea, and so it stays with me long after the emotional upheaval of a broken relationship has burned itself out.

Concurrently with all the above, life was proceeding on another level.

In fact, the summer of 1951 had started well enough. I had come to make a new start in writing, but how I wrote anything I don't really understand, for it was a time of many visits.

Not the least were two blessed descents of Eudora Welty from Jackson, bringing with her each time a friend she wanted me to meet. The first was Katherine Anne Porter, who had given a lecture in Jackson as part of a series featuring Southern writers. (I had myself been asked to participate, but was unbearably shy on a platform in those days and had declined.) Miss Porter was, as so often described, beautiful, with snow-white hair. Her small figure seemed delicate without being fragile. Her features were remarkable for showing no trace of slack skin; I was reminded of the trim, spare, expressive faces that Florentine sculptors knew so well how to mold.

I had the two of them over to my little apartment one evening. We sat and sipped drinks and talked. I will always be glad that Katherine Anne (as she insisted I call her) talked so much about herself. She felt like doing this, and she did it. Where else could I have heard her precise but soft voice say, "I would have been able to do much more, except for the many interruptions—by that I mean the time I've given to men." I think this is reasonably exact. It was honest and certainly not coy; she was anything but that. Another observation I recall: "I don't understand people who complain about art for art's sake. If we don't love her for her own sake, why else do we love her?"

She and Eudora were staying at the Miramar Hotel, just west of Pass Christian. It was a comfortably rundown old place; I used a made-up version of it in my novel *The Salt Line*. My feeling was that people who had made a habit of coming to the coast through the years had grown used to staying there and nowhere else. I remember sitting on the floor of a large room Katherine Anne had—I think she was propped up on pillows and trying to nurse away a cold or headache—and listening to her and Eudora talk.

A short time after this the novelist Elizabeth Bowen also visited Eudora. The two of them came by to see me before proceeding to New Orleans, where Miss Bowen was to lecture. We planned to meet for lunch at Friendship House, an attractive sprawled-out restaurant on the beach drive between Gulfport and Biloxi. The day was mild and the broad windows looked out on the sound and on the beach drive lined with oaks. The water lay placid and blue beyond.

I was charmed by the delightful sound of Miss Bowen's very English voice, not exactly marred by stuttering, but made a little comical when she came to speak of our wonderful b-b-buh-bourbon whiskey. Or related coming into the airport of some Western city (she had been lecturing throughout the United States), and how she had admired those numerous neon s-s-suh-signs. I wondered at her courage to undertake lectures at all, but am told that her certainly imposing looks—she was tall, strongly built, with red hair swept back—more than made up for the flaw. I came to know that she was one of Eudora's closest friends and had invited her often for visits to Bowen's Court, the family home in County Cork, Ireland, and that each lavished admiration on the other's work.

The two ladies were late in appearing that day, not having started early enough from Jackson. I had been seated in the restaurant foyer waiting for a good while when two young officers from the nearby air base came out of the bar and started to talk. Was I waiting for someone? Yes, two women friends from Jackson. Both from Mississippi? No, one was from Ireland. "Ah, a Jackson doll and an Irish babe!" When the imposing pair actually came through the door, regal in their tweeds, the Air Force wilted away.

At that time I had a new novel about to come out in the spring. Having finished a book creates difficulties in starting another. My work, taken up each day, seemed stubborn, inclined to limp along rather than run.

In spare afternoons, closing up the hope of a fresh start for yet another day, I used to drive to places I loved seeing. One by one they were there for me to find and re-find, always giving off to me their air of a past that I knew had occurred, but that I had no key to opening up. They could not help me to do what a writer most enjoys, visualize with confidence what has not actually been seen.

For instance, there was DeLisle, a town site inland from the beach drive, northwest of Pass Christian. Once you were out of sight of water, oaks gave room to pines, the tall longleaf pines of South Mississippi, and the road, largely unpaved, was carpeted in pine needles, quietened by a mix of sand in loam. DeLisle itself had been fairly populous once, and was all but entirely French, the descendants of the Acadians from Nova Scotia having settled here. French was used in school far into this century. A plain little church was still standing, and a few houses. The spaces where houses and stores must have stood were peaceful savannas, moss-hung round the edges, keeping memories not to be shared with me. A cloud of butterflies could be counted on to waft about like a length of yellow silk floating on air. A wooden bridge led over still, black water, Bayou DeLisle.

A few miles beyond, I would come to the really spooky place, Pine Hills, an old resort hotel, set in extensive grounds at the head of Bay St. Louis. It was begun during a boom year, 1926, and some people around Pass Christian had told me that it never opened, thus awakening in my mind images of fabulous châteaus, villas, castles, or mansions, richly prepared for expected guests, the snow-white linens starched and spread, the place settings of china, crystal, and silver all laid, the bedrooms expectant and fragrant, the staff coached, the management ready with smiles. Then—no one comes. All that is largely fantasy, of course; the hotel went down as an operating venture in the crash of 1929 and never reopened. Until a couple of years ago, it still stood, empty and expectant.

To go there alone past the entrance gates, to observe the small filling station with pumps for gas still in place and, toward the far right, outbuildings of every sort standing vacant—stables? garages? servants' quarters?—the tennis courts all weedy silence, and, most of all, to see looming straight ahead the massive hotel itself, windows by the hundreds with no one behind them, the curving entrance drive where no arriving guests would ever alight, no door ever swing wide to receive them—this was awesome.

It was told to me that the long room to the left of the entrance lobby had been the banquet hall. I once crept close enough to see if the tables were, as I had been told, still prepared for dinner, but I don't recall confirmation of that tale. Perhaps to anyone able actually to enter those dusky halls and cobwebbed lobbies, details would have opened out—a pen ready beside a blank registration page, a key forgotten in a cabinet for vases, one final ashtray left unemptied on a table. Who knows?

Rounding a corner of the hotel, one came suddenly into a full view of Bay St. Louis. Came only to learn that others before the hotel builders had felt the command and sweep of this site. A towering Indian shell mound, said to be the largest on the coast, still stood for marveling at. Even more than the hotel, it held its mystery: how it came to be put there, for what impressive purpose. At least the hotel planners had the sense to leave it alone. Perhaps they thought of it as a curiosity for the guests to look at as they strolled at twilight in full evening dress before cocktails and dinner. Now both monuments—hotel and mound—stand side by side, looking out over the bay. And the bay may well be asking itself who will come next to rear a monument and pass away.

My other favorite spot to visit—far over to the east in Ocean Springs—was, in contrast, very much a going concern. The Shearwater Pottery was owned and run by the Anderson family. It wasn't that easy to find. You had to know where to look.

You reached the house from a street in Ocean Springs, having searched carefully for a modest sign, a little plank nailed to a tree, saying SHEARWATER POTTERY and sporting the painted logo of a gull at wing. The drive to reach it wound through shaggy growth—small oaks, azaleas, Cherokee rose bushes, and camellias, all looking never to have been planted or tended, part of the wild. A turn and there was the Anderson house, modest, like the sign, but beautiful in its traditional Gulf Coast architecture: the gables, the slanted roof, the porch. The pottery itself was in a shedlike building. Nearby was the shop, where the various figurines designed here were displayed, along with vases, jardinieres, plates. The designs, taken from the natural life that lay all around, had in their movement and the humor and rhythm of their execution a totally original quality. Since those days, it has come into full light how considerable an artist was at work here. Locally known and protected—he evidently was the sort of eccentric people fear may come to harm—he was certainly prized by coast people during his lifetime. But I doubt if any friend or neighbor or visitor knew the extent, let alone the magnificence, of Walter Anderson's art. He seemed, like the Lord God before him, to be creating every day, fish, fowl, plants, flowers, trees, sea, and air, leaving behind him such abundance at his death that the Gulf Coast needs to find no other means to immortality.

I used to see them—him or one of his brothers, sometimes both, though which brother I never quite got straight. They were in and out of the shop, looking not so much distracted as alive to other matters than who came in to buy. Yet you could talk with them, ask questions, which were cordially and briefly answered. They went about in old dungarees, canvas shoes, denim shirts, a pullover in winter. This was right for them. I brought people there who came to visit me. Some of their figurines I bought—"widgets," they called them—have gone with me on many moves. A wing may break from a gull, or a foot from a dancing black man, and have to be mended, but the charm, the humor of execution remain intact. I have a watercolor painting by Walter Anderson of a brilliant rooster, standing on big yellow feet, flaunting his tail feathers of purple and gold.

Since Walter Anderson's death in 1965, exhibitions of his work have traveled to many cities, and books of his "logs" and art continue to appear.

So these were the poles, the Bay and old hotel, speaking of a dimly understood past, and the Shearwater Pottery, alive with the present mystery of art continuing on its course.

Many years later, Ship Island, the very spot where I had caught my breath to see the Gulf in all its expanse and glory, found itself in the target eye of a destruction so complete that the coast as we knew it could never be restored. Its name was Hurricane Camille.

Other hurricanes, memorable ones, had struck the area. One in 1947 burst the seawall to bits; it was replaced by a man-made beach of white sand. Betsy, in 1965, swept the beach away; it was built up again. But to Camille, all such efforts might have been sand castles left by a child. The statement was repeated too often to be false that here was the most powerful hurricane ever to strike the continent; none stronger was to be found in any record or in human memory.

In 1969 I was living in Montreal, but I saw more than enough of it on TV. I saw the few cars that crept through a world that was not falling down but bursting apart horizontally, trees, buildings, and telephone poles fighting like wildcats through the haze of wind and water to remain, slowly losing a night-long battle. I saw evacuation moving massively north along the highways, heard stations fading from the air, until all communication, like threads snipped one by one, was cut. I was left, in the distant northern night, to dream of other horrors still—my favorite old mansions crashing to flinders, piers lifted from their pilings to coil like whips in the storm's fury, giant oaks with their roots nakedly exposed. But whatever I could imagine would still be less than the actual disasters of August 17, 1969.

I returned to the area in the summer of 1970 to do a reading at Gulf Park, a junior college whose solid concrete buildings had survived the holocaust. I flew to New Orleans and rode to Gulfport on the bus. As we approached the coast through the marshy land west of New Orleans, I heard a woman talking behind me to someone she was sitting by. She had had to wait out the hurricane in Biloxi, at the hospital bedside of her father, who was too ill to be moved. "It was something more than natural," she kept repeating. "It was like one of them bomb experiments done got loose. It was just a lot more awful than anything natural could be." The tremor in her voice made me think that what had come that night would not leave her.

Not that I could blame her. The bus reached Bay St. Louis and crossed the bridge. To the right was open water, calm and innocent, but everything that had stood between the road and the water had vanished. The shoreline and the road were at least twenty yards higher than before. A wonderful alley of oaks, a cool tunnel of bearded moss, was simply gone, as were the noble white houses just beyond them, and all their gardens. Double staircases, high verandas like a dream of long summer afternoons, tall white-painted fences with wrought-iron gates, all were gone. Only walkways remained.

Back of the bare rerouted beach drive, I later saw whole groves of pine trees reduced to blackened stumps, as though the land had been burned over. I was told that sand driven by winds that had reached two hundred miles an hour (and probably much more: instruments at the time could go no higher) had blackened whatever it struck. How far back did the monster range, how far along the coast had it foraged? Sickened by the loss, I didn't want to hear any more statistics. The real message was written already in the ragged shoreline, the disappearance of the Pass Christian Yacht Club with its brave flags and trim marina, the few stricken and displaced houses that had somehow got through. This place was finished. "Gone with the wind" was waiting to be wryly said here. It may be in order to observe that Camille, with her demure name like a Southern belle's, did a better job than Sherman.

I knew I must write about all this someday. I had already done a number of stories about various points along the Gulf or in the Caribbean. The writer A. J. Leibling, who loved the area, insisted that the Caribbean was this hemisphere's Mediterranean Sea. I agree. Its ways of life, its mystery, belong to the sea and create lifestyles and outlooks that are totally, rhythmically different from what we think of as our own "normal" ways of living.

But it was the hurricane itself, its wild force and aftermath, that stayed with me and finally grew into the novel *The Salt Line,* which took many years in writing. I made a number of trips to the coast, lingering for weeks at a time. I heard hundreds of stories from people I knew who lived there. I read through innumerable accounts in the all-new library in Gulfport. I even went out once more to Ship Island. The lighthouse was gone, no victim of Camille, which she had somehow gallantly weathered, but burned down, I was told, by some boys on a lark. The island itself had been split in two parts by the storm. Now land that had offered the first harbor the French explorers had found and had been the scene of historic wartime events, decades of Sunday school picnics, and countless romantic afternoons was now two diminished little islands with the sea flowing between.

Back at Pass Christian the Gothic-style white-painted Episcopal church in its grove of oaks was gone—the rector, I learned, had seen his wife and child drowned in the tidal wave while he held to the front steps and reached out vainly to bring them in.

Ocean Springs, however, I found to my delight, was hardly touched. Best of all, Shearwater Pottery had been spared. It was still to be reached by its shaggy winding road, and there I discovered what others had found after the death of Walter Anderson. A hidden treasure was in a small cottage adjacent to the main house and the pottery, where he had lived in later years quite alone, his place of refuge.

This singular man had died soon after sitting through Hurricane Betsy in 1965 on Horn Island. He had gone out on purpose to get as close as possible to the invader. It is well known that Horn Island, like the cottage, was his special province. He rowed to it often, stayed there for weeks at a time, kept a journal about his experiences, and, of course, painted and drew its creatures, plants, flowers, sand, and sea. The hurricane to him must have been one more visiting live thing. He died soon after the experience of it, though not before rejoicing in his log:

> Never has there been a hurricane more respectable, provided with all the portents, predictions, omens, etc., etc. The awful sunrise—no one could fail to take a warning from it—the hovering black spirit bird (man o'war)—only one—(*comme il faut*) . . .

The cottage where he painted has now been entirely moved to the new Walter Anderson Museum in Ocean Springs. There one finds the walls set up as they were when he covered them entirely in brilliantly colored murals, all revealing his vision of the coast, its flora and fauna, its myth and its reality. The book that reproduces this astonishing work is called *A Painter's Psalm.* I know of no greater work anywhere in this country—it is safe to say that we must go to Europe for achievement to compare with it.

The character central in my novel *The Salt Line,* Arnold Carrington, also has a vision of the coast. Regretting Camille's destruction, he tries to restore by building anew what was typical of the old. Many of his feelings are echoes of my own:

> . . . the old pre-hurricane Coast: shrimp boats and ancient oaks, camellias in bloom, flags flying from the old white lighthouse, moonlight on the Sound, softly blowing curtains of Spanish moss . . . where to find this unity of house, shade and sun . . . the brick walk, the moss barely stirring to its familiar breeze of this hour, this peace and precious past . . .

But "gone are the days" is something all Southerners have had to get used to. Days are going all the time, taking with them places and times, leaving memories good and bad. I had taken a lot from the coast. For others to come, the sound is still there and the sea beyond the islands, opening toward unknown worlds.

23

NEW YORK AND BEYOND

IF the Gulf Coast was a presence in my life from the earliest times, New York had never been so until my first novel was accepted. That early visit had made me eager for more, but the brief passage through it after the *Île de France* docked in 1949 was hardly fulfilling. Every street I walked on or hotel I stopped in or play I attended made me feel its powerhouse of energies and possibilities, all to explore someday. But when?

In fact, to me the whole life of cities was a mystery. I thought maybe they were all pretty much alike, if I thought about them at all.

In the summer of 1950, while still at work on my second novel, *This Crooked Way,* I had the chance to go to the writers' conference held annually at Bread Loaf in Vermont. I received an invitation to be a fellow, and had heard favorable reports from a friend of those years, Caroline Ivey, herself a beginning novelist, whom I had known at Vanderbilt. There was also the lure of seeing Donald Davidson, who had a summer house in that very place.

Bread Loaf was a meeting ground for a goodly company, and many were pleasant to know. Richard Wilbur, then a budding poet, remains an admired acquaintance to this day. Young and lanky and soft-spoken, he made a nice contrast to another poet,

John Ciardi, whose style was flamboyant. Dick's calm manner made an art of cool understatement.

I was privileged to spend some hours in the evenings with the Davidsons. We went once on a picnic together up in the Green Mountains. I almost fell in a canyon, trying to recover something dropped. One evening Davidson, who played and sang well, entertained Mrs. Davidson and me with some ballads, the sort of music he loved, played on a curious old-fashioned instrument held flat on a table, something like a cithara or zither. I still remember "*The Golden Van-i-tee,*" its sad tale of an English ship of that name at war with "the Spanish e-ne-mee," dating back to Renaissance days.

Another evening he invited me to make a fourth at dinner along with Robert Frost. After a fine New England meal at the Middlebury Inn, we drove back and sat for a long evening, Mrs. Davidson and I listening while the two men conversed over the sad state of affairs in America. Frost was more relaxed in his views than was Davidson. Davidson was especially disturbed by some of the more liberal attitudes in Washington and in the literary and academic world. He was convinced that certain ideas were abroad which called for open opposition. "I want to fight," Davidson declared. Frost smiled gently. "You want to fight, do you?" They were both hearty conservatives in their views, and deplored much that was going wrong, but I think Frost's attitude was to take an oblique approach when it came to social comment, to use precise particulars which set some deeply known and loved local thing against the general drift. He was neither an essayist nor a polemicist.

Frost looked exactly like his pictures; his white hair and attentive regard made him seem benevolent. (Stories went the rounds that he was anything but.) He seemed to sense that I was shy of conversing with him, but asked me some respectful questions about novel writing. He said that he would never know how to go about writing a novel but thought once, when he saw an old house being torn down, the rooms that had once been private exposed to view, that this might make a good subject: who had spent time in those rooms, what had happened there, what had happened to them.

That was the time of the House Un-American Activities Committee, and the infamous McCarthy investigations were making scare waves everywhere. Anyone who *once* as a young person had attended a meeting of a Communist-front organization, or knew someone who had attended such a meeting, had reason to quake in his shoes. People were indignant and jittery. Reputations and jobs were at stake, and many had friends who had suffered.

Davidson was more than half inclined to approve of McCarthy. He said that evening, "If you read the *Congressional Record,* you will see what he's really saying. The newspapers make something else out of it."

"But he's somewhat extreme, don't you think?" Frost remonstrated.

The very evening Davidson had invited me to the dinner with Frost, a controversial figure named Owen Lattimore was to speak at Bread Loaf. He had written a book praising the Chinese revolution as a peasant uprising, not a Communist movement. I truly believe Davidson did not wish me to attend that lecture. He, of course, stayed away himself. He questioned Frost about Lattimore. Frost seemed to think Lattimore an "innocent idealist," someone easily deceived.

Davidson believed that a rather mild-mannered, talkative gentleman who hung around the dining room before meals was actually a government spy, commissioned to keep watch on a possibly subversive bunch. I never knew if there was any truth in this.

Each year for the conference, Frost was called forth to give a reading. His rendering of his own poems is still a vivid memory. He told something he remembered from meeting William Butler Yeats. He had asked Yeats how long it had taken to write "The Song of Wandering Aengus." Yeats had replied, "Seven hours of biting a pencil and sweating blood." Again he remarked, I think before reading "Stopping by Woods," that he wished his voice could do justice to a poem, but knew it could not. He paused and added, "But, oh, the voice that I hear in my head!"

The Korean War was on that year. A good number of my letters in recent months to Hunter Kimball, a young man who was then in the conflict, having been called there unexpectedly from Army duty in Japan, were returned, and forwarded to me at

Bread Loaf. I had reason to be anxious, for we had gone out together frequently, but reassured myself that better news would come. It never did. He was an early MIA and no search for him was ever rewarded. He simply vanished without a trace.

Bread Loaf, more than it liked to admit, was really an extension of New York. The editors and agents who came there to teach budding writers were actually on the lookout for talent. Applicants submitted their manuscripts and, if accepted as participants, paid for their own travel and stay. An editor or agent got to look at their work. Caroline Ivey had come on such an acceptance, but had had the honor of being taken up and actually published, as few who came ever were, or such was my impression. Her book, *The Family,* remains in print as a strong picture of Alabama life.

New York was in the offing, and I decided to stop a few days there. Ed Dodd at Dodd, Mead was eager to hear of progress on my second book, and David Clay was in touch. Robert Penn Warren was staying that summer with friends at Westport. Through David he sent an invitation for me to come to lunch.

Robert Penn Warren wanted to meet me! I was breathlessly happy to be noticed in this way.

After a restless night of anticipation, I went to Grand Central Station and asked for a ticket to Westport. I found the price extremely high and ventured to ask how far it was, how long it took. How could I possibly get there in thirty-five minutes? I had been given a ticket to Westport, New York, up near the Canadian border and nowhere near Westport, Connecticut. Well, no one had said Connecticut. One was supposed to know.

I sometimes still have the desperate fantasy that I am on that train. The time for being met anywhere is passing, passing, past. What can I do? No one meets me in Westport . . . it is growing dark . . . I have to telephone New York. Where did I go wrong? What can I do?

Straightened out by an unusually patient ticket agent, I did get the right ticket and the train to Westport, Connecticut.

Warren himself was waiting at the station. He came toward me at once, and what struck me was his drive, his clearheaded forward pace, direct and charged.

He was of medium height, and his red hair was mussed and coppery in the sun. One eye, I had been told, had been put out in a boyhood accident, but the one left was so strong an observer, I wonder if anyone could have supported two. He gave the effect of seeing simply everything. I thought of the opening description of Conrad's *Lord Jim:* "He was an inch, perhaps two, under six feet, powerfully built, and he advanced straight at you. . . ." Not that the details apply so much, but the vivid, light-footed advance of Red Warren ought to have been described by Conrad.

I remembered John Crowe Ransom, who had been present at the memorable literary meeting in Oxford. Brushed and quiet, gray-suited, with tie and socks and all else so decently in place, he seemed the opposite type from Warren. I couldn't imagine him in Red's clothes—the sneakers and slacks and T-shirt only barely clean and certainly unpressed. Each suited his own choice.

I spent an interesting day. Warren's friend and editor Albert Erskine and Albert's wife, Peggy, were there, and we shared an outdoor lunch. Warren was given to telling anecdotes in a rough, hasty voice, not at all unattractive, but sometimes hard to follow. It seemed his mind went faster than his speech.

He was flattering toward Mississippi writing in general and asked how I would explain the quantity and excellence of our output. I said I thought maybe it was because we were always being "picked on"—singled out for criticism was what I meant, as he understood.

"That doesn't make literature," he said.

I replied that it might make you articulate.

He laughed about people who would disparage regional writing. "*Madame Bovary,*" he said. "Pretty good for a local novel. Small-town France in the nineteenth century. Should have left all that and come to Paris." We enjoyed this sort of banter. He was good at it.

He knew that I had seen Davidson at Bread Loaf. I reported that Davidson was very much concerned about Communist infiltration into this country's inner workings. "I worry about them over there," Red said. "I think we can look after the ones over here."

Red was staying with friends at that time, being, as I learned later, in process of separating from his first wife and not yet married to his second, the extraordinary Eleanor Clark.

At a certain moment, as though by clockwork, everybody got up to go swimming. I hadn't thought to bring a bathing suit, but Peggy lent me one, and we drove to the beach. Mainly we lay on the sand in the sun and exchanged random remarks at intervals.

Red's interest followed me through the years. I felt his to be a complex nature, whose apparently friendly, straightforward, humourous, no-nonsense approach to life, to each encounter, made him seem truly involved with anyone of interest to him in a one-to-one manner. But while not a mask, and certainly not insincere, his manner of the moment could not be entirely trusted.

This impression carries no criticism. He meant what he seemed to mean, but hundreds of demands on his time were always coming, and everyone's time is limited. There is also the fact that the full range of his mind and heart could no more come out at any one instant or to any one person than a lion can be a house pet.

One can describe a gifted person as a genius much too easily. Red, I believe, was the real thing. His mind worked too fast, encompassed too much, and it was hard for him to speak it out plainly. This complexity often hampers the flow of his novels. One always must except *All the King's Men,* where for once he found a subject equal to his scope. But in his poetry and criticism he is always on track, and often superb.

His work seems underrated now, and perhaps is not as widely read as before, but ask any of us who followed him through the years what we could have done without him. To me he was a guidepost for the gropings of mind and heart. I think that without him we all would have got lost a lot more often.

How many of us rated his interest and attention! Welty, Porter, Bellow, Ellison. Friendships also with Peter Taylor, John Cheever, William Styron, and many others. His long connection to Yale and marriage to a New Englander led him to settle permanently in Connecticut, but so far as I can see, he never lost or scanted his Southern ties.

He said somewhere that he could not write fiction that was not based in the South. He had tried to write about New England, which he genuinely loved. But the "aura" was lacking, was how he put it.

So that was 1950—another brief visit to New York, which, like the two previous ones—no more than glimpses, all three—left me wanting to know more.

My next chance at that world came in 1952. It was at the close of the Gulf Coast year, when I was tidying up mind, spirit, and possessions as well as could be expected at the end of the affair, that I received word of an award from the American Academy of Arts and Letters "in recognition of the two novels" I had by then published.

New York again! And right at the time I needed it most. Coming back from the Gulf Coast, my car stuffed with the pileup of a year, I stopped in Jackson on my way back to Carrollton. Eudora Welty welcomed me with the news that she too would be going to New York, the Academy having just elected her to membership. We could certainly meet, have lunch and dinner, go to shows, enjoy a good time.

Eudora recommended that I stay at a hotel she favored, the Bristol, long since torn down. Its main attraction was that it was cheap. Neither of us could afford lavish living. It had a nice bar, and we used to telephone each other from floor to floor, arranging to meet for a drink before dinner.

Once the well-known novelist and short-story writer Jean Stafford dropped by. Intense, attractive, with a wistful face, saddened by heaven knew what, she seemed conversant with all the Vanderbilt group, and others I had heard about through them. She invited us both out to Long Island, an invitation I could not accept for some reason.

I remember Jean speaking with admiration of a new writer she admired—J. D. Salinger, who at that time was still living around New York, and was apparently accessible. She said he rode around in a beat-up convertible with an enormous dog for company.

Eudora had a lifelong friend in New York, Rosa Wells, one of the Jackson Wellses, best known as Dolly. She worked for John Fischer, an editor at Harper's publishing house, and knew all the Mississippi crowd who came through the city. Her apartment was on Twelfth Street, and we were often invited there for drinks first, then went out to dinner in the Village at Rocco's or the Grand Ticino.

I was at the time a client of Eudora's agent and dear friend Diarmuid Russell. He had seen my second novel, *This Crooked Way,* well launched and had found an English publisher for it also. He stayed in touch with me throughout the summer. He invited us both for a Sunday at his house in Katonah, up the Hudson. We went by train and spent a charming day with him and his wife, Rose. The hours passed quickly, sunlit and radiant with good talk.

Eudora was obviously Diarmuid's pride and joy, both as client and friend. He had seen her early work into publications that would scarcely pay a week's grocery bill, and now that recognition was increasing by leaps and bounds, it was certain to rejoice him.

Diarmuid was a commanding sort of person, imposing to look at, his accent distinctly not of this country, more crisply English, one would say, though there was a hint of Irish in it too. I was obviously young and new to the New York scene, but he didn't seem to mind that, and said things that fit with my thinking. He noted that it didn't matter how long it took to write a book, advising me not to feel threatened by time and deadlines, or to seek for a change in publishers because I knew some editor who wanted me on his "list."

The sort of talk that went on between new writers and those who sought them, while exciting to me, was old hat to him. What he favored in a writer was the steady course, attention to work in hand, a clearheaded judgment about what really mattered. His good relationships with English publishers was a great help to Eudora especially, and to some extent to me. She had won the attention of E. M. Forster, Elizabeth Bowen, and others, however, simply by the originality and worth of her writing.

Eudora left for home, but I stayed happily on.

The summer was a great one. I discovered Allen Tate had been on the committee that chose me for the award. He had written, in fact, some time previously to ask if I could accept appointment for the Prix de Rome, which would have meant a year's residence at the American Academy there. The Rome prize went instead to William Styron. My own award was a thousand dollars, and there at the Academy awards ceremonies was Saul Bellow, who had been given the same recognition as I. He and Anita invited me out, but another engagement prevented my joining them.

One thousand dollars is no grand sum these days, but I saw myself as expert in stretching money and decided to stay on in New York until I had spent it all.

It lasted all summer. I chanced to meet one or two young men with Southern connections who were starting careers in the big city. We made good company for one another, and I frequently got my dinners paid for. I found a room in a large apartment on Ninth Street. It was owned by a friendly widow, a Jewish lady, who wanted somebody "nice" she could leave in charge while she was on vacation. I thus had the whole airy place to myself, lots to read, a ringing telephone, and a small amount of cash, dwindling slowly.

Allen Tate called to invite me to lunch and then on another day to dinner. He took me after dinner to call on Philip Rahv and his wife, Natalie. Rahv was then editor of *Partisan Review,* and a powerful intellectual presence on the New York scene. We sat and sipped whiskey and I listened while they spoke of many literary personalities and did a run-through of the latest gossip.

I felt more than a bit out of place among these people. Though they were courteous, I felt I had entered the meeting of a highly special club, which I really had no wish to join. I found out again about myself what I had felt at Vanderbilt, that though knowing writers individually might be wonderful, literary groups were not for me. The "in" talk about poets' and writers' personal lives, sexual affairs, nervous breakdowns, drinking, ventures abroad, attempts at suicide or bigamy or Communism, was interesting, but I felt it was a bit like another Carrollton. I could go to North Carrollton and happily play in the band, but Carrollton had too often turned into a nest of vipers. I perceived the "literary life" as a little like that, a flowerbed where no one paid much attention to the bloom, but a swarm of other sorts of activity went on around the stems and roots beneath. (In these reflections I continued to make Eudora and Warren the exceptions, and so to this day—no vipers, they—they remain.)

Browsing in bookshops, I discovered Wallace Stevens's poetry; I still have the copy of *Harmonium* I bought that summer. I read Isherwood, whose *Goodbye to Berlin* was making a stir. Every other day I would come home with another treasure. Still on my shelves, these books speak to me of a glowing summer.

I saw a considerable amount of David Clay and his wife, Justine ("Dusty"). David was in a period between jobs, having left the company that had brought out my two books. It was my first acquaintance with the many mysteries of his career. I was grateful for his help as an editor and was not inclined to judge him. His close friendship with Red, dating from their student days at Vanderbilt, was of course a valued point of reference.

I helped him write some television scripts he was trying to sell as a series. We once sat up all night typing them in his apartment to meet a deadline. I assumed he knew he could make the sale—television was in an infant stage in the early fifties. He had a real interest in its possibilities. However, the series was rejected, and so far as I know, nothing came of it.

Such a story with David Clay became all too frequent through the years, but his confidence was such that no one listening to his way of speaking about some project could possibly doubt that it would materialize. Or so, to my trusting ears, it did seem. Whatever the problems, I keep a lifelong glow from that sojourn and for the Clays, as I knew them then, and for New York, as I knew it then.

At intervals, we often dined together with a friend from Memphis, who was starting out in newspaper work in New York. He had the unlikely name of Vartanig Garabed Vartan, or "Tonny," as we called him. He later became a leading financial reporter for *The New York Times*. His father was a well-known seller of Oriental carpets, who had a business in the lobby of the Peabody Hotel in Memphis. Mr. Vartan was known throughout the Delta as the best rug importer in the South. Tonny was a Yale graduate but had started work on a paper in McComb, Mississippi. He had been hired away from that small paper to work at the New York *Herald Tribune.* We had found ourselves to be neighbors on West Ninth Street, and we used to swap Mississippi anecdotes while sitting on the front doorsteps at twilight, or sometimes on a bench in Washington Square.

Like me, he was enduring the breakup of a love gone wrong; mine had come from Vicksburg, his from Memphis. There's nothing like bruised feelings to create new sympathies.

There was never the need to assign a special role in my life to Tonny Vartan, but I did often think that in him I had found a brother. Except for treasured intervals, I never succeeded in making any relationship with my own brother, who remained, except for those, one of the strangest people I have ever known anywhere. A sister, a brother, a father . . . one continuing part of my life has been a search for all three, a search many times rewarded, sometimes ending badly. Tonny was a fine reward.

Tonny was Armenian by descent, and his family story would make an encouraging American legend, the kind we all like to think possible. During the Turkish massacre of Armenians, his father was protected by a friendly Turk, who concealed him (according to Tonny, who loved good stories) in quarters reserved to the Turk's harem. He later was given passage to the United States. Helped by still others, he found his way into the Oriental carpet business. His clients were well-to-do people in Memphis and the Mississippi Delta. Most houses of any repute seemed to have at least one of Mr. Vartan's beautiful rugs. His only son, bright as a new coin, had a lifelong taste for good living that compared with the father's taste for rugs.

Tonny had a middle-European face that at first seemed blank, but was simply a good poker face, that of the listening first-rate reporter, inscrutable behind his familar Lucite-rimmed glasses. His beautifully rounded, totally bare head (I think he shaved it) held a scrolled-up wealth of everything he'd ever encountered, all processed and ready to hand. He could be sharply dismissive of whatever he judged not worth his time. He could be hilariously funny.

During that summer he was going to parties in the Village at Joan Williams's, she being at that time a special interest of William Faulkner's, and Faulkner himself was often there, though Tonny never mentioned this until many years later.

All of us were novelists, come to think of it. Joan Williams was writing her own, and Tonny lived to write two novels, *50 Wall Street* and *The Dinosaur Fund,* which clarify that opaque aspect of American life more than anything else I've read.

I think back to Tonny and myself now and see two young people sitting at twilight on a friendly, uncrowded New York street—there were such things back then. How tiny, how speck-of-dust-size we are in that huge all-accepting, all-engulfing pile of steel and cement, tunneled perpetually by anonymous crowds! Yet it scarcely worried us. Life was before us, and we did not question what good things it could bring. We were often laughing.

One phone call away was Allen Tate's invitation to come for a weekend at Princeton with his daughter Nancy and her husband. I thus took part in one of the long-running, heavy-drinking parties the Tates were famous for giving. A guest would start out in the house, an old residence on a Princeton street, hearing talk of how Princeton was the "Harvard of the South," how those wonderful black waiters who turned up at the inn were descendants of the faithful body servants young Southern students would bring with them from home.

All this was lore and gave one a lovely glow of feeling to be on the right side of everything, among those who understood a Southern heritage and "how it all was."

Then as more liquor was consumed and food partaken, the party would drift out on the lawn. Consciousness began to come in luminous segments. Conversing in the hammock with Nancy's husband, Percy. Dancing to records in the living room. Reminiscing over one's Southern childhood with Allen on the sofa in the library. Inspired by some thought we had exchanged, he suddenly sprang toward the bookshelves, seized a copy of his novel *The Fathers,* and impulsively autographed it to me. I have it still and find the inscription: "To Elizabeth Spencer on the occasion of her 1st visit to P'ton, where Tenn-Miss prevails . . . with great admiration of her and her 2 books Allen Tate August 1, 1952."

My feeling toward Tate and my final rejection of his friendship, which was no doubt meant sincerely, is something of a mystery to me to this date. For one thing, I did not find him an attractive man. He obviously wished women to find him so. There is nothing wrong with that wish, and by all accounts many women did. He could be genuinely charming and quietly considerate in conversation. His major appeal to me was that he sought out and supported talent. He had no regard at all for "success." In fact, to him a popular success was suspect. His critical judgment both in his writing and his talk still seems awe-inspiring. He could pierce at once to the very heart of any matter.

The thing, I believe, that put me off most about him was his tendency to gossip. He started out with genuine interest, but as details about a person amassed, he would suddenly turn destructive and derisive, even about his friends. Later, he might counter a harsh observation with something redeeming, but the damage had been done. One had to be careful of a chance remark that might be quoted. It was not comfortable to be around him.

The extraordinary influence that Tate had on the entire American literary world seemed to come as much from his wide acquaintance as from his brilliance as a critic. I was never swept away by his poetry, though I suspect the best of it rises very high on the scale, but to read his criticism is to be in the real presence of his mind—and what a presence that is! One could read through a whole library of comment on Dante, for instance, and never find anything so penetrating as what Allen Tate was able to say in a few pages.

Tate's wide connections were not exclusive to the South, or even to the United States. He was in friendly correspondence with Eliot, could quote remarks dropped by Hemingway in Paris, had almost come to blows with Scott Fitzgerald, had known leading figures on the French scene, and could find points of welcome anywhere in the world he chose to be. The poet Karl Shapiro once remarked to me, "When people ask about your standing as a poet, it's enough to say you know Allen Tate."

I returned to teaching at Ole Miss in the fall of 1952. Following that memorable summer in New York, I seemed to myself to be set for better days ahead. I had projected a new novel, the one that finally became *The Voice at the Back Door.* I had submitted the project in my application for a Guggenheim Fellowship. I had never stopped longing to return to Italy, and with sponsors like Red Warren, Stark Young, and Hodding Carter, the well-known editor of the *Delta Democrat Times* at Greenville, I felt I might even succeed in getting the grant and striking off on my own.

In the spring of 1953, however, a massive misfortune overtook the whole family. My uncle Joe, he who through the years had been surrogate father, trusted confidant, charming lover of tolerant living and fine good times, died suddenly in a gun accident.

The fact that no one knew if the death was accidental gave an unbearable twist to this tragic event. His first wife, Aunt Esther, had died slowly and painfully of cancer—a home death, grievous to contemplate. He himself had been tormented by an illness to which this dread diagnosis had not been given, so far as we ever knew. But we knew he was depressed and unwell, having expressed a degree of blank despair in living, or so I was told later, that hardly seemed to be possible for him, of all people, to feel.

However, the accident may certainly have been just that—a nervous state, a lack of caution, a fall with a loaded gun.

All of us were struck numb. How much we had all depended on his wit, his caring, his good faith! And not only the family itself, but a wide circuit of friends everywhere. I attended the home funeral at Teoc, and saw the faces crowding the yard beneath the great live oaks, a mass of black ones among them, many streaked with tears.

I returned to teach, but found that one wound tears open another, and life was becoming a source of despair for me as well. I had gone suddenly from light to darkness. I experienced a daily blank feeling I had never known before.

My decision was to work, and work I did, harder, harder and harder, but nothing seemed to go well, and for some reason related to my despair, I stopped eating. If able to force a few bites down for each meal, I felt I had enough. Colors and sounds grew vague and hard to separate. I seemed to expend an enormous amount of energy simply meeting a one-hour class. When walking, I seemed not to touch ground. I think I was becoming gravely ill without caring to recognize it.

Something had to give. Shortly after receiving the letter from the Guggenheim Foundation, congratulating me on my appointment as a fellow, I became altogether unable to carry on, and bad times had struck in earnest. I had to delay acceptance of the fellowship until the fall, and go through a long spell in hospital.

But at last, in October rather than June, with mind and body stuck together once more but feeling they might still come apart, reduced to ninety-eight pounds and lacking in daily energy, laden with the multiple anxieties and total disapproval of my parents, I went to New York and boarded an Italian liner to go to Italy. At sea I used to lean on the rail and reflect that if I fell in, I was so frail I might not even sink.

We landed at Naples.

I came up to Rome by train and found lodging, quite by chance, at the same hotel—the Inghilterra on Via Bocca di Leone—where I had spent my last night in Italy in the summer of 1949.

I took the coincidence as a good omen for great days and better health, and hope was floating all around that room on happy little wings as I fell asleep, exhausted.

24

RETURN TO ITALY

KARL Shapiro and his family of that time were in Rome in 1953. I had met Karl at a literary meeting he had come to Mississippi from Chicago to attend. He was at that time editor of *Poetry Magazine*. I had liked him and liked his lecture, and we had discussed meeting in Rome.

I made contact with him and his wife, Evalyn, almost at once, and along with the hustle of finding cheap quarters, packing up, and moving in, I was also running out to meet them for lunch and for the evening gatherings they began immediately to have.

I settled at the Dinesen, a hotel/pensione on Via di Porta Pinciana, near the Veneto, well known in those days. It was run by a Danish woman who had come as a beautiful young tourist to Rome well before World War II. She had immediately been scooped up by an Italian, married him, had sons by him, and survived in some way during the Fascist era.

At the time of my stay she was still beautiful, an old woman wearing plain, flowing gray, who appeared infrequently in the parlors and dining room. Her sons were running the hotel. A good many Scandinavians stayed there for their Roman holidays; also the English and Americans seemed to know of it. It was a former monastery, belonging to an order of Lebanese monks, who took over the dining room once a year to dine together, and who could be heard at times, chanting in booming, bell-like tones in the building next door.

The food there was extremely good, and before many days had passed the Shapiros had come there to eat with me. Also, by chance, at the foot of an elevator shaft in another building entirely, where I had found a temporary lodging, I had heard a voice rising up that I felt I should know. It was speaking French, but where else could "*mah bah-gaage*" come from but straight from Mississippi? I was right. The speaker was Frank Lyell, whom I had heard about but never met, though I knew his brother, Louis. He was from Jackson and was a close friend of Eudora Welty's. He also began eating at the Dinesen.

Frank lured me into sightseeing with him, during the few days he spent in Rome. He was simply lightning when it came to getting places. Here was the Colosseum, there the Forum, out here the Lateran Palace, and now we could go and lunch in Piazza Navona at the Tre Scalini and watch the Bernini fountains play before the church of Sant'Agnese (façade by Borromini). I felt I had not a chance to remember all that he was telling me. He lectured in literature in Texas and seemed to be infinitely well-informed about everything.

Many movies were being shot at that period in Rome. It was the era of Gina Lollabrigida ("La Gina"), Sophia Loren, Claudia Cardinale, and numerous other beauties. The Italian craze was on, and many of the movies that Italian directors like Vittorio De Sica and Roberto Rossellini were making turned out to be enduring classics.

But Hollywood had caught it, too, and during those days that fall the talk was all of *The Barefoot Contessa* (*La Contessa Scalza*). In one day Frank reported sightings of Humphrey Bogart, Ava Gardner, and Gina Lollabrigida. All these could be easily seen on the Via Veneto, with its fashionable Doney's and other sidewalk bars. I was getting dizzy with Frank's whirlwind of discoveries. At the lunch table one day he told me the entire story of Eudora's novel in progress, *The Ponder Heart,* later published in *The New Yorker.*

Not only the Shapiros, Frank Lyell, and multiple movie names were attracted to Rome, but swarms of cognoscenti were gathering from everywhere. I had no notion that this would be the case. Robert Penn Warren had kindly written letters to Laurance and Isabel Roberts, the gracious couple who ran the American Academy in Rome, out on the Gianicolo.

Their residence was the beautiful eighteenth-century Villa Aurelia. I almost immediately received an invitation to dinner or lunch, I forget which, as I was so lavishly favored by their hospitality that the occasions run together, like bright, dazzling colors.

But at the same time, the Shapiros, having settled with three young children in an apartment not far from the Dinesen, were having in their list of guests. It was through them that I once more encountered Peggy Erskine, last seen on the beach at Westport. Her marriage to Albert Erskine was ended, and she was then living in an apartment on the Via Margutta, an address somewhat the equivalent of Bleecker Street in Greenwich Village.

Peggy gave a good many parties, beginning before dinner. The guests sat crowded together on sofas in a medium-sized *salotto,* looking out on rooftops. She frequently passed an iced pitcher of martinis. Everybody drank a lot, and groups were formed, who later trekked off to dinner at some nearby trattoria.

At the first of these occasions, who should appear but Allen Tate and his wife of that time, Caroline Gordon. They had unerringly been given a fine apartment connected with the American Academy, a terrace overlooking the city from the Gianicolo, and a cook who was a former chef at Ranieri's, the famous Roman restaurant. Lovers of all social occasions, they often invited me to lunch and to dinner.

Caroline Gordon, an enthusiastic convert to Roman Catholicism, thought vastly little of anyone who was "outside the Church." She seemed to me hospitable, as was Allen, but rather more opinionated and quarrelsome than he. She liked contradicting any passing opinion she did not choose to honor. She spoke continually of books and writers one could or could not like. *Moby Dick* was "not a novel," *Huckleberry Finn* was "not a novel." Graham Greene was nothing but a "gifted amateur." When young writers like myself, she went on, told her they liked Graham Greene, she despaired of the future of literature. Henry

James was a "real novelist." I mentioned admiring Turgenev; she said I should read Chekhov.

I used to ask her questions at first out of interest, but later to draw her into what I considered absurd statements. To me it was a form of teasing, as I dislike authority. But I doubt she caught on. I was a Protestant and hardly worth her notice. She'd never read "any of my stuff" but told me at length what I had to value and what rules I must observe.

Both the Tates grew almost hysterical in their praise of Flannery O'Connor. Caroline told me that Flannery was doing something that had "never been done before." She was examining the South from a Roman Catholic viewpoint. Since the entire culture of the South is basically Protestant, I wondered then what I wonder still: What right does anyone have to do this? To examine Catholic Ireland from a Protestant viewpoint would seem presumptuous in the extreme. (It may be that O'Connor was not really doing what Caroline Gordon spoke of her as doing. Her stories frequently puzzle me, and solutions as to what they are saying are not easy to find.) At any rate, the Tate gospel, being proclaimed everywhere, was that O'Connor was all that mattered among present-day American writers.

I learned later that Caroline and Allen were at that time on the verge of a second divorce. They had gone through one, but remarried. However, in those days in the fifties they generously gave halcyon times to all they invited.

One such guest was the Principessa Caetani, founder and editor of the prestigious magazine *Botteghe Oscure*. It was hard to believe in appearance-conscious Rome that here was indeed a real princess. To lunch she wore a plain cotton print dress and low-heeled "sensible" summer shoes. Her face was distinguished, intelligent, and self-assured in a pleasant way. One learned without surprise that she was a New England woman who had brought considerable wealth into a noble family. When I was introduced to her, she said vaguely, "Oh, yes, someone has spoken to me about you." All the chatter of a Tate gathering swirled about her, and for that matter about me also. Allen complimented her: "Marguerite has one standard of judgment for the manuscripts she wants to publish: 'I like it.' "

Hidden under all the exchanges with which the Tates' lunches and dinners abounded, there were doubtless reservoirs of genuine worth. I still reproach myself for the adverse state of mind they used to plunge me into.

Meanwhile back at the Dinesen, things were not bad at all. One evening early in my stay, an American couple walked in for dinner, the husband looking vaguely familiar. The name Mattingly rang a bell. Wasn't he . . . ? He was. A book of my aunt's that I had read with great interest in Carrollton was Garrett Mattingly's *Catherine of Aragon.* I was delighted to meet him. There immediately returned to my mind a letter Catherine, exiled and abandoned, had written to Henry VIII. "Above all things mine eyes have most desired to see thy face." Maybe I was into some schoolgirl crush, but the words had stuck, and gave me an excellent start on conversing with the remarkable pair, "Matt" and "Gert" (Gertrude), who were to become my fast friends.

We often ate together at the Dinesen, went to parties together, visited sites together. Matt, like me, was on a Guggenheim, engaged in research for his fine book of two years later, *The Armada.* On the strength of this book and *Catherine,* I remain convinced he, though an American, is among the most noteworthy European historians.

There was other company: Charles and Darr Klappert, an antique dealer and his wife from La Jolla, California; and a charming old character named Martha Wright, a widow from Chicago via Texas, recently in Guatemala, whose whiskey-deepened tones could liven any conversation. There also appeared a pair of annual visitors from England, Daniel Cory and his wife, Margot. Daniel had been the philosopher George Santayana's private secretary for many years before his death, and still spoke affectionately of the old gentleman. He was an engaging man, perpetually smiling, his neat hair white above a youthful face. He was American by birth but had lived abroad so many years he seemed Anglicized, and his voice, with its slight attractive stutter, would keep pleasingly on in one's head after he departed.

The exchange among us all during those after-dinner groupings over coffee in the *salotto* made hours race past till bedtime. I think of the conversation as moving like a loom, with threads feeding easily into place, warp and weft interlacing.

Of course, we drank too much at times, but there was much shared affection and high spirits untouched by meanness, and the days flew. Working through the mornings in my narrow monk's cell (the Mattinglys had a whole apartment, but most rooms were simply former cells), I began to see my novel take shape and march along.

One day a strange thing occurred. I was sitting alone in the late afternoon, writing a letter in one of the two *salotti,* when through the door came a robed man with a black beard. He walked uncertainly toward me and sat down. He asked in very limited English what I was doing. I said I was writing a letter. He seized my hand. "I luff you," he said, several times over. I extracted my hand with difficulty. He asked to go to my room. I said I had a letter to write. Presently, he got up and wandered away.

I guessed that he was one of the Lebanese monks from whom Madame Dinesen leased the hotel. But I had altogether forgotten the incident until, at dinner, where we were all busily eating, the door burst open and here came the monk. He was walking even more uncertainly and began to wander about the dining hall.

A lady staying there was the daughter of a New England Congregationalist minister. Her name was Alice Carter-Foy and she had a character to go with her snow-white hair and gentle smile. The monk approached her. She leaned forward graciously ready to attend to his every need. He grasped her hand. Within seconds Mrs. Carter-Foy had recoiled with a crimson face, there was general consternation, and the dining-room steward was summoning the manager. My guess was that he had announced he luffed her, too.

When I think of him I recall Chekhov's story "The Black Monk," for certainly there was something Russian-looking about him, an exotic step beyond the many robed figures we saw daily around the city.

One morning I received a call from Peggy Erskine. A friend of hers, an Irishman named Harry Craig, had been one of those at her apartment the night before. We had had a good conversation and gone out to dinner. I had been presented to Alberto

Moravia, the Italian novelist, at Peggy's, and I believe he was part of the group.

Peggy told me that she, Harry, and Moravia wished to take a trip across Italy to the eastern coast. There was a phenomenon one could visit there, then being talked about all over Italy. An Italian priest, Padre Pio, had received the stigmata, and going to a daily mass to see him and view his visible, though bandaged hands, stained with blood, was the goal of the trip. Their motive, I did not have to be told, was curiosity rather than piety. We would drive through the Abruzzi to the Adriatic, down through Puglia, returning by way of Naples.

I was still not entirely well. I could not walk for any distance, or eat as much as I would like. A return to normal was occurring, but the pace was slow. Yet it did seem a wonderful offer, a grand opportunity to spend time in company with Italy's most celebrated novelist and to rove freely among remote places. Peggy's interest was in art history, which she was then studying in Rome on a Fulbright fellowship. She later became a lecturer in art at an American school in Rome. She would be certain to seek out places of artistic interest and know what to make of them. I took a deep breath and said I would go.

We set out eastward on a crisp autumn morning, traveling first toward Tivoli and along the Aniene, but soon passing out of a well-traveled area into the Abruzzi. The sophisticated atmosphere of Rome and its environs, along with aqueducts, ruins of imperial palaces, monastery gardens, and country villas, dropped quickly away. Here were no amiable crowds meeting, no elegance, neither sightseers nor sights to see.

Instead we drove through dry hills with olive groves, stretches of fields planted in wheat, a few vineyards. There were little villages perched high on hilltops. Roads wound tediously up to them. We found simple places to eat, while everybody stared at us.

From the villages the people descended every day to work in wheatfields, gather the olive harvest, tend sheep, plow oxen. The oxen in fact were the sights to see—large white and dun-colored farm beasts with their marvelously wide spread of horns, unknown in our country. There were donkeys as well, all working animals. The farm carts were impressive, with wheels higher than their beds. Harnesses for working animals were em-

bossed with designs in silver, sometimes hung with bells. The donkeys took fine regalia as their due: enormous ears and eyes said so. This was a farming world.

There were few trees. An occasional villa, having seen better days, would rise up lonely on a barren hillside.

Peggy's car was a Volkswagen, sturdy but scarcely comfortable. We were somewhat crowded, bags stashed under the hood, motor toiling in the rear.

Throughout the trip what I listened for most was Moravia's voice. His opinions and reminiscences were free-flowing and moved by association and memory from one topic to another. He did not exactly converse but seemed conversant constantly with his own mind. He held opinions but did not insist on agreement. I found him rather fascinating. He could not understand my accent—he was slightly deaf, his English was not so good, and my accent was strange to him. I was content to listen.

He was not very tall, but above the Italian average. His hair in those days was dark, sprinkled with white. He had beautiful eyes—large, intelligent, gray—with thick brows and lashes. One could scarcely call him handsome, but the face was arresting. He did not seem very much attached to his own ego. He was intensely curious about the sexuality of everyone mentioned.

It was habitual in those days, to an extent that seems at present much reduced, to have to know immediately about anyone's sexual preferences. Homosexuality in the United States was still something of a "closet" matter, though perhaps not so in larger cities. In what was often called the Age of Anxiety, the macho extreme was evident everywhere. Was someone or wasn't he . . . ? What was a woman doing even talking with a man thought to be "queer"? Someone was always waiting and spying, armed with suspicion like a branding iron. Some have called it the sexual witch-hunt, implying a resemblance to McCarthyism and the Red scare.

Moravia's prying, however, was not offensive. His attitude seemed to be that sexuality was so important that knowing anything at all about a person naturally involved a question of sex. He had tolerance for most anything human, disliking, so far as I could tell, only people who did nothing, especially wealthy people who seemed to be without purpose in life. He held interesting viewpoints on Mussolini. To him, the good of Mussolini was in his having sprung from the Italian peasantry. His roots in "*il popolo*" had made him popular in Italy. But this was only in the beginning. Later, the Fascist element took over, which led to the grievous end.

To support himself Moravia had often worked writing dialogue in Italian to be dubbed into American films. Several of his own books had been made into films, notably *La Ciocciara,* which was released in English as *Two Women.* Sophia Loren took the part of a strong peasant woman who had to see her daughter raped before her eyes.

He related being at lunch with Anna Magnani and Roberto Rossellini, Magnani's lover at that time. Rossellini had just received a letter from the actress Ingrid Bergman. (Later, the two became involved in an affair that made worldwide headlines.) Alberto recalled that Rossellini read aloud from the letter: "I am just a little Swedish girl who admires you so much and wants to act in a film of yours." Magnani took up a plate of spaghetti and threw it in Rossellini's face.

Peggy's friend Harry Craig was Irish to the point of obsession, and quoted long stretches from Yeats's poetry. Alberto inquired if Yeats was homosexual. "Heavens, no!" Harry all but shouted.

Moravia had odd opinions on American literature. He did not care for Faulkner except for *Sanctuary,* the most sexually shocking of Faulkner's works. He thought Carson McCullers, who deals notably with characters outside the norm, was the best American writer.

He would often smile indulgently at us when relating some event. It was a moment of outcries and even riots in Italy against the British. Only days before our trip a British commanding officer in Trieste had ordered soldiers to fire on a crowd of demonstrators, and six Italians had been killed. A free city at that time, Trieste was the cause of intense disputes between Yugoslavia and Italy. Later the same day, the commander was photographed at a cocktail party. Italians were outraged and demonstrations flared up everywhere.

The car we traveled in had a British license. Harry Craig kept identifying himself as "Irlandese," but the distinction was a rather fine one for the average Italian in some country village. Several times we received poisonous stares and shouts, and once found a hostile group of young men encircling our car when we came from eating lunch. Moravia was immensely helpful. His fluent colloquial Italian kept trouble at bay. Peggy and I were "*donne americane studiose, simpatiche*" . . . Harry was "*uno scrittore ben conosciuto.*" We were going to find Padre Pio, "*vedere un miracolo italiano.*"

Alberto told us of an incident during the recent demonstrations in Rome. A crowd marching down the Via Veneto had remarked Allen Tate, also driving with a British license, and had set upon his car with clubs and fists. Allen sat at the wheel with his hands over his English-looking face, shouting "*Sono americano! Sono americano!*" "He was mob-bed," Moravia drily remarked with his characteristic laugh.

He was extremely intelligent in his appraisal of the Italian Communists. He himself had flirted with Communism at one time, enough to learn, with a novelist's typical curiosity, how party cells worked, what methods of inquiry they used, how they impressed guilt, confession, and belief on the individual spirit. He claimed to have been refused a visa to visit the United

States, though I was told by someone at the embassy that this had been a temporary ruling in his case, and was later cleared.

On we drove through open country increasingly dry and barren. "Sheeps," Moravia used to remark. And of a village, "*Ecco* so-and-so. You like it? You want to live here?" He used to say that there would be no cultural interest in such a village. Who did one talk to? The doctor might walk in the afternoons with the priest. The druggist might play cards with both. It would be a monotonous life. Yet always I felt that his true interest in Italy was with *il popolo,* the common people. He showed little interest in art galleries, cathedrals, and palaces. He spoke of poverty and a stubborn love of living. He seemed to know what it was like.

Moravia also confided that his enemy was boredom. He often traveled to keep up an interest in life. When he traveled he was less bored. He walked with a slight limp, and told how as a young man he had spent time in a sanatorium for tuberculosis. He asked me if I saw his books anywhere in America. I told him many were out in paperback and could be seen on shelves for sale even in drugstores. He smiled. "It is hard to believe," he said.

When night came on in this country, a good hotel was an idea to give up right away. We had to put up in a sort of inn, two rooms available with curtains strung out between beds and a single toilet down the hall. It was cold. It still seemed around midnight when someone shouted what sounded like "Radio!" but I later learned was "*Sveglia!*"—"Time to get up." We took a sleepy cup of *caffelatte* and some hard rolls for the road. Workers were descending to the fields in the early light. Our car threaded among them, the donkeys and horses in their proud harnesses, the wagons drawn by the oxen, women and children riding to work with the men, all moving among the beasts with the same rhythm. The village was emptying, would stand like a ghost town until evening. A kind of dusty mist was rising from the fields below.

Foggia, a fairly large town on the Adriatic, was our goal, for near there lay San Giovanni Rotondo, the town of Padre Pio. If San Giovanni had once been only another country village, that was true no longer. Splashy new villas stood along the outskirts in rows, each with a garden, a driveway, ornamental sculpture. Shiny cars were running about. There were a huge new hospital and new hotels. Padre Pio's stigmata had brought prosperity. The contrast to the villages we had seen along the way was almost ludicrous.

The truth was, I had very little interest in Padre Pio. I don't doubt miracles—why should we doubt them? Things seem to be one way; then something happens that is not to be explained rationally, and they change. The hands of a priest in a remote village begin to ooze blood, and his feet and side do the same. The wounds of Christ crucified appear on his own person. People flock in to see. He holds a daily mass.

We had all decided to rise early and go to the mass. I slept badly. The hotel was new and had evidently been put up hastily, with flimsy materials, for I could hear doors close, people speaking, water running, and toilets flushing from floors above and below. The sleep I finally fell into was from exhaustion, and continued with contentment long past the time of the service.

The accounts I heard were of some interest. Crowds of elderly women had been the main part of the congregation. According to Moravia, "The smell of piety was strong." The padre wore his hands bandaged and covered with gloves, but pictures of him holding up his palms for all to view were available on postcards. There were also booklets on sale, detailing the miracle.

From San Giovanni, we drove down to Gorgona, in the province of Puglia. Gorgona juts out into the sea, a little hump on the Italian boot. Here to our surprise we found forests. I did not realize how much that dry, picked-over, impoverished country could affect my American spirit until I saw these trees—live oaks, beech, and cypress—some turning golden with autumn, damp from recent rain, their great strong trunks and soaring height showing what it should have been like everywhere in a denuded land. On a marble tablet we read a passage from Dante describing that locale. Moravia remarked that a poet was a great thing for a country.

Our goal now was west to Benevento and beyond that Naples. It was an easier drive. Moravia loved Naples. He became excited when we drove into the city. "Naples is the sweetest town," he kept saying. He liked its way with poverty, its frankness and combative spirit. Sightseeing again, we all drove out to Pompeii, and then for some harebrained reason decided to ascend Vesuvius.

A long road led upward to a certain point, but the summit had to be gained by way of a ski lift. The volcano itself—its crater actively smoldering away, a raw inflamed throat, a giant's satanic yawn—opened below the footpath. There was no protective railing. Anyone who wanted to could have jumped right in. Dante must have seen this sight before he wrote his *Inferno*. The surrounding lava felt soft from the heat just below, but down the slopes it had hardened into grotesque black shapes, the last thing one would want to fall on. Falling seemed a real enough danger, for the ski lift had no support for our feet. I rode side by side with Moravia, holding on to a rather fragile bar and traveling at an angle I do not care to remember. That day we were the only visitors.

Peggy and Harry left Naples to spend a few days in Procida, an island near Ischia, so Alberto and I took the train to Rome. Along the way he began to talk volubly, telling me how during the war he and his wife, the novelist Elsa Morante, had gone from Rome into the countryside to take refuge and to avoid capture by the Nazis.

They had taken the train down from Rome to go toward Naples, but knowing themselves followed, had left the train at a small stop midway. From here they managed to mingle with crowds of fearful people, and to escape on foot into the mountains. Hiding out, they lived mainly on the countryside, but peasants brought food to them, and no one gave them away. His account of how they lived through this difficult time was swift and vivid. I felt I could have been reading one of his forceful stories. When I think of that train ride, his voice comes back, just as memories of that time and place were coming steadily back to him.

People of great talent and value to a country can suffer more than any others when politics go against them. They are to be silenced, or driven out. That trip was an education.

The fall of that same year was notable for William Faulkner's visit to Rome. A Nobel laureate, he was being asked by the State Department to go to various capitals and make himself available to all and sundry who wished to meet a famous American writer.

I was more nervous about his visit than were people who knew nothing personal about him. I felt that the South, especially Mississippi, was on trial. I wanted him to be on good behavior. But I knew this was something no one could predict.

Along with an impressive guest list I was invited to the cultural attaché's lovely apartment in the Renaissance quarter for a reception in his honor. The Tates, of course, were there. Faulkner seemed cordial, though reserved, saying very little to those who ventured to try talking with him. Just as he had at Ella Somerville's reception in Oxford, he stood near one corner holding a glass but did not drink. There was some considerable muted excitement in the room.

As we were leaving, Allen and Caroline asked me to join them and "Bill" for dinner at a nearby restaurant. I went along with the Tates by cab, but in a chauffeur-driven car a heavily made-up woman wearing some extraordinary burnoose-type headdress was bringing the guest of honor. "You great man, you!" she burbled to him, as the car arrived. She turned out to be Anya Seton, a popular novelist whose books had evidently made whatever money was needed for chauffeurs, burnooses, and so on.

Allen was quite excited at the dinner and talked with considerable charm. Faulkner said little. Allen raised his glass and asked Bill to toast "the old South." He complied. I recall that Faulkner did ask Caroline Gordon what had happened to Mr. Maury. He was referring to her splendid book, which he evidently admired, *Aleck Maury, Sportsman.* One could see his threshold for that approving query. His own hunting stories are among his best.

At a certain point we all looked up as a stunning black-haired girl entered. She joined us at the table. She had not been present at the reception. This was Jean Stein, Faulkner's companion at that time. He chose a moment after introductions to remark, "The two most beautiful words in the English language are 'pretty girl.' " One had to think of Henry James's similar comment, his choice phrase being "summer afternoon." The parallel seemed a good summing-up of both men, and a courtly compliment in this case to the girl who had joined us.

So far so good. But at a luncheon given by Clare Boothe Luce, the American ambassador, in Faulkner's honor, he behaved badly, Moravia said, driving his hostess to despair by his stubborn refusal to say anything at all. Alberto left feeling awful, and asked me later why this man would behave as he did. I had no ready answer.

However, in the interviews that appeared, Faulkner seemed to have been cooperative enough, showing a wide knowledge of European literatures. A French woman who met him told me that his French was excellent.

During the summer of 1954 in Italy I went up to pass some months in Florence. I thought I needed to be around Italians, and hoped to progress further in the language than I had been able to do in Rome, with its ceaseless round of invitations to occasions where English was spoken.

I had hardly settled in when Allen Tate showed up. He was attending a Roman Catholic conference, and called to ask me to various social events. The poet John Frederick Nims and his family were living in a palazzo famous for its connection with James's *Portrait of a Lady.* (It did seem that everything Allen had to do with was famous for something.) Caroline was not with him.

Allen invited me to spend some time with the Nims family, also in company with Father D'Arcy, the well-known English Jesuit, who had come to the conference and lent a memorable presence to the evenings. He was very thin, with thick hair turning gray, a face strongly accented with high cheekbones and heavy brows. I thought of those Gothic saints on the walls of French cathedrals, upright, skeletal, steadfast. He spoke not at all of the names associated with him as Catholic counselor—Graham Greene and Evelyn Waugh, among others—but I felt drawn to his humanity and fine quality, his awareness of every person in his presence as an individual. Later, I sought out some of his writings and had a continuing impression of him as someone to whom Christianity had the meanings it was meant to have. His ideas on grace as a sign of God's love are central to those meanings.

An annual event in Florence is the celebration of La Festa di San Giovanni, the patron saint of the city. There is an opening parade of the nobles, with the descendants of distinguished families dressed in medieval costume and mounted on horseback. Pages in Renaissance tights wave pennants and all converge on the Piazza della Signoria in front of the Palazzo Vecchio, where bleachers have been set up and the surrounding buildings decked out in banners displaying all the local devices.

The major event, a game of *calcio* (soccer), also began with ceremony. The players dress in medieval suits but otherwise are as fiercely intent as in any other match. I had tentatively been invited to go with an Italian sculptor I had been seeing, but he had not telephoned to set the time of meeting. When Allen Tate called to ask me, I declined at first, but when he insisted, I consented. (I had to refuse the sculptor who called soon after.)

Allen and I had good seats, and it was from there I observed a strange accident. The little medieval cannon that had fired to signal the opening of the game took a notion to fire again. Everyone stopped in astonishment, and a man who had been leaning on the cannon fell to the ground. He did not succeed in getting up, and two men soon approached with a stretcher and took him away.

At the apartment where I was staying, I asked a few days later what had happened to him. He was still in the hospital, I was told. Later they told me he had died of blood poisoning. There was some mention of neglect; no penicillin had been given him. However, one heard strange stories about Italian medicine and the details passed on to me may not have been true.

Long after, when I came to write a story set in Florence, called *The Light in the Piazza,* I made use of the event almost as it had happened. I am convinced that unforeseen accidents determine life. A chance meeting, a missed appointment, a gunshot . . .

Living in Fiesole above Florence was Elisabeth Mann Borgese, daughter of Thomas Mann, and widow of the remarkable scholar Antonio Borgese, who had lectured for many years at the University of Chicago. I met Elisabeth through a mutual friend at the cultural office in Rome, who had given me a ride to Florence when I came. She was a hospitable, friendly person, with hair bobbed short and a world of energy.

I was happy to be invited to her home a number of times. She was trying then to write fiction and I think finally published a volume of stories, but did not seem able to give much sense of reality to her material. She said little about her father and her family, and I did not try to draw her out about them. I knew too little about German literature to carry a conversation forward. She mentioned some writers that her father had encouraged—Hermann Hesse was, I believe, among them. One felt her family attachment, and her devotion to her two little girls—nicknamed Nikki and Gogol—was obvious. One Sunday noon this inventive pair were holding a birthday party for their cats.

New acquaintances also were a whole family named Scaravelli. The family had a beautiful villa at some remove from Florence, in the surrounding hills. Professore Scaravelli was a lecturer in philosophy at the University of Pisa. His houseguest for what seemed an indefinite stay was the Indian philosopher of later fame, Krishnamurti. He was a frail Indian with a refined, sensitive face, who was struggling with the language as industriously as I. He was a vegetarian, so we generally dined on omelets. Signora Scaravelli liked to entertain young people resident in Florence for study or work. After dinner we spent evenings before a huge fireplace exchanging talk mainly in English, as most of her discoveries were Americans abroad. Much later that year, back in Rome, I learned with a shock that the professore had committed suicide. On reflection I began to see the signora's invitations in a new light; her eagerness to bring in a lively crowd must have been related to her anxiety for him.

Friends from the Dinesen were also in Florence for a stay, and we had some happy evenings. It was cool; a late spring was trying unsuccessfully to come. I shivered each morning and worked wearing a heavy sweater. It was a good break at day's end to meet the Mattinglys or the Klapperts at the Excelsior Hotel bar for warmth and drinks.

Allen Tate went up to England after his time in Florence. He knew that I was going there to see an English publisher, Victor Gollancz, who was bringing out my writing with some enthusiasm. He had asked me to be in touch and said he would like to introduce me to T. S. Eliot and whomever else in London I cared to meet. He no doubt meant this offer kindly, but I did not take it up. A chance to meet the great poet passed me by.

By good luck, Eudora Welty happened to be in London at that

time, and advised of each other's presence by the faithful Diarmuid Russell, we found each other and often met for the theater, tea, and shopping. Eudora loved English ways and took a childlike delight in such things as having tea served during the interval at the theater.

I felt disappointed in London, having got used to Italian food and the sun. It was at times unpleasantly cold. In July I once saw snowflakes in a gust of wind. Victor Gollancz, the publisher, favored me with affectionate regard, and invitations to his country house at Brimpton were welcome. But the seeming aimlessness of Italian life, like a sort of eternity entered into in advance, had taken hold of my personal rhythms. I worked well in Italy because nothing seemed to pressure me to do so. My feeling was that nobody really cared. I was left to find my own way, and if that included writing a novel, I could go right ahead with it.

So I fretted through the days in London. I had met an Englishman I at first liked, but what seemed the promise of a relationship turned as cold as the weather. My self-esteem dropped along with the mercury.

When I returned to Florence, I fell back to writing diligently again on the novel that became *The Voice at the Back Door.* I spent each day alone at the typewriter in a spacious apartment out near Piazza Beccheria. The contessa whose residence it was worked in public relations for the Italian fashion industry. She went off to work on a bicycle rather early and was never present during the day. Much of the novel had already been written during the past winter in Rome, and I could see the road ahead. But I still believe the portions of the novel written in Florence were the best part of the book. Perhaps my personal discouragement of the moment made concentration an escape I needed.

The odd thing about writing this novel, so totally centered in Mississippi small-town life, filled exclusively with home voices, home manners, characters whose thoughts and lives were all centered there and nowhere else, was that these various things came clearer to me from a distance than they might have done at home. I was surrounded by a language I was barely learning to comprehend, but I could catch in my inner ear the precise intonation of someone saying all the phrases I was brought up hearing. Whole conversations flowed easily onto the page. Much of the talk in this book, centered on local Mississippi politics, is among men, and I wonder to this day how I seemed to have got it pretty nearly right. The only source must have been my habit, as a little girl, entirely unnoticeable, of trailing along behind my uncle or my father in all their many contacts with people from every walk of life. In the rural South, you never have to say "Here comes everybody," when "everybody" is around all the time, high and low, rich and poor and all the in-betweens. A society like this gives the fiction writer a wonderfully broad base; the wide net is already spread.

Each afternoon after lunch I would walk down to the Arno. I met a Florentine there who was temporarily out of work as a typesetter. He and I would walk out on some rocks and sit with our feet in the river and talk for an hour or two. It was a pleasant time, warm and full of light. My Italian improved. My self-image revived a little and began to give off a feeble glow which got brighter as the summer passed.

But ahead, as Ferragosto, the August holiday, passed, lay another winter. I began to have longings for Rome. Through the autumn of 1953 and on through the winter it had lost its strangeness and become a second home. I was never to feel this for Florence, which I loved in a different way. Not that I can ever see works by Michelangelo, Donatello, Botticelli, Filippino Lippi, or Della Robbia without feeling the sheer thrill of them. One glimpse of Cellini's *Perseus* is still enough to cause me to feel what Stendhal talked about as "the illness of beauty."

But the enclosure of the city and the round of seeing the same faces at the same sorts of occasions made me feel that I was growing into a routine in a place not even native to me.

So at the first bite of cold weather, I said goodbye to the contessa in much better Italian than when I came. Also to the typesetter, who had gone back to work and to being a husband.

There was another cause of restlessness. I knew that I was lonely in a basic way, that I needed a real relationship. I had enjoyed pleasant flirtations and brief encounters with enough men of different nationalities to form a sizable committee for the United Nations. Scandinavians passing through Rome stayed at the Dinesen; smooth-talking Englishmen emerged out of nowhere; some transient American had been given my name to look up. There was a lawyer in Rome and a sculptor in Florence. But after a few outings, nothing of real rapport seemed to develop between myself and these guys, and many in any case were on their way elsewhere. More fascinating company were those intelligent men like Garrett Mattingly, Charles Klappert, and Daniel Cory, who had their charming wives firmly attached.

I tried to shake off my sometime depression by enjoying friendships, by seeing more art and learning more Italian. But could I seriously believe all this would work?

Only a week ago I came across a box of letters my mother had saved. They were full of accounts of my time in Rome and Florence. In a letter dated September 1954, I note the first mention of a man from Cornwall I had met in Rome, who was teaching English to Italians. He had begun to stop by my *pensione* for a visit or to telephone me in the afternoons. I said that John Rusher was not so well off, didn't have a car, but was good company and interesting to talk to.

Dinesen friends of the year before had flown away home. My literary socializing dwindled. I moved into a room in a large flat. Work on the novel, after a few crankings and sputterings, began to move again. I had a terrace to myself, a desk for my typewriter, a shelf for books, and hanging space for clothes. Each afternoon the phone rang. It would be John, telling me news, arranging to see me.

Before I knew quite how it happened, I had entered one of my happiest years.

John had already been in Italy for a year or more. By teaching English to foreigners in London, he had devised a way to get to Italy for the same purpose. He had worked for a time with the Berlitz school of languages in Rome; then, finding a core group of enthusiastic pupils eager to continue studies with him, he broke away from the school to teach them on his own. His hours were eccentric, but he could often take time in the afternoon for tea or a walk. The English, I soon learned, adore both tea and walking. I felt myself growing stronger on the sound of his encouraging voice: "Oh, now you know you can walk a little further. Come on. Try."

On some warm afternoons in the fall we would sit in the park on the Pincio, watching people pass, and recounting how life had treated us. One day we fell to quoting from *Alice in Wonderland*, first the Mad Hatter's tea party, discovering we remembered whole chunks of it verbatim. The Humpty Dumpty passages from *Through the Looking-Glass* most delighted him.

"... There's glory for you!"

"I don't know what you mean by 'glory,' " Alice said.

Humpty Dumpty smiled contemptuously. "Of course, you don't—till I tell you. I meant 'there's a nice knock-down argument for you!' "

"But 'glory' doesn't mean 'a nice knock-down argument,' " Alice objected.

"When *I* use a word," Humpty Dumpty said ..., "it means just what I choose it to mean—neither more nor less."

"The question is," said Alice, "whether you *can* make words mean so many different things."

"The question is," said Humpty Dumpty, "which is to be master—that's all."

We found we knew many of the nonsense songs by heart:

In winter, when the fields are white
I sing this song for your delight—

In spring, when woods are getting green,
I'll try and tell you what I mean....

John said he often pointed out Lewis Carroll to his students. I said he might utterly confuse them with such nonsense, but he said people should be confused occasionally.

Our best times were at night when he had finished his work, usually rather late, and would call me to meet him in Piazza San Silvestro, a busy downtown square near the post office, where a good trattoria gave three courses for six hundred lire—about a dollar in those days.

Many of John's pupils were interesting to meet. The variety was astounding: a principessa, a count, a member of Parliament, a policeman, a waiter in a restaurant. All needed English for their daily toil. And being English and always going about Rome, it seems he met all the other wanderers and sojourners from England whose various pilgrimages led them through or to that ancient city. The English, I was learning, through their long acquaintance with wars and work in foreign lands, can fit easily into any society. They never seem to lose their own culture—tea and Alice would only start the list of their typical preferences—but neither do they insist that others become like them.

John related how life in London, where he had held a clerical job after the war, was dreary and depressing. Like many another, he had longed for sun and fogless air. So far his scheme was flourishing, and my fellowship funds, carefully measured, were holding out. We paid our rent—I for my room and terrace near Piazza Buenos Aires; he in his neat little quarters on Via Merulana. We did our work and had fun.

Via Merulana itself was made for experiencing a poor but lively section of Rome. Once in a nearby park, we saw a stuntman riding a motorcycle high up the perpendicular walls of an enormous sunken cylinder. Another time, looking out the window, John had seen the whole Roman zoo—elephants, lions, tigers, and giraffes—parading past. They were en route to the Baths of Caracalla for a performance of *Aida.*

On late evenings we sometimes went to find a French or English movie at a distance from the center. We would take the tram that circled the city, the *circolare,* and come to some tucked-away spot, where we sat on hard benches. Since everybody smoked in the cinema, at intervals they would open up the roof and let the smoke out. Late night in Rome in those days was tranquil and silent. One could feel safe then in almost any quarter. Once, out late on a winter night, we walked through a silent fall of snow. So few were abroad, it was not even noted in the press, though it was most unusual.

Times when we caught the train from Stazione Termini to some nearby town like Orvieto still lift my spirits to remember. There was a sense of discovery and exciting departure, even though we would be buying the cheapest tickets to ride along with peasants, their sacks of produce, crying babies, and sometimes live chickens. Once we rode facing an ample woman dressed in black with a face so kindly it seemed nothing could defeat it. We conversed a little; then she leaned back and looked at us both as though we were her own children: "*Una bella còppia,*" she said. "A handsome couple." I had fully registered that John was extraordinary for his good looks—"*testa d'aquila*" (eagle's head), as an Italian friend had said—but I was glad to be associated with him in her compliment.

. . .

I finished a draft of the novel in the spring. My problem then was how to stay on for the summer. My Guggenheim funds, never so ample to begin with, were all but exhausted. The foundation sent a small extra sum. I put my plight to my parents and my father consented to a meager allowance. However, the "plight" was really nothing more than a desire to enjoy Rome, life, and leisure. After a long stretch of hard work, and the slow recovery of my health, I thought I had it coming.

I had no eventual plan except to return to Mississippi, to go back to the native soil. Still I lingered. The skies grew bluer, the air warmer. Rome burst into flowers and sidewalk living.

We grew more acquainted with a friend John had made previous to meeting me. This was Gloria Scala, who had come to Italy from Chicago to renew family ties with her relatives near Turin. From some cousin or friend she had acquired a car, one of those tiny Fiats everybody of modest means drove. Generously, she would ferry the two of us out to Fregene, a favorite Roman spot on the sea. We would rent a bathhouse, change, and swim in the crisp water, lunch on bread and wine, cheese and salami, at outdoor tables in the pine grove. Skins tingling with salt and sun, we would drive back to Rome in the dusty afternoons.

All this time we were growing closer. I think back on the many ways of falling in love, a good number of which I can report on firsthand, and I conclude that the falling part may sometimes happen too fast for savoring the experience, or doing anything to stop it in case of danger signals flashing with lurid force. This latter kind is rather like Alice down the rabbit hole, only with no time even to snatch a jar of marmalade from a shelf. I think the best way of falling may be in slow motion, extended over (not too much) time, taking in many hitches, little and big, quarrels and even fights, with reconcilings to follow, and the ever-heightening joys of choice occasions and good friends. Many threads get woven in; for a long time you may not know what to call it.

Karl Shapiro returned to Rome en route to lecture in India. Friends from Ole Miss days began to pass through on their way home from Greece, or on summer tours in Europe.

September had nearly come before I could bring myself to face facts: I had to leave.

The last Italian Line boat to sail from Naples was the *Conte Biancamano*. I booked passage without enthusiasm. I felt that my venturing days were done.

"*Arrivederci, Roma.*" No one needed to make things worse by singing that. When I took the train to Naples, John, who had come to see me off, stood in the middle of the platform sadly waving his familiar rolled newspaper, the London *Daily Mail*. Long after his tall figure had vanished from my sight, I kept seeing it. I cried all the way to Naples. The Atlantic grew much saltier from that passage.

Had I done right to leave such a happy relationship, to leave Italy, and return to native things instead of marrying into an uncertain life abroad? Of course, I had. I knew I had.

25

HOMECOMING

AFTER two years away and so much that had happened in my small world, I had good hopes about returning to Mississippi. I had written long, single-spaced, multiple-paged letters home, telling of every sort of occurrence—people, places, trips of every description. My improving health was a constant subject; the progress of my work was frequently mentioned.

I had a problem ahead in that I wished to spend some time in New York to find a better publisher in case the new novel looked promising enough to merit that. My feeling, shared by many, was that Dodd, Mead, a small and rather unimpressive house, could be left for greener pastures.

My mother had written that my father wished to help me! He would be glad to see that I got to New York, she wrote, to do whatever I needed to do. She further said, thinking no doubt of my recent illness, that they did not see why I should work at all! By this I took her to mean that I should no longer seek to hold a regular job.

I knew that my father had now achieved a state of real affluence. He had acquired large properties—a seven-hundred-acre farm in the rich Delta country, a cattle farm near Carrollton, in addition to many other parcels of land and smaller moneymaking ventures. He was a founding member and prime mover in a hunting club on the river near Greenville. He and others of prominence in the state had banded together to acquire a beautiful pre–Civil War mansion, called Belmont, which they used as a lodge, inviting many from other parts there for the various hunting seasons, and for fishing in nearby Lake Lea. They also owned an extensive island, formed in the river during one of its changes of riverbed, where they hunted deer and other game in season.

Through the years my father had dispensed large sums to see my brother through medical school, to support his wife and child, to establish him in practice. He was now giving lavish support to his grandson. Though he had generously met hospital and other medical expenses during my illness, I had so far not seen much of a profit from being a daughter. But I reasoned that everyone's turn does come round, and I was happy to feel that this, by all I was told, was now occurring.

I reached home in the still-lingering high temperatures of a Deep South September. After two years abroad when I'd had little extra money to refurbish my wardrobe, my clothes no doubt looked worn, and the presents I brought, though all I could afford, were scarcely impressive. But none of the above could quite have been the cause of the fierce rejection I encountered.

There is little to be gained, such a long time later, in recounting all that transpired. I was brought up short in every passing comment. I might as well have been eight years old and told to go sit in a corner. Italy, an unimportant place full of Eye-talians, should not be mentioned. My work was not discussed.

Nearby, not many miles over in the Delta, and quite near my father's farm, a terrible thing had just occurred. A boy named Emmett Till had come from Chicago to visit relatives. He was black. He had whistled at the attractive wife of a man who ran a small highway grocery. That evening her husband and her brother-in-law had taken him out for a whipping. They had finally let him go—or so they said. However, the mutilated body of a boy identified as Till was recovered some days later from the Sunflower River. He had evidently been beaten to death and his body weighted down with a hundred-pound metal fan, a piece of gin machinery, tied around his neck.

For years my father had been a source of pride in my thinking.

Though difficult and autocratic and many times lacking in any understanding of my feelings, he had at least been forward-looking about racial matters. He had deplored the strict segregationalist bent of my uncle, who though vastly humane in his feelings, based all his theories of race on Southern tradition. To him history had established a set of values not to be betrayed.

My father, however, subscribed to and read Hodding Carter's

liberal paper, published in Greenville, the *Delta Democrat-Times.* On the place he had bought during the 1940s and had worked steadily to bring to a high level of production, he had held contests for the black tenants to improve their gardens and houses. He had based his actions on an oft-stated principle: "We've got to treat them just like white people. Nothing else will do now." He encouraged those who wanted to "go North" to go right ahead if they thought they could do better.

It was to this fair-thinking person that I thought I was speaking when I deplored the murder of Emmett Till.

Everybody around Carrollton and elsewhere in our part of Mississippi was on edge after this crime. Every day was scorching hot, and the news of the murder and the talk of it and the refusal to talk of it seemed to be throbbing intensely in the air. My mother in her anxiety often said that "something ought to be done to those men." She did not say what should be done. She would then go on to say "that boy may have been just fourteen but he was grown, he was a *man,* and he shouldn't have been looking at any white woman."

My father reacted to the crime the way a stone wall might if hit by a BB gun. He refused to discuss it or to hear any discussion of it. He said that "we had to keep things in hand." The attitude of the business communities, now forming themselves more and more into the so-called citizens councils, was that the principal task of the white community was to "maintain order." So far as anyone could see there was no threat whatsoever to order, but stories revealed that the councils were vigilantes bent on keeping blacks from registering to vote. For even attempting to register, a black man could lose his job.

My cousin May Spencer, she of always delightful memories, called up, wanting to see me. She had taught grammar school when she stayed with us years before, but she now had a doctoral degree in history and was visiting her family in Winona. I did not, I realized, dare to ask her home. Of course she would have been welcome. My parents loved her dearly. But she was a thinking relative, good for exchange of ideas, for excited talk over books, for speculation on current situations, whether political or otherwise. We would be dying to talk about Emmett Till and the present climate of thinking at Ole Miss and in other

Southern states. She would also want to talk with me about my work, and ask many questions about Italy.

If she had come to dinner or even for a longer visit we would not have been allowed any exchange at all. We agreed to meet at a highway restaurant and have our catching-up. The encounter was welcome and restored some equilibrium.

But the fact remained that things got so bad at home that my mother suggested I go up to Oxford and visit some of my friends at Ole Miss. I knew that she was nervous and anxious, not only for me. She felt her accepted ideas were being threatened by an event that could only serve to dramatize what was there already. (I'm convinced to this day it wasn't so much the Emmett Till case that upset everyone—who really cared very much if this uppity black boy from Chicago had got himself killed?—but what it brought into the public glare for all to see.) But I also knew my mother was aware of what had been promised me and would intercede for me with my father.

So it was that after two years away, I found it necessary to leave home after two days.

When I went up to Oxford for a visit, my ears were still ringing with parental abuse. The visit was a pleasant one, Oxford being much the same in its quiet sense of fine things, good talk, openhearted welcome. My dear friend Morton King, head of the sociology department at Ole Miss, was cordial in finding a whole empty apartment for me. Ella Somerville extended open arms. The English department head, Alton Bryant, was ready to offer me a teaching place once more.

William and Elizabeth Willis talked earnestly to me. Of course, I would see the Till murder in terms of tragic mistakes that happened in many societies. Of course, I would see every reason for coming back to the fold with those I loved. *Of course,* I thought, *of course* . . . Even the redoubtable A. Wigfall Green, our scholarly Renaissance lecturer, unbent enough to tell me I would need to be thinking of a house of my own in the wooded hills nearby.

All this, I had every reason to feel happy about. But I had unfinished business to attend to—my unrevised novel, not yet under contract, my hopes for seeing the work through in New

York. The slow labor of two years was tucked away dormant in my mind, just as the actual typescript was packed, tied and still unwrapped, in the corner of my baggage.

I went back to Carrollton but things were pretty much the same. My mother had indeed argued with my father on my behalf. His pronouncement finally came: He would give me two thousand dollars in cash for going to New York. After that was spent, he didn't know what I would do. I took it at once, as I was so glad to leave. I didn't myself know what I would do when it was spent, but whatever it was, it would be done without further reference to Luther Spencer or to Carrollton, Mississippi.

Yet it took a while for me to come around to verbalizing the extent of what had happened. I knew it in my bones, in the sick empty feeling there inside long before I could say to myself what I had been given to understand.

You don't belong down here anymore.

26

LEAVE-TAKING

MANY a black person had already taken the train ride that I took north in that fall weather of 1955. Many of both races in the years just beginning would follow. Mississippi was pulling inward, the wagons were making a tight little circle, the feather had showed up behind the rock, every night sound was a threat. The closed society was bolting and barring every door and chinking every window.

On the road ahead lay the forced integration of Ole Miss, when the state government refused to obey a federal order to admit the one black student, James Meredith, who had dared to apply. The refusal led to President Kennedy's decision to send in federal marshals. The Ole Miss riots were the result.

Also ahead, in the years coming swiftly on, lay the Freedom Riders, the murders of Medgar Evers and the civil rights workers, and the personal turmoil that came into every family, everywhere. All unsuspecting, I had walked early on into the opening pages of a conflict as lengthy and ramified as those depicted in *Gone with the Wind* or *War and Peace*.

Many were determined to hold on to, defend, the dear old South, Mississippi the way it had always so beautifully been. What of the other Southerners open to a new and better future?

My friend Morton King, then firmly in place at Ole Miss, resigned the year following my own return from Italy. He served on the student-faculty committee directing the annual Religious Emphasis Week. An Episcopal priest from Ohio had agreed to come and speak on "Religious Insights in Modern Drama." A state legislator, learning he had contributed to the NAACP, demanded the invitation be withdrawn. The committee refused, but the chancellor overruled them. Morton resigned forthwith.

Later, when the Ole Miss riots occurred, William Willis was one of the faculty members in their midst, attempting to maintain reason and civic order. In one nasty episode he was almost dragged down by a mob from the foot of the Confederate soldier's monument on the Oxford square. He and Rev. Duncan Grey, the Episcopal rector of St. Peter's Church, were trying to address a crowd. The entire Willis family, seeing the enormous expense of time, effort, and feelings always demanded, at last decided to leave Mississippi behind forever.

James Silver, chairman of the history department and prominent among those favoring the Meredith admission, exerted himself tirelessly. He was constantly abused and misquoted in the press. He, too, finally resigned and accepted an appointment elsewhere.

In later years I was to learn that Dr. McDill of Belhaven memories had left for much the same reason. When pressed, he had announced in favor of integration. "I could take threats to myself," he told me, "but when my wife and children were threatened, I felt it time to leave."

No wonder William Faulkner spoke of "the human heart in conflict with itself." In his or her heart of hearts, the Southerner who was wedded to tradition hoped that someway, somehow, the day would never arrive when black would have to be accepted on an equal basis with white. When U.S. marshals first seemed about to enter Oxford to implement the federal court order, William Faulkner vowed that he would be out there in the street shootin' at 'em. He later took back his statement: "No sober man would have said it; no sane man would believe it." In other words, I was drunk but you are crazy. Yet the feeling was there.

But in the long run Faulkner came through publicly with great force, and his eloquent cry "What are we afraid of?" condemned the prevailing attitude in the state.

Now the truth is, I don't know whether I was struck down to ground zero in my own family specifically because of ideas about racial equality. The typescript of *The Voice at the Back Door* was never taken from its package, nor was it discussed. What was repeatedly said was that I had "gone off to Italy and gotten hold of some funny ideas," but whether this applied to racial matters or to other ideas all across the board, or to any ideas at all, was never clear. Nothing was to be discussed.

James Silver later wrote a book about the insurrection at Ole Miss. He called it *Mississippi: The Closed Society.* A passage from his book is revealing:

> The best of Mississippi's men born between 1820 and 1845 were lost on the field of battle. Many of the more ambitious who survived went north and west, and they have been going ever since. . . . In fact, ex-Mississippians today play a role similar to that once performed by migrants from poverty-stricken Scotland—to a surprising degree they have achieved positions of eminence in all phases of American life. The only native to reach the pinnacle of renown while remaining in the state was William Faulkner, and I have personal reason to believe that he would have completed his removal to Virginia if he had lived another year. . . .
>
> The exiles are among the most ambitious, the ablest, and the most adaptable to change of all Mississippians. Such constant attrition of potential leadership is generally regarded as one of Mississippi's great unsolved problems and must be a major cause for the state's unwillingness to give up its ancient folk-ways. . . . Mississippi has for more than a century been driving away a substantial proportion of its brightest young people who might otherwise have played a leading part in bringing the state abreast of the times. The professor who sorrowfully departed from the University in 1963 as a protest against the workings of the closed society was in effect banished from the community, as surely as the sensitive youngster who, having had his eyes opened to the outside world by an inspiring teacher, decides that he would prefer to live in that world.

> . . . One can but wonder to what degree Mississippi's story might have been different if a sizeable number of those thousands of bright, perceptive natural leaders among the men and women who have been forced from the state had in some way found it possible to return.

Another side of the question may well apply to the whole South. No less devout a Southerner than Allen Tate has thrown light on this subject. What, really, about art and the South? What does the South feel about the many fine talents she has nurtured?

Times in this respect have certainly changed. Once William Faulkner was safely in his grave, having won the Nobel Prize and also having become a world figure, Oxford people found they had always cherished him. It may seem mischievous to mention that they now found him a source of increased income. Many visitors came from everywhere. Genial stories multiplied. People were invited to go on platforms to tell all about him. It is all so folksy to paper over the real story. But William Faulkner was a recluse in the years I was in Oxford, and the hatred of him personally and of the things he was said to be writing—though probably few who criticized so violently had bothered to read him—was widespread.

The day the announcement came that he had won the prize, I was still teaching at Ole Miss, though living out in the town. I was passing at twilight by a screened-in porch where people were conversing. A woman was saying, "If William Faulkner thinks he's so smart, let him pay that grocery bill he's been owing me."

Maybe in a French village, or a Greek town, or an Italian *paese,* a similar thing having occurred, the same sort of thing might have been said. Vox populi . . . But now in Oxford the name has sacred status, so all is forgotten.

These days a genial light is shed on the fame that Southern writers achieve. Eudora Welty's subtle and discerning work has brought her the affection of all of Jackson, Mississippi. Yet one must not mistake her naturally gentle spirit, her constant effort to seek out sources of laughter and signs of love, as approval for what was going on. She had, in fact, a great deal to say in nonfiction about what she felt. And in a short few pages, published in *The New Yorker,* titled "Where Is That Voice Coming From?," she took hold of the mind of the man who shot Medgar Evers, all this on the evening it became known, with no one to tell her the details. Yet so well did she know the killer's mentality—"I done it for my own pure-D satisfaction"—that the piece stands today as a revelation. She even guessed the kind of car he was driving, what it looked like.

Business ruled supreme in my father's heart. He gave to the church, where he was an efficient Presbyterian elder. He believed in "helping people" who would "amount to something in the community." He evidently had some benign vision of a world where good Christian feelings prevailed, where everyone worked hard and earned his way and raised a good family and was addicted to "sound thinking." I should have said "good Protestant feelings," for he hated the Roman Church with a passion.

He did not want anyone to be helped to be anything at all in the arts. For one thing, as an economic base for life, art was an uncertain calling and therefore apt to be a losing proposition.

It is this set of ideas that Allen Tate, in his important essay "The Profession of Letters in the South," calls the "cash nexus." It drives men into politics to hold fast to their own interests, but it cannot leave space for the arts. I think my father's trouble with the arts came not only from their economic uncertainty but from the fact that he could not control them.

To quote Tate regarding the fate of Edgar Allan Poe when confronting his adoptive father, John Allan, who drove him out:

> It was obvious . . . that here was no dabbler who would write pleasant, genteel poems and stories for magazines where other dabbling gentlemen printed their pleasant, genteel stories and poems. . . . If there is such a person as a Southern writer, if there could be such a profession as letters in the South, the profession would require the speaking of unpleasant words and the violation of good literary manners. . . . Only cranks and talents of the quiet, first order maintain themselves against fashion and prosperity.

Are we even talking only about the South? I saw a carefully made TV documentary on the disappearance in New Guinea of Michael Rockefeller. He was seeking examples of wood carvings among the aborigines. On a trip by boat to claim some fine examples he had been promised by a remote tribe, he vanished. But his delight in the art he had found among these primitive people was evident in all he said. He said he wanted to die among them. I was forced to guess that he had escaped the "cash nexus," the creed of the plutocrat. A Rockefeller naturally had to go a maximum distance to escape.

There would have been plenty of reasons other than disagreements over race to get rid of a contrary, opinionated, nonconforming daughter who not only read books but wanted to write them. All these reasons and doubtless others were in my bulging family dossier; no doubt many were valid. Certainly they were operative.

My mother, in all this unpleasant back-and-forth, did not always keep her head. Her emotional outbursts might sound like one train of thought at one time, the opposite at another. But it must be said for her that she kept her deepest feelings intact. Her love was never to be doubted. She was a fragile spirit, but the strongest among us often seem deceptively fragile. Her heart stayed in place.

It came to me many times then and in future years that I might have found some way to go back—knowing what I knew, forearmed, as I would now be—and live within a separate peace, communing with a network of many friends and supporters in different small nooks and crannies. There was always the fact, however, that our "connection," assembled from both sides of a long-time rooted family, seemed to make up about half the population of the state. One year alone I had eleven cousins either teaching or studying at Ole Miss.

But the South had been my subject as a writer, my ground of operation, and my constant spur to putting things down. How could I let it be snatched away?

Another Southern state then?

It did not turn out that way. On that ill-fated visit, I had not even unpacked everything before I was packing up once more.

And though I was to return many times as a visitor, I must have sensed I would never be coming home again. These events bring to mind, of course, Wolfe's famous title *You Can't Go Home Again.* I am sure, however, of what the trouble really is: It's not that you can't go home. Rather, there isn't any home to go to.

27

WRITING IN NEW YORK

In New York, I was immediately given welcome, understanding, and moral support by David Clay and his wife, Dusty, and through them, though at a distance, by Red Warren. Dusty and I set about at once finding me an apartment I could afford, checking the *Times*, making phone calls, visiting possible addresses. I finally found a walk-up on East Twenty-second Street.

A series of new one-bedroom units were being opened for rental, three floors of them above a restaurant. The rent was ninety dollars a month. The Jewish-Hungarian rental agent, who himself had "always wanted to be a writer," agreed to let me have heat during the day, a real concession as everyone else would be out to work.

(As I was signing the lease a young Negro woman came in and asked about the apartments. She told him she was Indian. He said they were all rented, which I knew to be untrue. Naïvely, I told him after she left that I had lived around Negroes all my life, and did not mind it. He said I was obviously a nice person.)

I had to have furniture. I set aside two hundred dollars, and got together a couch that could serve as a bed, a desk and chair, a dresser, a lamp, and a dining table. I went daily to Third Avenue secondhand-furniture shops and found a fascinating conglomerate of New York souls, speaking in thick Middle European accents, quoting prices one could usually negotiate, making weirdly funny remarks, usually ready to help pick and choose and deliver. I even had enough money left to buy a rocking chair.

Then, settling down, I finally reopened the typescript of the novel and began the slow but rewarding process of polish-and-revise, revise-and-polish.

No one could have been more helpful in this task than David Clay. He had had considerable experience in working directly with writers, tactfully but persistently insisting on the reworking of a bad passage, the deletion of unnecessary matter. His focus on my pages was like a magnifying glass directing sunlight. Nearly all was there, the characters in place as they had always been, and no real structural change was necessary. But revision means refinement, and having a good sounding board is of measureless worth for a sometimes uncertain writer like myself.

But on the whole the book was done already, and the work that went on steadily for about three months was mainly the writer's normal reluctance to let something go that had all but become an organic part of her system.

It was fun to be back in New York. I had scarcely enough money to buy a decent meal, but the Mattinglys, living up near Columbia University, where Matt had returned to lecture, extended frequent invitations. Sidney and Frances Alexander, whom I had known in Florence and Rome, were living not far away from me. Sidney's fictional biography of Michelangelo was then in progress and finally came out in three richly detailed volumes.

Tonny Vartan was there to be counted on. He was moving further uptown all the time, making his way as a financial reporter who commanded respect, and occasionally adding another Oriental carpet. By the time he died, much too soon for all who knew him, he had a steady byline in *The New York Times* and was living on Sutton Place. His elegant carpets were wall-to-wall, he had a fine New England wife, and his little boy, growing to manhood, was named Kirk Spencer.

It was easy in those days to catch a bus to the theater district for a Saturday matinee. A single balcony seat could usually be had and cost only a few dollars. Here, on a rainy winter afternoon, I saw Gertrude Lawrence and Yul Brynner in *The King and I. Cat on a Hot Tin Roof* was also playing with Barbara Bel Geddes in the role of Maggie. She spoke her lines in a slightly hoarse voice, with a skilled up-turning "Southernness" that makes any statement sound something like a question. I can still hear her say "those no-neck monsters?"

Sometimes on Saturdays I would take the cheapest trip of all—the subway to Brooklyn Heights and the St. George Hotel. I believe it has since been seriously damaged by fire, but then it was an enormous structure, with shops and a swimming pool in the basement. This was no ordinary pool. It was long and wide, and surrounded with glittering mirrors. Loud, it was true, with echoing voices, but it cost only about a dollar to plunge in for as long a swim as one would want. Showered and dressed, I would wander into the basement drugstore for a twenty-five-cent milkshake. I felt agreeably alone after a good week's work, observant but pleasantly uninvolved with anything I saw. New York has offered solace to thousands by extending this sort of anonymity. Who cares? Why, nobody cares. Be yourself. Be happy.

But then, of course, the threat is loneliness. It comes to you when you see, through the window of a smart restaurant, two friends eating together, or when you simply turn into a residential street and note flowers on a windowsill, homeward steps entering an opening door. It comes on crowded buses where everyone is looking straight ahead, lost in separate thoughts, no common ground sought for or offered. It comes after you have gone alone to the theater or a movie and want to talk about what you've seen. Then a small cloud settles over you—small, but in that immensity of stone and steel you also are small, and the cloud is just big enough to cover you.

There was a church nearby—Calvary Episcopal at Twenty-first Street and Park Avenue. I went there as a regular habit and found a good spirit of welcome among the parishioners and the clergy. They also ran a very simple lunchroom where meals could be had for less than two dollars. My kitchenette was serviceable, but cooking and consuming one's own meal is an invitation to the cloud.

Once when Eudora Welty was in town, I invited Red Warren and his wife, Eleanor Clark, to dinner in my apartment.

The Warrens had frequently asked me up to visit them at their interesting house in Fairfield, Connecticut, which they had converted from a lofty New England barn into a residence of considerable charm. Once, at a dinner party, I had sat on a sofa next to a small, attractive man with a flat Bostonian way of speaking, inclined to spill out words all together, giving a witty turn to whatever he said, often interrupting himself with a deprecatory laugh. He had just won the O. Henry Award for the year's best story, but when someone complimented him on that, he said wryly that he thought the story was "slick." The story was "The Country Husband," and the writer was John Cheever.

I had read his stories in *The New Yorker* and liked them. I asked him about a volume that brought them together, as I had not come across one. "Elizabeth," he said, "my stories sell so few copies not even my best friends can find them. I have to go out and look for them myself to give them away." His cheerful acceptance, the downbeat view of life in general, his love of exaggerating whatever came along—all this seemed pure Cheever.

Voices. His pretty wife, Mary, had her own girlish way of speaking. Anywhere you saw them, you would have picked them as a pair, assured of love.

Cleanth Brooks was there as well, and his wife, Tinkum. The fire crackled. Red seemed delighted with us all. He must have started out to dress elegantly, for he had got as far as a pair of evening pumps, but for the rest, a colored shirt, knit tie, and a green tweed jacket had to serve.

I had met Eleanor Clark before, once in New York with Red before their marriage, again briefly in Italy when I had returned to Rome from Florence. I knew her also as the writer of *Rome and a Villa,* the most brilliant of all encounters with Rome one could possibly find in writing.

She was quite beautiful, strongly and positively a New England woman. She was prone to assert her own ideas, and her judgments, which she made without apology, could be severe. But unlike Caroline Gordon, I felt, she was always in good contact with whomever she spoke to, and I had no sense of having to be on guard. I especially admired her on that evening in Connecticut. She had had to get two young children fed and settled, to ready a dinner party for at least twelve people, and to make the guest of honor, a French priest who was also a literary scholar, feel at home, in his own language. No one could have managed better. And no one could be in that house without feeling the solidity of the marriage and the great enveloping love the two shared for their children.

The time had grown later than anyone realized, and some of us had to be put up overnight, then dragged out sleepy-eyed to catch the train to New York in the morning. The Cheevers and the Brookses lived nearby.

On the evening of my small dinner on Twenty-second Street, I remember, Red charged in and looked about the space I had to live in with the bewildered expression of a large animal clapped into a stall. He asked for the bathroom. I pointed to it. It was tiny; only a few feet separated the bathtub from the door. Red entered at such a pace he all but fell into the tub; except for the tub, he might have smashed into the wall.

I had cooked a lamb roast in my tiny oven, and we made a nice meal, what with wine, potatoes, salad, cheese, dessert, and the wonderful talk you might expect from those extraordinary three.

Eudora was in New York on that trip to see the Broadway play made from *The Ponder Heart*. She invited me with her to one performance. Though scarcely exactly what she had written, it was a creditable, down-home treatment, with David Wayne as Uncle Daniel Ponder. He did an exceptional job of holding things together. Eudora said that the main problem in the production had been the fireball. We were both brought up on stories of fireballs, strange phenomena connected with severe thunderstorms. Once at school in Carrollton, lightning had struck close by and a ball of fire had rolled across the pupils' desks.

In the story, Bonnie Dee Ponder died during such a storm. She was sitting on the sofa with her husband, Uncle Daniel Ponder, when a fireball rolled through the room and scared her to death.

The stagecraft crew had managed someway, for a Mississippi fireball appeared on cue to dazzle the Broadway audience, who could choose to believe it or not.

Winter passed and the book was done.

I had met various editors and publishers who had some interest in knowing what I was doing on a new novel, wished to see it, read it, possibly make an offer to publish it.

David was working in some TV-related job at McGraw-Hill and through him I met the extraordinary editor Edward Aswell, who headed the trade department at that time. Aswell had been Thomas Wolfe's editor after Wolfe had quarreled with Maxwell Perkins. He showed a marked enthusiasm for my manuscript and wanted it.

David negotiated with him for a favorable advance—five thousand dollars. In fact, it was so favorable I could only sit down in my little apartment, holding the check on my lap and staring at it. I had lived on miserly allotments of dwindling money for so long it seemed impossible that the check would even be genuine. My father had indeed sent a small sum from the sale of stock in a fertilizer co-op, and I had gone out and bought two new dresses. To have anything new was such a rare occurrence that I still remember that gray silk with the pleated skirt and small white collar, the black linen with the low-cut neckline. But here was real money, and the book was out of my hands, and spring was coming on.

The Warrens went off to Italy and the Clays moved to their house in Fairfield. I was to live in the Clays' apartment and try to sublet it for the summer. It was while I was alone there, showing it to occasional people who had seen the sublet ad in the *Times*, that I received a call from Dorothy Cater, a woman I had known in Rome.

Dorothy was the granddaughter of the theatrical producer Henry Miller. Her father, Gilbert Miller, also in theater, was usually resident in London. Divorced, she had an apartment in the Parioli in Rome, a fashionable quarter, and had often invited John Rusher and me to cocktails or dinner parties.

We had lunch together in the Miller apartment on Park Avenue, a huge flat with dustcovers draped over all the furniture, even the piano. We had to eat in the kitchen, fishing food out of one or another of the mammoth refrigerators. But why was Dorothy so intent on seeing me?

She was really bringing me word of John Rusher. I had thought of him often during the months in New York, and felt it was mainly because I missed his steady company and affection that I found no real thrill in going out with various men who had shown interest from time to time. I said that I was missing Rome, and tried to convince myself that this was true, but it didn't quite satisfy. We had exchanged letters, and I had even mentioned returning to Rome *if* I could place my novel, but I suppose both of us had naturally to wonder, *What then?* I had been adamant before I left Italy about seeing my life ahead in the South, though I had recently modified that to read "in the United States."

Over salad and cold cuts in the Miller kitchen, Dorothy told me that John seemed pretty desolate without me. It was something I needed to hear. She said he was going up to London to take a summer job, since his pupils in Rome were notoriously lax during that season. I knew, of course, of his plans, but had thought of him only in connection with Rome. It would be too late, I said, to plan anything for London now; boat travel was still the way most people went abroad, and all berths had been taken for weeks.

"If you decide to go," Dorothy said, "the Miller office can get you passage."

Still, I was not too certain. Surely even going there would put things back to square one. But just to see John again might turn out well, and London would seem much better for me with him as a companion than it had the one time I visited it in the past. I wrote rather tentatively to say I had my advance on the book. Many letters were suddenly exchanged.

Thanks to Dorothy, I found myself with a reservation on the *Queen Elizabeth*. Should I take it or not? Indecision kept me awake on a regular basis. One thing only was certain: I did not want to go to Mississippi.

One afternoon, coming into the Clays' apartment with an armload of groceries, I saw a telegram lying on the floor in front of the door. I knew what it was, but not what it would say. Either way it would define something. For a long moment that rectangle of yellow paper was the most important thing in my world. It sometimes seems I am still standing in the hallway of the apartment complex on the East River looking down at it.

It was from John, as I knew it would be. It said he would meet the boat train in Waterloo Station on June 6.

28

PLACES TO COME TO

ENGLAND was such a place in the summer of 1956. I took the boat train from Southampton to London. Alighting in the gloomy, smoke-smelling reaches of Waterloo Station, wearing, as promised, a big hat, I was thus easily spotted by a man hastening toward me, all but concealed by a huge bunch of red roses.

What did we do all that first day? Some of it is hard to recall. I do not quite know how we wound up strolling around in Richmond Park, but distinctly remember the deer, who were quite close, looking us over, finding us neither alarming nor unfamiliar.

John was eager for me to go down to Cornwall to meet his family. He had already been in touch with them, and a letter for me was waiting.

I had been brought up hearing that all of "us" were of Anglo-Saxon descent and therefore more kin to the English and the Scots than to any of "those others." It would have been hard going for a freedom-loving Southern spirit to get mired down in an Italian family, and of "those others" I've no idea. But certainly the Rusher/Stevens/Walters connection seemed ready-made for a Mississippian's safe entry.

They lived for the most part on a family estate on the north shore of Cornwall. The gales blew, the gulls screamed, and twice daily the ocean rushed up to the garden wall. But otherwise one might have packed them up and shipped them to the South and found they fit right in.

There were a half dozen aunts and uncles, cousins dropping by, shops where everybody knew the family on sight, eccentricities to spin out as stories through any number of evenings. John's father, a retired brigadier, had been captured in the fall of Singapore and spent some horrendous years in a Japanese prisoner-of-war camp. A high-ranking British officer, enjoying all the perks of empire in both England and India during the years between the wars, was demeaned to working in rice paddies under harsh Japanese command in Manchuria. A panel filled with medals honoring Brigadier Rusher's services to the nation was modestly displayed behind glass in a corner of the sitting room.

John's mother, who during the war had got stranded in India, had never really recovered from the strain of those years, though certainly she had admirably managed to "cope."

Relatives in Kenya and Australia were spoken of. An uncle had run a ranch in Western Canada, which relatives had traveled cross-country by sleeping car to visit. Another had been an Anglican missionary to the Indians in New Brunswick. A first cousin, Anthony Stevens, serving with the Foreign Office, was at that moment settling some "problems" on Cyprus. He was later to be transferred to Belfast in Northern Ireland, another problem area.

I began to get a keyhole view of the extent of British overrule—all those pink countries on the map I studied in grammar school now figured in a living way through John's kin.

Those at hand were also of some interest. An eccentric great-aunt, who had lived with her late husband in British Honduras, was found in her living room, standing knee-deep in leaves blown by a gale into her thatched-roof cottage. She railed at us for not having come to tea the day before, though she had forgotten to invite us.

Two ancient aunts who lived in nearby Newquay kept tender memories of their late brother, a local hero, who had among many other feats excavated a whole prehistoric village on a spit of land in front of the Rusher garden. Uncle Will Stephens had also discovered a smart boy who was a tin miner's son and had brought him home, given him books to read, and made him welcome. A. L. Rowse climbed rapidly in school and became a fellow at Oxford and a well-known British historian. An early edition of his book *A Cornish Childhood* was dedicated to Will Stephens.

As many of the family as could rise and walk came to our wedding in St. Columb Minor, a church built the year before Columbus sailed in search of China. John's brother, Jim, and sister Jenifer, both employed in London, came by train. Another sister, stationed with her husband on Gibraltar, sent a wire.

The two ancient aunts, having "cut sandwiches" the night before, immediately set off on a bus tour of Wales.

I loved all this ramified local life, distant from London, as Mississippi always felt at a remove from the Yankee world of big

urban centers; and I loved the fact that they had taken me in, as though it were a natural occurrence to have a heard-about-but-never-met "Amedican" woman walk in and marry their son (or brother, or nephew).

But our sights were set on returning to Italy in time for John to pick up his work in the fall. We went by the slowest imaginable stages, through Salisbury and by Stonehenge, London, and thence to Paris for a few days, then back into our city of so many memories.

As in the past, Rome was bursting that year with a literary crowd. John Cheever had made a movie sale of one of his Wapshot books, and had come to Rome with Mary, his daughter, Susie, and son, Ben, determined to live it up. He had no trouble doing so, and before anyone knew quite how it happened he had secured a whole apartment in Palazzo Doria.

Even after some years in Rome I was impressed with the splendor the Cheevers were living in. They had an *entrata* which opened into an enormous *salotto*, as big as a ballroom, with decorated ceiling, marble floors, and a fireplace at the far end. There was room here for everything—dining, "receiving," parties, and family living. There were cooking and sleeping quarters as well.

The Cheevers soon found how difficult it is to be well off in Rome, let alone affluent. (John and I had flourished as *poveri amanti*, lovingly observed and helped by all, but the minute we set up a middle-class lifestyle in an apartment, with a maid and a *macchina* (auto), the wolves began to get wind of us and sniff about.) The Cheevers, Mary pregnant with Federico, were thrown into despair early on. Mary called me one day to ask if I could recommend a good maid to her. I had inherited one from our landlady, Iole Felice, a strong, kindly woman, very managerial by nature. I told her to go over to the Palazzo Doria and ask for *la famiglia di Signor Cheever*, to see what she could do.

Only a few hours had passed before Iole called me to say she was sending me her sister as a maid. Her reason was simple: *"I Cheever hanno bisogno di me."* "The Cheevers need me." As indeed they did. She began to rail at tradespeople and drive down the grocery bill, to shop, cook, and clean and see the children off in time for school.

The relation became a permanent one. In time John and Mary took Iole back to the United States with them, where she flourished. For many years, though married to a greengrocer in Ossining and living in her own house nearby, she remained on call to prepare wonderful meals, and help out for "occasions." Mary told me that many of John's stories set in Italy were Iole's stories. I know that she figures prominently and recognizably in "Clementina," a fine story about an American couple who take their Italian maid with them to the United States.

We got on just as well with the other Felice sisters, one of whom, Maria, became a necessary part of our life in Rome.

Another call for help came from the Cheevers. This time it was John, asking us to stand as godparents for Susie, who was being baptized as a preliminary to confirmation at the American Episcopal church in Via Nazionale. John Rusher and I had long gone there, he being more inclined to a Low Church service, as held in the American church, than to the High Church leanings of the Anglican congregation. On a cold day in wintry Rome, we stood in the back of the church near the baptismal font and saw Susie safely christened.

I eventually learned from John Cheever that he and Mary had been sending Susie to a school in Rome run by nuns and that she was rapidly turning into a Roman Catholic. I never heard John pronounce against the Roman Church, but he was then, and remained, a good lay Episcopalian. In the United States years later, I once asked him if he still attended church. "Elizabeth," he said, "every Sunday morning I'm right there on my knees."

Susie won't mind my saying, I think, that back then she was a shy, awkward girl, hard to get a word out of. I used to write her frequently, and I still get word from time to time from a different Susie, blossomed into a literary life of her own. Her *Home Before Dark* is a fine memoir of her parents and her own growing up.

Red and Eleanor Warren had returned to Rome that fall from their cherished seaside fortress at La Rocca, where the weather had become too cold for them to stay. They stayed at the American Academy and we were invited there by them or by Isabel and Laurance Roberts, so that we often saw each other. In evidence, too, were Ralph and Fanny Ellison.

I had never met Ralph, though I had joined with everyone else in admiration of *Invisible Man.* He had taken notice of *The Voice at the Back Door,* and seemed to like it, though it is always a good question as to what the African-American really thinks when a white person writes about a racial issue. I suppose my goodwill in the writing must have counted for something. He and Fanny always remained on good terms with us, through all the years. Ralph delighted in recalling a memorable picnic we went on together on the Aniene above Tivoli, when some gypsies camping nearby sent their children sneaking close in to swipe his fine fishing gear and were routed by my husband.

I felt Ralph's intensity, his intelligence, but most of all, his sense of value. He seemed always to be measuring life in terms of those American values he cherished.

As for *The Voice at the Back Door,* its adventures, separate now from my own, were pacing along. It was published in the early fall of 1956. David Clay, with whom we stayed pretty constantly in touch, sent the notices. On the whole it was well received, some reviews being positively ecstatic. I remember most of all a review of Brendan Gill's in *The New Yorker.* I should be ashamed to admit that I read it so often I could almost quote it by heart. *Time* gave the book a strong review. To my surprise reviewers all over the South, including Mississippi, found it an impressive novel. It eventually went on to win the first Rosenthal Award of the American Academy. I was told that it was a strong contender for the Pulitzer Prize. The fact is that none was given in 1957.

My mail from readers and others got so heavy that other renters in our palazzo began to ask why so many people were writing me. Most letters were pleasant, some were not. One or two threatened retribution should I dare to come back to Mississippi. I heard through friends that a good many people were "getting very upset with me."

But both Warren and Eudora Welty had given "quotes" for the book jacket, and many more were forthcoming from other writers as the weeks went by. Before many months had passed, David

Clay, acting as my agent, had made a movie sale of the book to MGM. The sum immediately became the kind of nest egg that any couple needs to feel they have put away somewhere.

Paperback rights quickly materialized, as did English publication, and numerous translation rights. It was selected by Time Inc. for its Reading Program and came out in a handsome edition. The movie, through one mischance after another, was never produced, though it was scripted and even cast.

As I see it going on bravely through the years, seldom out of print, I wonder at it as an expression on its own, vital and determining for me, but also joining the deepening current of national realizations and conflicts over race, which continue at full force to this day.

"What's to be gained by talking about it?" I was asked over and over regarding questions of race. Well, everything is to be lost by *not* talking about it, I could have replied. And though I had to speak from a young Southern woman's sheltered experience, my ear was sound, and I knew what I had heard. I also could still hear Laura's voice, calling at the back door on that fateful night in Carrollton. Some might reckon that her voice goes on calling in these pages.

I said often that I did not write the book to reform anybody except myself. For I also had subscribed to the "Southern way of life," had thought that my parents and grandparents could not be wrongheaded, that they had lived a correctly reasoned approach, had died in clear consciousness of having done the right thing during time of slavery and war and all the difficult years that followed.

But an accumulation of experience, known or known about, had gradually begun to pile up on the scales and outweigh my received ideas. I wrote to straighten myself out, letting my story and the characters in it lead me on.

I am convinced that writing anything of value takes place in this way. A writer undertakes a work of fiction under a strong impulse, not completely understood, and pursues that original drive through an act of composition, short or long. At the end, if an end can be reached, she stands back and knows that something is there which was not there before, and further knows that she herself is also different than before. Roger Angell, my editor for several years at *The New Yorker,* once said, "You don't write because you know but because you *don't* know." He was right.

Foreigners without relations in Italy should always have some outside source of income. We were learning this as a reasonably comfortable life got ever harder to support. We loved Rome, always around us, and the friends we made to enjoy and to keep, but more and more it began to seem that our future should be elsewhere.

John's mother's family had originally been early New England settlers, but at the time of the American Revolution had moved north to Canada and were among the founding fathers of St. John, New Brunswick. One grandmother had married an Anglican cleric and so returned to England. John's sister, now living in Montreal for some years, wrote us glowingly about the life there.

I began to scheme. If we could go there instead of to England, so far away from American turf, why could we not, little by little, think of living in the United States, somewhere in the South? I thus thought it worth a try for my own reasons; John for others.

We left from Southampton by Cunard liner, the *Saxonia,* in the midsummer of 1958.

Someone has remarked that you should be careful what you wish for because you might get it.

As a little girl, on a winter night, I would go out with my grandfather and stand in the front yard and ask if it would snow. "Maybe," he would say, wanting what I wished for, "maybe it will." We would both stand squinting up, thinking we saw flecks of white sparkle in the blackness overhead. About once in four years, we would all wake up to white icing on the magnolia leaves, bunches of snow in the cedars big as squirrel nests, snow spread evenly over the yard and fields beyond.

In Montreal nobody had to wish. When snow came howling out of the north like a vast shaggy presence, it came to stay. The winter of 1958 was one of the worst for blizzards. As I looked out the window of the small apartment we had rented in midtown into the gray air swarming with flakes, I grew aware of distance, more distance from all else in the world than I had ever imagined. Before they had the telephone and mail service to help out, what had those early people felt when the last boat sailed away eastward on the St. Lawrence before all passage froze?

Yet here was a lively, cultivated city, and even with ice forming on the river and fields of snow, knee-, waist-, and chin-deep, piling up all around, the faces peering from furry hoods were open and friendly. There were many newcomers like ourselves, from all over Europe, as tribally numerous as Indians. Booted feet came plodding, stamping off the snow. Piles of footgear stood in doorways. For evening parties, mountains of coats piled up in bedrooms.

The U.S. border was only forty miles away, but driving to New England revealed a country suspended in winter, smoke rising from farmhouses, but little sign of life outside. Montreal was the opposite. On the coldest days, it burst with crowds, walking, meeting, shopping. Boys played makeshift hockey in the parks, while children skated in caps and scarves, bundled in padded playsuits.

Our first concerns, like those of pioneers of yore, were purely practical. Down to the nitty-gritty, calculating how far money would go, could we afford a car (at first we took buses); how to risk life in a one-room furnished apartment with kitchenette and let-down bed (much more of this could certainly lead to divorce); was there a fur coat in my future. Fortunately, John soon had work with a firm that manufactured elevators, but after that landed a better slot in Kingsway Transport Company, a trucking line that covered Canada from Halifax to Vancouver. Here he was to work in an office on the western outskirts of the city, near a town named Lachine. After another year of apartment camping, we saw our way to a down payment on a house in that pretty town, part of larger Montreal, but with an interesting history of its own. It lay on the western side of the Lachine Rapids, where the St. Lawrence River runs powerfully over rocks. As this proved a hindrance to the early boating traffic coming into Montreal, a town and commerce grew up there, and exploration parties, one headed notably by Sieur de La Salle, took off from Lachine (China) in hopes of finding the Northwest Passage to the Orient. He found the mouth of the Mississippi instead, and finally died in Texas.

Our house was on one of the older streets, with large lawns and friendly neighbors. A well-kept bowling green was only a block away, and cricket matches were still played in a park just to the east. The movie house in Lachine was named The Royal Alexandra after the wife of Edward VII, and just as in England, "God Save the Queen" was played after each showing, with film clips of the lady herself, "trooping the color." The prevailing emphasis was still on Empire.

As for the French-Canadians, they were scattered all among us. The highest concentration of spoken French, however, was definitely centered in the eastern part of the city.

After much hassling with furniture and mortgage contract and all the familiar problems of ownership, old stuff to most couples our age but new to us, we moved into our house. Our bohemian wanderings had left us far behind in the home-ownership game; it was like learning a foreign language to deal with fixed-term and adjustable-rate mortgages, surveying lines between properties, and township rights of way. But once all this was cleared and we were actually at home for the first time, exhausted but enclosed in our own four walls, I had not slept so soundly since I was a girl.

Our back yard was a deep one, and since we soon acquired a beagle, all the neighborhood children, mostly forbidden to have pets, were constantly coming over to play. Their mothers called me in alarm. "Diane walked right into your house without knocking." "It's okay," I would reply. "She's just come to see Rascal."

Fall lingered long the first year. It was early December and roses were still blooming on the Fairchilds' lawn across the street. I could look over and see Diane among them, posing in a frail fancy frock she was to wear in a wedding. Who said this was a cold country?

But the fatal night would come; I somehow knew it in my bones. Sure enough, one calm evening there came a moaning sound from away to the north, seeming to die away, then reviving and coming each time nearer. Hours later we felt for the first time the majestic force of Canadian winter. It seemed an enormous hand had been laid to the side of our house; the walls shuddered. Outside, the black night was riddled with white streaks, coming first at a slant, then shooting in horizontally, an inexhaustible supply. The moan turned into a howl, not just from the north, but from everywhere. We woke to a strange country, which wore a shroud of white. Shovels, storm windows, snow tires, and furnace heat, in addition to bundles of clothing, boots, and fur-lined gloves, were now part of daily life. The dog, still a puppy, ran out in the yard and refused to believe what he saw. He barked at it. Wouldn't it go away? No, it wouldn't.

Before a year had passed, John's grandmother had died; soon his mother's death followed. He was left a small legacy by each and decided to open his own school again, this time offering a full slate of languages. French was becoming more and more a necessity for doing any sort of business in Montreal. There were many also who needed English for the same reason, and others certainly would appear who had needs for other, more remote, languages. After considerable planning, he located vacant offices on Sherbrooke Street, near the center of the city, and soon had turned them into a rabbit warren of small classrooms clustered around a central reception area. So was born the Cambridge Language Centre, which continued for many years as a fixture of the Montreal scene.

All the time, there was my own work, too, proceeding along with the early days of our settling in.

When we were still in Rome, an editor at *The New Yorker* had written to know if I had any short stories I might want to submit to the magazine. I hadn't written any short fiction in years, but I dusted off one that the magazine had rejected back in the 1940s. It was accepted, so I wrote another, also accepted.

In the face of so much change, I was reluctant to undertake another novel. How could I get at an increasingly scattered-out experience better than by writing stories? Memory was sharpening what I knew about the South, lifting up some subjects and kinds of people as possibilities for stories, letting others slip away. But did I have to cling to writing just about the South? Would the same process not happen with respect to my Italian experience? It, too, was becoming memory as the days got gloomier and shorter and thoughts of Italy made images of brilliant light and sharp shadow come thronging to my inward eye.

Daily, I used to leave the apartment and go down to a public library on nearby Atwater Street. There were long tables there and no one bothered a visitor who wanted to sit for hours writing on a ruled legal pad. It was thus that I started my first story set in Italy—with the thought of light.

It began in a favorite piazza—where back in 1949 I had been struck with Italy's glory—and with a favorite work, Cellini's *Perseo*. But there had to be a who also. I felt more at home writing about Southerners, wherever they might show up. So here came the two who were central to the story, a girl named Clara Johnson and her mother, Margaret, from Winston-Salem, North Carolina.

The Light in the Piazza came close to writing itself, with little interference from the author. I had envisioned a thirty- or forty-page short story, but traveling on its own momentum, it grew to a longer work, well over a hundred pages. I had wanted the episode of the exploding cannon that Allen Tate and I had witnessed at the soccer game to take a central place as unforeseen accident; instead it became a pivotal moment, and later volunteered to serve as metaphor.

I would write through some hours at the library, then come back to the apartment and type up the day's scribbling. I would read the results to John in the evening. His one comment was "Keep going." The original typescript took about three or four weeks to complete. What I thought of it was that it was a freakish sort of story with some nice moments, though the plot was such an odd one, nobody could possibly want to publish it. I sent it to David Clay with a note, "A crazy story, but you might find it fun."

Within days he was on the phone, extolling what I had done. In his enthusiasm he rushed into making a premature submission to *The New Yorker,* where it was turned down with a long letter of apology and regret.

I was ready to put the manuscript in a drawer with other beginnings and tries that never worked. But David stuck with his belief that here was something good. He urged a few revisions on me, a little smoothing out here, an expansion there. Did I think this scene was a little long, this one sketchy? Most of these suggestions I simply never took. But one or two were telling in their effect. Just a touch of the lens and a focus came about, rendering the whole as sharp and clear as what I had in mind.

To my dismay, for I dislike inviting anyone who says no once to say it again, David resubmitted it to *The New Yorker*. In days, I had received an enthusiastic letter from my editor. The story was published in a single issue in the following year. It had "a happy reception," which Red Warren, when he saw the galleys, predicted, and a long and happy life thereafter, which still continues. First came the magazine; then, with a little expansion (mainly reinstating bits I had taken out to speed the narrative as a story), publication by McGraw-Hill as a separate novella. After that came a book-club selection, paperback and translation rights, and a movie.

Olivia De Havilland became Margaret Johnson, Yvette Mimieux her daughter, Clara. Rossano Brazzi was wily Signor Naccarelli and a youthful George Hamilton the eager Fabrizio. The producer was Arthur Freed. Florence appeared in Cinemascope in all its beauty. Perhaps the movie was not quite what I had written—it lacked the irony that a writer's voice is able to give and glowed with a little too much picture-postcard prettiness—but on the whole one had to be pleased with such a faithful effort.

Proceeding as a writer after such an unexpected success should have been easy as falling off a log. Instead, I felt faced with dilemmas. Did I write more about Italy? Should I go back to earlier things? I now had a larger number of readers, this being the only very good thing, besides a welcome flow of cash, that a writer's success can mean. Yet it carries its own dangers: If one is expected to say "something important," what can come out might not be important after all. Asking myself questions, I listened for answers but heard nothing at all.

I finally let nature take its course and stuck to what I felt best at doing—storytelling. My stories, laid either in the South or in Italy or wherever they might happen, kept being welcomed by *The New Yorker* and other magazines. And what I had to say seemed to manage to unfold its own importance out of its own nature. And this was what I wanted.

A novel evolves naturally out of time, out of lived experience, preferably in one place. As Jane Austen wrote to her niece back in 1814:

> You are now collecting your People delightfully, getting them exactly into such a spot as is the delight of my life;—3 or 4 Families in a Country village is the very thing to work on—& I hope you will write a good deal more, & make full use of them while they are so very favourably arranged.

All true, as long as one lives in one place, going by the settled rules of a stable world. But ways are different now; throngs of people wander about like terrapins, wearing their culture shells on their backs.

A native is one not by choice but by birthright. This is especially true of a women. Habits of cooking, of home decor, of manners and hospitality, of reckoning up friends and foes, all stem from a way of life that sets in early. Any Frenchwoman, for instance, living no matter how many years in Brazil, or Turkey, or the United States, will be certain to maintain a style of cooking, a way of dressing, an innovative touch with local fabrics and art.

So much, too, for "Southernness." It would be there, whether thought about or not. I could no more become one of the expatriate tribe than I could turn into an Aztec.

The next novella I wrote, *Knights & Dragons,* was also set in Italy. The attempt was to internalize the experience of one woman, who set out on a psychic voyage of some peril. I had seen life bounce along on charming surfaces and proceed to a happy ending in *The Light in the Piazza,* Now the effort was to find a darker side of what could happen abroad. Many who expected me to write another version of the first story did not care for the second. But somehow this story has found its enthusiasts and keeps a hold on those it speaks to.

The characters in *Knights & Dragons* were not from any especial ground in the States. In the next novel, *No Place for an Angel,* the wanderers in Italy and elsewhere were mainly displaced people from the South—Texas, Mississippi, Maryland. Their lack of fixity in life gave them need of angelic messengers, but none came to their aid, and spiritual strength seemed hard to come by. Their varied experience did not lack vitality, or so I believe, but the theme was pessimistic, and may have reflected some of the personal difficulties I felt besieged by at that time.

Most important of these was the slow deterioration in my relationship with David Clay and his wife, Dusty. Their obsessive devotion to Christian Science made it increasingly difficult to speak with them on any subject. To the Clays, no one was ever born, hence age did not exist; no one ever got sick, sickness was unreal and not to be mentioned; no one ever died; one divine mind was all that everyone was part of.

At times our conversations became ludicrous. When John Kennedy was assassinated, Dusty told me by phone that none of it had "happened." To the Clays I knew nothing about something called "divine intelligence," so how could I know what was true? Communication slowly faded into a sense of unreality, of stumbling through an unlit room to seek persons much esteemed but hard to locate. Then, in one burst of total misunderstanding, it was over. Over, that is, except for my unceasing gratitude for kindnesses innumerable, cumulative from the past.

What do people with fanatical religious belief see that others do not? Some will exile, torture, or kill anyone who disagrees, all the while professing the utmost faith in Christian principles. Others simply set out to correct any casual utterance, to warp and bend every conversation to suit their own conclusions. All fanatics must be seeing things in a way opaque to the everyday world and the common vision. It was such a complete absence of a common point of view that doomed an important relationship.

With President Kennedy's death and other deaths occurring during the sixties, other unforeseen transitions, abrupt and harsh, came tramping over the spirit.

One day in Lachine when I was returning from the grocery, a neighbor came out of her side door and asked if there wasn't some writer named Faulkner from my part of the world. She thought she had heard on the radio that he had died. She was right.

The assassination in Dallas occurred when Tonny Vartan and his wife, Cynthia, were visiting us for Thanksgiving. We were returning from lunch in the city on the second day after they arrived, when that same neighbor came out the door once again and called to us: "Turn on the TV, I think something's happened to your president." We did turn it on and stayed there transfixed for the entire weekend, compelled by terrible images forming from moment to moment, by now indelible in our history.

As we were driving through some verdant Vermont woods in summer, the radio let us know that Ernest Hemingway was dead, an apparent suicide. "Stop the car," I said to John. I walked into the woods, finding no path, and sat down at some distance beside a brook. The cold water itself could not have made me feel more numb than this announcement. But how beautiful those trees were, and in the clear water there might have been trout, lurking deep but visible, their tails poised against the current.

As a writer from somewhere else, I always felt welcome in Canada. Many Canadian writers come from somewhere else—Michael Ondaatje from Sri Lanka; Joseph Skorevky from Czechoslovakia; and even earlier, the strong and vital poet Irving Layton, so identified with the Canadian scene, had emigrated from Romania as a babe in arms. I was quickly accorded a place among the English-speaking writers and never felt especial rejection by the French.

Yet Canadian writers during the sixties and seventies were doing a very natural thing in which I never found any part to play. They were building a Canadian literature, an identity for that literature and for themselves distinctly different from that of the elephant of a neighbor to the south or the British and French across the ocean. Books like Margaret Atwood's *Surfacing* and her work of Canadian criticism aptly named *Surviving* were breaking open new paths for others to follow. Groundwork had already been laid by such writers as Hugh MacLennan and Margaret Laurence. I could reflect that in the South writers had done much the same thing, making a literary identity so viable it became a living tradition that shows no sign of waning. Yet one writer I met and became friendly with, Alice Munro, defined herself as "a Southern writer from Canada." She read exhaustively in Southern books, and the small-town Ontario she often describes show their influence.

My own writing, with some few exceptions, was never grounded in Canada. The 1991 novel *The Night Travellers* dealt with characters from the United States who had found refuge there as a result of the Vietnam conflict. They experienced much of the sense of distance that I myself felt during the first years.

Working pretty much on my own, I began to see fiction, and especially the novel, in new ways. Leaving aside the mysterious question of why one is compelled to write anything, or for that matter why one is drawn to one character or story rather than any number of others, I took the choices that came my way—did they, as Willa Cather once remarked, choose the writer, rather than the other way around?—and began to explore from their vital center outward, through the phenomena of place and time and circumstance. So how does one know this "vital center"? For me it is usually a person, someone who matters, who can best carry the whole considerable weight of an unfolding plot. Like a magnet, this person will draw me to tell about it, how it all was.

I began to try this method out in various short stories, many of which have found a lasting place in collections. The editor I had for a time at McGraw-Hill was a most singular writer called William Goyen. A Texan, he had known many of the same people as I, and we found common lines of experience to form a base for work and discussion. Bill's constant helpfulness furnished a spirit to lean on in the years after I lost the Clays. He was there to be counted on. What can one say of his work? He built a solid following, and many of his books are still with us. His *House of Breath* is a fine novel. His quirky, elusive stories read like no one else's.

Bill's powerful fantasy life made it possible for him to live on two tracks at once. Sometimes the two ran together, and like puzzling crossovers of rails on a railroad line, they would reverse positions. With Bill, the act of fiction could take place in midsentence. Most writers have this tendency. It was hard to know when John Cheever was recounting an event or building a fantasy version of it. Plain old fact became the pinhead the angels danced on. Red Warren could never resist "making a good story." It was built into his spirit, his exuberant idea that life is fun.

But once I could see how Bill's thoughts worked—electrical charges skip-hopping through connective wiring—we got on well through many sessions. His attractive wife, the actress Doris Roberts, was good at keeping us down to earth.

A regular job could hardly be held by a less suitable person than William Goyen. He soon left his editorial work, but not before he had made an important friendship for me with the poet and critic Robert Phillips. Then working in advertising and living up the Harlem River line in Katonah, Robert delighted in moving in New York literary circles. He also was an avid reader of his friends' work. Whether poetry or prose had been published, there Bob would be at the party, cheerfully ready for comment and serious discussion. If there was a PEN gathering when I happened to be in New York, Bob would see that I got to it. A reading at the "Y"? A need for a cheering letter? A phone call? A suggestion for sending something to a new magazine? He was on the editorial staff of many. His own poetry, wry and engaging, full of sassy modern reference twined with serious meaning, came to me regularly, as it still does.

Bob's problem in those days was commuting. In mid-dinner, mid-party, mid-sentence, you would find yourself addressing the place he had vanished from. He had to catch the last train from Grand Central to a waiting family.

It was Bob who encouraged me to collect my stories in one large grouping and submit them as a volume. I had little belief in this. Publishers seemed to dislike doing short-story collections; the theory was that they did not sell. However, when an editor at Doubleday was attracted to a story in *The Southern Review* and wished to see others, I sent them. *The Stories of Elizabeth Spencer* came out in 1981. It made the front page of *The New York Times Book Review* with a welcome review from Reynolds

Price, and was widely praised. It earned the Award of Merit Medal of the American Academy. The dedication was to Robert Phillips.

Writers object to labels: "Southern writer," "Jewish novelist," "historical novelist," "one of The New England poets." Now I had got known as a "short-story writer." But what about novels?

New Orleans as a place came vividly to mind, out of many visits there as a schoolgirl and later. A murky crime that had occurred during the fifties was still accessible to me from a stack of old newspaper clippings I had saved. They dated from the year I had lived on the Gulf Coast and had followed these curious events daily in the *Times-Picayune.* A few extended visits to that unique and wonderful city, long talks with friends there who knew the place much better than I, numerous books of fact and fiction, and I was well away into *The Snare,* which appeared in 1972.

Once while working in New Orleans, living out on St. Charles Avenue in a rooming house called The Columns, really an enormous, old-time mansion that had seen better days, I chanced to meet a New Orleans lawyer prominent in political circles. This was Ben C. Toledano. Ben was an avid devotee of Southern literature and writers. He invited me to dinner at his home and later with his wife, Roulhac, and daughter, Gabrielle, we went for a visit to his weekend house in the bayou country.

The first evening Ben C. asked me if I had ever met Walker Percy. I said no, but I expressed admiration for his work. Before I knew it, or could stop him, he had impulsively picked up the phone and called Walker. Walker expressed a similar desire to meet me. He and his wife, "Bunt," drove down to New Orleans from Covington the very next day. We spent the first of several happy meetings at lunch together, running over familiar ground and mutual friends. I had known his closest friend, Shelby Foote, for years; he lived in Greenville, across the Delta from Carrollton, and I had also seen him once during my summer in New York.

Walker invited me to stop off at his house in Covington on my return north to Carrollton. It was there he suddenly, to my surprise, remarked, "I am not a Southern writer." No one could have looked and behaved more like a courtly Southern gentleman than Walker Percy. *The Last Gentleman,* title of one of his novels, could have been written as a logo under his signature.

I later thought of what he had said and began to understand that his problem in writing had been similar to my own, that we both knew new ground had to be broken. His own direction was philosophic, an existential exploration of modern life in terms of Christian belief. This, so far I know, was new in Southern fiction. And Walker's achievement, in the long run, took him far beyond a label like "Southern novelist," though to say why that should be thought a limitation for him, as for me, is difficult, and would require a good many pages.

Briefly, I think of the South as no longer an entity, although it is a region certainly still unique for its history, its weather, its natural beauty, pronounced sense of family, variety of characters, and so on ad infinitum. But interests and manners and all other aspects of daily life are now thoroughly encoded by the whole of American experience, and points of reference that were once so "different" as to be thought of as ours exclusively no longer really exist. If Southerners insist upon them anyway, it all becomes a sort of put-on. The Southern belle pretense, for one thing, has not only lost its charm, it is all too easy to see through and dislike.

What then of Southern literature, which still goes on in book after book? Great ones may still come our way, and many good ones are written. But to me the last distinctly and thoroughly Southern novels were Eudora Welty's *Losing Battles* and William Faulkner's *The Reivers.* In both, it is important to note, the writer went back to a time remote from the present, when the South was still there, confidently its own self and nothing else.

The same approach as I had taken with *The Snare* also led me through *The Salt Line,* its central feelings at first springing out of my grief at the damage hurricane Camille had done to a much-loved place, then centering on a character who embodied that place and time.

In both *The Snare* and *The Salt Line,* I felt free to draw on traditional Southern sources of family and history without being tied to them. What then is their centrality? A spinning center that builds its own force is not sufficient to meet the human need for meaning, and just as it was a necessity for me to vanish into the story of each work, so it was also needful to know what human values were at stake to be lost or found. This centralizing knowledge makes a demand as strong as gravity, or a work can grow as meaningless to the reader as some distant beautiful star or as talk about a "black hole," heard about on good authority but never seen. I sought for the human and the humane, the decency that struggles against the indecent, the values of love, fairness, and justice that cannot live unless they are lived.

29

THE ROAD BACK

In 1970 we reluctantly sold our house at Lachine. We already kept a *pied-à-terre* in central Montreal. John's work was centered there, and most of our friends were living in or near the center or in Westmount, just to the west. We took a spacious apartment on rue St. Mathieu, and what with new writing income constantly arriving, I was able to rent a small studio for myself over on rue Prince Arthur, east of McGill University.

It was during the sixties and seventies I began to return South quite often in response to invitations to meetings and conferences and short campus residencies. I was also wanted for frequent visits to Carrollton, always there and constantly revealed in letters from my mother as a place where people got born, married, and died. Houses changed hands; some people moved away; the church had a new minister. Cousin Wanda's roof got blown off in a storm; the town turned out to help. The fish were biting. The cotton needed rain.

People got sick. Most of my summonses were for sitting around in hospital rooms or taking over the house in Carrollton when there was no one else to do it. I once was asked to fly all the way to Mississippi because the cook had got sick and my mother could not cope. My brother had returned to Navy service during the Korean War and was now with the medical contingent in Vietnam. My nephew was a Navy pilot, stationed on aircraft carriers, sent on frequent missions to bomb the enemy.

In Carrollton I stumbled on an unexpected friend. Will Neill, the local banker, had for years been a familiar landmark, a gruff-spoken, old-fashioned, confident gentleman, a little frightening to a small girl he had no reason to remark. But he had been my uncle Joe's best friend, and together, as single men between marriages, they had gone about discovering wondrously happy times together.

Now, my uncle gone, Will seemed intent on discovering me. He said that seeing me brought back old times. He must have noticed me more than I had thought. A traditional Southerner, he surprised me by praising *The Voice at the Back Door.* "You got this country down pat, Lizzie" was how he put it. He was well read and kept up with many of the Southern writers I admired. He and William Faulkner had exchanged letters.

Will and his wife, Mary Dora, took me frequently to Lusco's, a favored eating place and one of my uncle's haunts, in Greenwood. Their back yard in summer was a place to sit with a drink while the light slowly faded and the trees turned to black silhouettes against a pearly sky. After a few drinks, however, Will would come forth with a curious idea. He believed, he said, that in the whole country there would be armed conflict with the blacks. "It will be a shooting war," he said. "Now," his wife chided, "you know Benny would never shoot at us." (Benny, aged, jet-black, and kindly, was the family cook.) "The hell she wouldn't," he would say.

Nevertheless, with Will I felt accepted. The gift astounded, but that made it all the sweeter. He understood much without being told. He dated back to a past I could know only by hearing about it. He was an active spirit in the present.

Another discovery was cousins. One was the son of my first cousin Louie Spencer, who was in turn the son of my father's brother Uncle Louie. Louie the Third started coming to Montreal in the interest of an international business project. He told me later that he had "dared" to ring me up. What tales he had possibly been told, I never knew. He came one summer afternoon with a friend. I gave them strawberry shortcake. To hear him speak of it later, he must have thought a "writer" had to be a wild woman in purple tights, swilling martinis.

After a few minutes, we were talking easily, and on subsequent trips he came to know John as well. His father was a respected businessman in Greenwood. Through Louie, I found the way open to renewing his father's acquaintance. Uncle Louie had died some years before. Louie Jr.'s help and support during my father's last difficult years were all one could wish for. Through such contacts as these we became friends. When he died of a fast-moving cancer in the early eighties, I felt I had lost someone more a brother than a cousin.

Many doors were suddenly opening. Cousins who had been in the South all through the years of stress, trial, and confrontation were graduating into a saner, freer, easier world. Especially after my parents' deaths in the mid-seventies, I needed them in a practical way. I also delighted in finding them accessible to friendship.

May, of long remembrance, was as bright an intelligence as ever. My cousin Jamie, practicing law in Jackson, a respected city judge for many years, was his funny old self, ready for a talk, a laugh, or serious family advice.

In 1969 one of my literary invitations was to the University of North Carolina, where I got to know such figures as Doris Betts, Max Steele, and Daphne Athas, fine writers and formidable creative-writing teachers, also Louis Rubin, the eminent Southern critic, novelist, essayist, and teacher. Through the years that followed Louis became a prime mover in seeing me invited to various gatherings of Southern writers, in Mississippi, Louisiana, and North Carolina. But it was not until the eighties, after a good many years so unexpectedly but for the most part happily passed in the land of ice and snow, that we felt it was time to move.

One reason was the deteriorating political scene in Canada, a constant English-French conflict that turned a beautifully welcoming international city into a battleground of name-calling and demands for change. One referendum followed another. Many of the oldest English-speaking residents moved elsewhere;

the FLQ (Fédération Libération de Québec) became known as "Folks Leaving Quebec"; the food in Toronto improved from the influx of French chefs. Quebec, it was loudly said, must be "liberated." Coming to visit a world's fair, "Expo," in the late sixties, Charles de Gaulle cried out "*Vive le Québec libre!*" The French applause was thunderous. Ottawa rescinded its invitation to the general. But he had struck a match to tinder.

Quebec has never separated from the rest of Canada, but the festering grievances go on to this day; concessions are voted in, negotiations proposed and compromises rejected. The outsider, once so happy to be part of an open-minded, evolving country, one delighting in the arts and building new centers for performance and exhibition, now had a box seat on a conflict in which he felt no visceral interest. Did it really matter if a clerk in a store spoke in English rather than French? It mattered to the clerk, who could be reported and fired.

Yet the conflict was bound to be of interest to a writer. The source of it, it seemed to me, was the Québécois fear of losing their language. Already in a multiracial city like Montreal, English was slowly prevailing. "*Joual,*" a kind of street argot, was spoken all the time in poor areas. Lists of odd expressions could be drawn up. A car was repaired? *"Oui, madame, ça runera."* A room is dark? *"Switchez la lumière."* It is fearful, like losing a part of the mind or the body, to think that your language is being taken away. The violent assertion of French identity seemed motivated by this fear of loss.

But it was a long struggle, which would take more than one lifetime to reach resolution. Canadians doubtless have the good sense eventually to move beyond, but for us the struggle had no special personal significance. About this time my dormant health problems flared up. In a specialist's judgment, the Canadian climate was not the best place for me to be. John, with his usual generosity, said my turn had come. We would seek a place in the United States, farther to the south.

In 1985 I had been with Louis Rubin at two conferences, one in Baton Rouge to celebrate the fiftieth anniversary of the founding of *The Southern Review,* the other an international literary conference in Miami.

The *Southern Review* conference, hosted by Louisiana State University, was of especial nostalgic interest. Red Warren, who along with Cleanth Brooks had started the publication in 1934, was present, though his health was obviously deteriorating. His throat ailment made it impossible for him to finish his scheduled reading. He gamely struggled through one poem, then asked for someone else to read. At our applause, he waved cheerfully from his silent seat in the background. I listened through tears. It was the last time I saw him.

Cleanth Brooks was present also, with Tinkum, his beloved wife, so soon after to die of cancer. Eudora Welty was there to read stories that *The Southern Review,* edited by these discerning two, had published when she was a beginning writer. Walker Percy and Bunt were present, Walker under heavy siege by autograph hunters.

But I myself felt hardly present at times, for I was running a constant fever and had to survive on liberal doses of codeine and cough syrup. The same ailment, a sort of "walking pneumonia," had cropped up again when I went to the conference in Miami. Louis Rubin remarked all this with a worried frown and we talked of a possible move. Not long after, I received an offer to come to a part-time teaching job at the University of North Carolina.

After thirty-three years of displacement, the long road had turned a wanderer southward. I rejoiced to see that road was no longer mined and booby-trapped, but broad, smooth, and welcoming.

In 1986 we came to Chapel Hill. It was midsummer. The weather was scalding hot. Two mornings before we had wakened in the cool mists of Gananoque, a border point on the St. Lawrence River near the Thousand Islands. There were huge gray boulders along the highway. Trees, vines, and grass were a rich green. Beneath the bridge, one of the world's great rivers ran blue and quietly powerful on its way to the sea.

At the border, the customs declared our car not to have proper smog control by U.S. standards. The officials examined John's many papers of immigration, so tediously amassed out of interviews, photographs, medical examinations, and records of health and employment. They must also have read our faces. Searching hard, they read fine print and found a "one-time only" exception to the regulation. Then with handshakes and smiles, they wished us good luck and waved us through.

Our passage over the high arch of the Thousand Islands Bridge marked more than the start of a new chapter. It would require a whole new volume, and will have to await another time for telling.

INDEX

About the Author

ELIZABETH SPENCER was born in Carrollton, Mississippi. She received her undergraduate degree from Belhaven College in Jackson, Mississippi, and her graduate degree from Vanderbilt University in Nashville, Tennessee.

After working briefly as a reporter for the Nashville *Tennessean,* she taught literature and writing at the University of Mississippi. In 1953 she received a Guggenheim Fellowship and went to Italy, where she lived and worked for some years before moving to Canada with her husband. In Montreal, she taught writing at Concordia University until she moved to North Carolina in 1986.

Ms. Spencer is an active member of the American Academy of Arts and Letters, having received the Rosenthal Award and the Award of Merit for the Short Story, both from the Academy. She has also received the John Dos Passos Award for Literature, among other honors. Her work has been widely translated. She resides in Chapel Hill, North Carolina.

About the Type

This book was set in a version of Sabon, a typeface designed by the well-known German typographer Jan Tschichold (1902–1974). Sabon's design is based upon the original letter forms of Claude Garamond and was created specifically to be used for three sources: foundry type for hand composition, Linotype, and Monotype. Tschichold named his typeface for the famous Frankfurt type-founder Jacques Sabon, who died in 1580.